Disrupted

Disrupted

My Misadventure in the Start-Up Bubble

DAN LYONS

hachette
BOOKS

NEW YORK

Hachette Books
Hachette Book Group
1290 Avenue of the Americas
New York, NY 10104
hachettebookgroup.com
twitter.com/hachettebooks

First edition: April 2016

Hachette Books is a division of Hachette Book Group, Inc.
The Hachette Books name and logo are trademarks of Hachette Book Group, Inc.

The publisher is not responsible for websites (or their content) that are not owned by the publisher.

The Hachette Speakers Bureau provides a wide range of authors for speaking events. To find out more, go to www.hachettespeakersbureau.com or call (866) 376-6591.

Library of Congress Cataloging-in-Publication Data has been applied for.

ISBNs: 978-0-316-30608-9 (hardcover), 978-0-316-30607-2 (ebook)

Printed in the United States of America

RRD-C

10 9 8 7 6 5 4 3 2 1

FOR TEAM SHRED: L.S., M.B. & P.B.

THE BEST PALS EVER

Author's Note

I've spent the past decade writing satire about the technology industry—first on a blog, then in a novel, and most recently on a TV show. But nothing I ever dreamed up in those fictional accounts could compare to the ridiculousness I encountered when I took a job at an actual tech company, a software maker called HubSpot. This book is the chronicle of my time at the company, and it's not satire. Everything in *Disrupted* really happened. With some individuals I have used real names, but in most cases I have invented pseudonyms and nicknames. Some current and former HubSpotters agreed to be interviewed for the book, but only on condition that our conversations remain off the record. Some people were afraid to talk to me at all. At the time I thought their concerns were silly. But as things turned out, those people may have been right to be afraid.

Regarding terminology: When I use the term *Silicon Valley* I do not mean to denote an actual geographic region—the sixty-mile peninsula between San Francisco and San Jose, where the original technology companies were built. Instead, like Hollywood, or Wall Street, Silicon Valley has become a metaphorical name for an industry, one that exists in Los Angeles, Seattle, New York, Boston, and countless other places, as well as the San Francisco Bay Area.

The term *bubble*, as I use it, refers not only to the economic bubble in which the valuation of some tech start-ups went crazy but also to the mindset of the people working inside technology companies, the true believers and Kool-Aid drinkers, the people who live inside their own filter bubble, brimming with self-confidence and self-regard, impervious to criticism, immunized against reality, unaware of how ridiculous they appear to the outside world.

HubSpot, where I worked from April 2013 to December 2014, was part of that bubble. In November 2014, the company floated a successful IPO, and it now has a market value of nearly $2 billion. But this book is about more than HubSpot. This is a story about what it's like to try to reinvent yourself and start a new career in your fifties, particularly in an industry that is by and large hostile to older workers. It's a story about how work itself has changed, and how some companies that claim to be "making the world a better place" are in fact doing the opposite.

Myths and mythmaking are rampant in Silicon Valley. I wrote this book because I wanted to provide a more realistic look at life inside a "unicorn" start-up and to puncture the popular mythology about heroic entrepreneurs. HubSpot's leaders were not heroes, but rather a pack of sales and marketing charlatans who spun a good story about magical transformational technology and got rich by selling shares in a company that still has never turned a profit.

At the heart of the book is my own sometimes painful and humbling journey of self-discovery, as I attempted to transform myself from a journalist into a marketing professional at a software start-up. My hope is that my story offers an overdue behind-the-scenes look at life inside a start-up during a period when the tech industry had temporarily lost its mind—and when I, for better or worse, did the same.

Contents

Midway on our life's journey, I found myself
In dark woods, the right road lost.
                                    —Dante Alighieri

I used to be with it. But then they changed what "it" was.
Now what I'm with isn't it, and what's "it" seems weird and scary to me.
                                    —Grampa Simpson

Prologue

Welcome to the Content Factory

If you made a movie about a laid-off, sad-sack, fifty-something guy who is given one big chance to start his career over, the opening scene might begin like this: a Monday morning in April, sunny and cool, with a brisk wind blowing off the Charles River in Cambridge, Massachusetts. The man—gray hair, unstylishly cut; horn-rimmed glasses; button-down shirt—pulls his Subaru Outback into a parking garage and, palms a little sweaty, grabs his sensible laptop backpack, and heads to the front door of a gleaming, renovated historic redbrick building. It is April 15, 2013, and that man is me. I'm heading for my first day of work at HubSpot, the first job I've ever had that wasn't in a newsroom.

HubSpot's offices occupy several floors of a nineteenth-century furniture factory that has been transformed into the cliché of what the home of a tech start-up should look like: exposed beams, frosted glass, a big atrium, modern art hanging in the lobby. Riding the elevator to the third floor, I feel both nerves and adrenaline. Part of me still can't believe that I've pulled this off. Nine months ago I was unceremoniously dumped from my job at *Newsweek* magazine in New York. I was terrified that I might never work again. Now I'm about to become a marketing guy at one of the hottest tech start-ups on the East Coast. There is one slight problem: I know nothing about marketing. This didn't seem like such a big deal when I was going through the interviews and talking these people into hiring me. Now I'm not so sure.

I reassure myself by remembering that HubSpot seems pretty excited about having me come aboard. Cranium, the chief marketing officer or CMO, wrote an article on the HubSpot blog announcing that he had hired me. Tech blogs wrote up the story of the fifty-two-year-old *Newsweek* journalist leaving the media business to go work for a software company.

But when I arrive at HubSpot's reception desk, something weird happens: Nobody is expecting me. The receptionist, Penny, who could pass for a high school student, has no idea who I am or why I'm here. She frowns and looks me up on her computer: nothing. This seems odd. I wasn't expecting a brass band and balloons, but I did assume that someone, presumably my boss, would be there to meet me on my first day at work.

"I'm going to be working for Cranium," I tell Penny.

Cranium is a big, hulking, baby-faced guy in his late thirties who once was a college football lineman and still looks the part. In his official HubSpot management team photo, he wears an open-collar oxford shirt and a white T-shirt, like a beefy-faced frat boy. Officially he is the person who hired me, but the decision was made by HubSpot's co-founders—Brian Halligan, the CEO, and Dharmesh Shah, the chief technology officer. Halligan and Shah didn't recruit me; I recruited them. I found HubSpot through a job posting on LinkedIn, had two interviews, and finally met with Halligan and Shah, who offered me a job as a "marketing fellow." The title was unusual, but also pleasing, with a quasi-academic ring to it and an implication that my role would be to serve as a kind of *éminence grise* at the company. My job description was vague, but I believed I would be writing articles for the HubSpot blog, advising executives on media strategy, writing speeches for the CEO, and attending conferences as a kind of brand evangelist.

Penny makes some calls. Finally she tells me that Cranium is not in the office today. I check the calendar on my phone and glance through my email to make sure I've arrived on the correct day. As far as I can tell, I have.

"How about Wingman?" I say. Wingman is Cranium's sidekick, a thirty-one-year-old director of something or other. I've met Wingman, and he's nice enough. I don't really know what he does, but basically he seems to be a mini-Cranium. Wingman actually looks like Cranium—round-faced, with short hair—and dresses like him, wearing a "business casual" uniform of jeans, sport coat, open-collar oxford shirt and white T-shirt.

Penny makes some calls. Wingman, too, is nowhere to be found.

"Maybe you should take a seat," she says.

I sit down on an orange couch and gaze up at a big flat-screen TV that shows TED talks on a loop. Orange is the official color of HubSpot, and it's everywhere: orange walls, orange ductwork, orange desks. HubSpotters wear orange shoes, orange T-shirts, and goofy orange sunglasses. They carry orange journals and write in them with orange pens. They put orange stickers on their laptops. HubSpot's logo is an orange sprocket, a circle with three little arms sticking out, each with a knob on the end. Sometimes the word *HubSpot* is rendered with the sprocket where the O should go. I have no idea what the sprocket is meant to convey, nor do I know if anyone realizes that the three arms with bulbous tips look like three little orange dicks. Those orange cocks are all over the place, including on the hoodies, hats, and other pieces of HubSpot apparel and swag that are on display nearby, available for purchase either in person or through the company's online store, the HubShop.

I'm still waiting on the couch, and now it's nine on a Monday morning and HubSpotters are streaming into the office, many wearing HubSpot clothing, like members of a sports team. Most are in their twenties. Attire for the guys skews toward bro-wear—shorts and flip-flops, untucked button-down oxford shirts, backward-facing baseball caps—while the women cultivate a look that a friend of mine calls "New England college girl going on a date," meaning jeans, boots, sweaters.

A woman shows up and reports to the reception desk. She's wearing a suit—here for an interview, no doubt. Penny tells her to take a seat.

The woman sits down next to me but then, in a minute, gets scooped up and called to her meeting. Meanwhile, I sit. And sit. Penny looks at me. "I'm still checking," she says. I smile and tell her it's no problem. Penny keeps making calls, glancing up at me and then glancing away, trying to figure out what to do with this gray-haired guy who just showed up claiming to be an employee.

Finally, a few phone calls later, a guy named Zack arrives. He's sorry that Wingman and Cranium aren't here today, but he wants to give me a tour around the offices. Zack is in his twenties. He has a friendly smile and gelled hair. He reminds me of the interns at *Newsweek*, recent college graduates who did background research for the writers. I figure he must be someone's assistant.

The building we're in also houses a venture capital firm and a few other small companies, including Sonos, which makes wireless home stereo equipment. But HubSpot keeps growing, spreading out, and colonizing more of the building. The engineers are on one floor, marketing on another, sales on another. HubSpot has five hundred employees and is hiring like crazy. It has been named one of the best places to work in Boston, with perks like unlimited vacation and Blue Cross health insurance that is fully paid for by the company.

The offices bear a striking resemblance to the Montessori preschool that my kids attended: lots of bright basic colors, plenty of toys, and a nap room with a hammock and soothing palm tree murals on the wall. The office-as-playground trend started at Google but now has spread like an infection across the tech industry. Work can't just be work; work has to be fun. HubSpot is divided into "neighborhoods," each named after a section of Boston: North End, South End, Charlestown. One neighborhood has a set of musical instruments, in case people want to have an impromptu jam session, which Zack says never happens; the instruments just sit there. Every neighborhood has little kitchens, with automatic espresso machines, and lounge areas with couches and chalkboard walls where people have written things like "HubSpot = cool" alongside inspirational messages like "There is a reason we have two ears and one mouth. So that we listen twice as much as we speak."

On the ground floor, an enormous conference room doubles as a game room, with the requisite foosball table, Ping-Pong table, indoor shuffleboard, and video games. The cafeteria next door boasts industrial refrigerators stocked with cases of beer, cabinets with bagels and cereal, and, on one wall, a set of glass dispensers that hold an assortment of nuts and candy. It's called the "candy wall," and Zack explains that HubSpotters are especially proud of it. The wall is one of the first things they show off to visitors. It's kind of a symbol of the fun-loving culture that makes HubSpot unique. It's a young place, with lots of energy. Teams go on outings to play trampoline dodgeball and race go-karts and play laser tag.

Dogs roam HubSpot's hallways, because like the kindergarten décor, dogs have become de rigueur for tech start-ups. At noon, Zack tells me, a group of bros meets in the lobby on the second floor to do pushups together. Upstairs there is a place where you can drop off your dry cleaning. Sometimes they bring in massage therapists. On the second floor there are shower rooms, which are intended for bike commuters and people who jog at lunchtime, but also have been used as sex cabins when the Friday happy hour gets out of hand. Later I will learn (from Penny, the receptionist, who is a fantastic source of gossip) that at one point things got so out of hand that management had to send out a memo. "It's the people from sales," Penny tells me. "They're disgusting."

Later I also will hear a story about janitors coming in one Saturday morning to find the following things in the first-floor men's room: a bunch of half-empty beers, a huge pool of vomit, and a pair of thong panties. The janitors were not happy. They get even more distressed when, one morning, a twenty-something guy from the HubSpot marketing department arrives wasted and, for reasons unknown, sets a janitor's cart on fire.

Everyone works in vast, open spaces, crammed next to one another like seamstresses in Bangladeshi shirt factories, only instead of being hunched over sewing machines they are hunched over laptops. Nerf gun battles rage, with people firing weapons from behind giant flat-panel monitors, ducking and rolling under desks. Standing desks are the hot new thing for tech companies, and HubSpot has installed them everywhere. People hold standing meetings and even walking meetings, meaning the whole group goes for a walk and the meeting takes place while you're walking.

Nobody has an office, not even the CEO. There is a rule about this. Every three months, everyone switches seats, in a corporate version of musical chairs. HubSpot calls this a "seating hack," and says the point is to remind everyone that change is constant. If you want privacy, you need to book one of the meeting rooms that are strung around the edges of the working spaces. Some meeting rooms are named after Red Sox players, others after "famous marketers"—I take a moment to let that sink in. Some have beanbag chairs instead of actual furniture, and in those rooms people sprawl out, with laptops propped on their knees.

Sure, it's kind of kooky, and it all feels a bit forced, as if everybody is working just a little too hard to convince themselves that their job is cool and they're having fun. But who cares? It's my first day. I'm excited to be here. I think it's a hoot. In the past few years I've visited dozens of places like this, and I've wondered what it would be like to work at one.

As we make our way around the building Zack tells me a little bit about himself. Just like me, he's a newcomer to HubSpot. He only joined a month ago. In college he majored in English and wanted to be a sportswriter. But after graduation he decided that journalism seemed too shaky and took a job at Google instead. I tell him he did the right thing. Publications are struggling, and reporters are getting axed in droves, which is why people like me are now showing up in places like this, trying to "reinvent" ourselves by working in PR or marketing. Those jobs supposedly draw on the same set of skills that you develop as a journalist, meaning that you can write and you can work on deadline. And frankly, by the standards of corporate America, you're cheap.

Zack thinks it might be helpful if he explains how the marketing department is organized. We go to a conference room and he begins drawing an org chart on the whiteboard. Zack, I will discover, loves to write on whiteboards. At the top of the marketing department he puts Cranium, the chief marketing officer. Below Cranium are Wingman and three other people. Each of these people has a team or set of teams organized underneath them. On and on Zack goes, creating a tree structure that keeps getting bigger and soon fills the white board. There's product marketing, web marketing, email marketing, social media marketing, customer marketing, conversion marketing. There are people who do demand generation, others who do customer advocacy. There are people who do sales enablement and lead nurturing. There's something called the funnel team, and another group called brand and buzz, which oversees the public relations team and runs the annual customer conference.

Finally, off to one side, is the content team. It comprises the people who write for the blog and another group who write e-books. That's where I will be working.

I notice something: On the chart, Zack's name is located *above* the content team, right below Wingman. I'm no expert in corporate organization, but based on the arrangement of this chart, I think—or, rather, I fear—that this guy who I thought was some kind of administrative assistant might actually be my boss.

"Wait a minute," I say. "I'm confused."

I look at Zack.

"Zack," I say, "what do you do here? What's your job?"

"Oh," he says, "I run the content team."

"So if you run the content team," I say, in a halting voice, "does that mean that you're my boss?" I'm trying not to sound alarmed. "Do I work for you?"

Zack says he doesn't know if he would actually call himself my *boss*. Strictly speaking, as he understands it, my official manager will be Wingman. But on a day-to-day basis, well, it's true that I will be working on the team that Zack manages.

Fuuuuuuck, is what I say to myself.

"Okay, cool," is what I say out loud.

Zack wants to take me to see where I will be working. I get up, feeling dizzy, and follow him out of the conference room, down a hallway past people who suddenly all seem way too young, like high school kids. They're everywhere, all over the place. They're rushing around carrying laptops, sitting in groups in little glass-walled meeting rooms, drawing on whiteboards, looking at PowerPoint presentations on giant monitors, drinking coffee, taking notes. I think I may be having a panic attack. Or an acid flashback. Part of me wants to dash for the door.

Fuck fuck fuck fuck fuck, a little voice inside my head keeps saying as I follow Zack and his gelled hair down the hall, my pulse thrumming in my temples.

Nine months ago I was the technology editor of *Newsweek*. In that job I did not even notice people like Zack, or Wingman, or even Cranium. They are the kind of people whose calls I would not return, whose emails I deleted without opening. Even Halligan and Shah were such small fry that I probably would not have taken time to meet them for coffee, and I certainly would not have written about them. And Zack? Good grief. He's five years out of college, and his work experience consists of two journalism internships and three years in an entry-level job in a regional Google ad sales office.

Zack takes me to a cramped little shoebox of a room, about fifteen feet wide and thirty feet long, where twenty young women are packed into two rows, staring at laptops. This is the content factory. That is literally what they call it. These people are content creators. That is literally what they called themselves. "Hungry for more content? Click here to get some!" is something they write on little boxes that they place next to blog posts, hoping that the promise of "more content" will entice readers to stay on the site.

I smile and shake hands and go down the line, past a blur of Ashleys, Amandas, Brittanys, and Courtneys, realizing as I do that I am literally twice the age of these people, in some cases more than twice their age. "So where were you before this?" I ask some of them, who give me a strange look and say, "Uh, college?" I stop asking that question. They're all women, they're all white, and they're all wearing jeans and sporting the same straight, shoulder-length hair. They all seem baffled by my presence. What is this old guy doing here? I smile and realize that I already cannot remember anyone's name.

Next, Zack introduces me to the blog team, the people I will be working most closely with—Marcia, Jan, and Ashley. I've read their work already. They say things like *totes magotes* and *awesomesauce*, and produce blog articles like "5 Ways to Make Your Landing Pages Awesome," and "7 Tips to Improve Your Lead Quality." They write in a folksy style: "Hey, blogging's *hard*, right? You don't have to tell us!! But didya know there's a remedy for those summer blogging blues? Well, there is, and we're gonna tell you about it, so read on!"

I'm not sure what my relationship to these women will be. I'm not their boss. Zack is. Zack points to an empty desk. "I guess you can sit there," he says. Instead of a chair, there is a big rubber ball—orange, of course—on a rolling frame. I'm not quite sure what to do. If I ask for a chair, I risk looking like an old fart who doesn't know how to sit on a bouncy ball or like a prima donna demanding some kind of special treatment. But if I do sit on this thing I'm pretty sure that I will immediately fall off. I imagine myself, age fifty-two, toppling off an orange bouncy ball and onto the floor, as a bunch of young women look on and try not to laugh. Some awkwardness ensues as I ask Zack if it might be possible to find an actual desk chair. We scavenge a chair from a desk in another room. The crisis is averted.

Zack goes to his desk and gets to work on whatever it is that Zack does, while I take my seat at my little desk, which is empty save for a new MacBook Air. Is this really it? Is this my job? Will I really go to work every day and sit at this shitty little desk in this shitty little room? Are these people now my colleagues? Will I have to sit in meetings with them and listen to them talk? What exactly is my actual job? Once I finish doing all the first-day paperwork, once I have my picture taken and get my ID badge and set up my parking garage pass, what am I supposed to do? Zack seems to have no idea. He's so new that he hasn't even figured out what his job is, let alone mine.

I spend the day filling out paperwork and trying not to freak out. Surely, Halligan and Shah would not have hired me and then just stuck me in a room, working for Zack. There must be some kind of mistake. When Cranium gets here, he will sort things out. Then again, is it a bad sign that Cranium made such a big deal out of hiring me and then wasn't here to meet me on my first day?

Stay calm, I tell myself. Take deep breaths. But no matter how hard I try, I can't block out the sound of that little *fuck-fuck-fuck* voice, which keeps telling me that I've made a very big mistake. Soon I will discover that the little voice is correct.

One

Beached White Male

Nine months earlier, it's the summer of 2012, and life is good. I'm fifty-one years old, happily settled into married life in a suburb of Boston, with two young kids and a job I love. At *Newsweek*, I get paid to meet amazing people and write about subjects that fascinate me: fusion energy, education reform, supercomputing, artificial intelligence, robotics, the rising competitiveness of China, the global threat of state-sponsored hacking. To me, *Newsweek* is more than a company—it's an institution. And being a magazine writer seems like the very best job in the world.

Then one day, without warning, it all just ends. It's a Friday morning in June. The kids are at school. I'm sitting with my wife, Sasha, at the kitchen table, drinking coffee and going over the plans for our upcoming vacation, a three-week trip to Austria. It's a bit of a splurge for us, but by using frequent flyer miles and staying in modest hotels we can just about afford it. Our kids—twins, a boy and a girl—are turning seven in a few weeks, and they're finally old enough to handle an adventure. Sasha has just left her teaching job, because she's been suffering from chronic migraines and spending too much time in emergency rooms. She needs time off to take care of herself. A few weeks in the Alps seems like a good way to start. We'll miss her paycheck, and her insurance, which is first-rate, but I can get decent insurance from *Newsweek*, and in addition to my salary I've been making some money on the side by giving speeches.

So we're good. Sasha can quit her job and we can still afford the vacation. It's all going to be great. That's what we're telling each other as we pull up the website for one place where we'll be staying, a cluster of chalets perched on a hillside in a remote village surrounded by mountains. A local guide takes tourists on day hikes and offers a rock-climbing class for kids. A nearby stable offers trail rides on sturdy little Haflinger horses with shaggy blond manes. We leave in three weeks.

My phone beeps. It's an email from my editor, Abby. She wants to know if I can get on the phone. I go upstairs to my office and call her at the office in New York. I figure Abby wants to give me an update on the tech blog we're launching. But unfortunately that's not it at all.

"I have some bad news," she says. "They're making some cuts. Your job is being eliminated."

I'm not quite sure what to say. On the one hand this should not come as a surprise. *Newsweek* has been losing money for years. Two years ago the magazine was sold to a new owner, who promised to turn things around. Instead we are losing more money today than we were two years ago. Subscribers and advertisers are drifting away. I suppose some part of me has been expecting this call. Still, I wasn't expecting to get it today.

Abby says it wasn't her decision to fire me. I ask her whose it was. She says she doesn't know. But someone, somewhere, has made a decision. Abby is simply the messenger. There's nothing she can do, and no one to whom I can appeal. This is obvious bullshit. Abby knows who made the decision. I'm betting it was Abby herself.

Abby is an old-time *Newsweek* person. She left the magazine before I joined, but three months ago she was recruited to come back as the executive editor. I was overjoyed when I found out I would be reporting to her. We're old friends. We've known each other for twenty years. As soon as she arrived we started talking about launching a tech blog, which I would run. I figured I would have a year, maybe more, to get the blog off the ground. That's why I thought my job was secure and why I am now sitting here, staring out my window, feeling as if I have been clubbed over the head.

"I think they just want to hire younger people," Abby says. "They can take your salary and hire five kids right out of college."

"Sure." I'm not angry. I'm just dumbfounded. "I get it."

From outside comes the roar of a lawnmower. I glance out the window and see that the guys who mow our lawn have arrived in their truck. I make a mental note that this is one small luxury that we now will have to live without, because surely an unemployed man cannot pay someone else to mow his lawn. I'm not even finished getting fired yet and I'm already thinking about ways to save money. Should we get rid of cable TV? Will we stop going out to dinner? Can we still go to Austria?

Abby says she really likes me, and this was a really hard phone call for her to make, and she hates to do this because we've known each other for so long, and nobody ever wants to call up their friend and tell them this. In a way I actually start to feel bad for her, even though I'm the one getting fired.

I tell her I understand. I'm a business reporter, after all. This is the stuff I write about—legacy companies getting disrupted by new technologies, slowly going under, laying off workers. If I were running a magazine that was losing money, I would be looking to cut costs, too. I'd get rid of the expensive old guys and hire a bunch of hungry young kids. It makes sense.

I went into this job knowing that it probably wouldn't last forever. Back in 2008, when I joined, *Newsweek* veterans were being offered buyouts and early retirement packages. And it wasn't just *Newsweek*. Newspapers and magazines were dying out all over the place, disrupted by the Internet. Despite all that, *Newsweek* was still an amazing place, and even if the magazine only had a few years left in it, I still wanted to work there.

Now, on this sunny Friday morning, it's over.

My last day will be in two weeks, Abby says. I will get no severance package, just two weeks of pay and whatever vacation time I'm owed. At the end of two weeks I'll also lose my health insurance, but the HR people will help me figure out how to set up COBRA to continue my benefits.

Some of my colleagues who left when the magazine was sold in 2010 received packages equal to a year's salary. I'd expected that if or when I got cut, I'd be given enough severance to provide a cushion. Two weeks seems inordinately harsh. I try to bargain. I ask Abby if they will keep me on for six months while I look for a new job. That will let me save face and make it easier for me to find my next job. Sorry, she tells me, but no. I offer to take a pay cut. That won't fly either, she says. How about I take a different job, I say. It doesn't have to be much, but it will keep me on staff, with benefits, while I look for something else.

Abby is not having any of it.

"Abby, I have *kids*." There's a quaver in my voice. I take a breath. I don't want to sound panicked. "I've got twins. They're six years old."

She says she's sorry, she understands, but there's nothing she can do.

I tell her that my wife has just left her teaching job. I've just finished sending in the paperwork to move us from Sasha's insurance to the insurance plan offered by *Newsweek*. The HR department at *Newsweek* must be aware of this. That was the "qualifying life event" that enabled us to join the *Newsweek* health plan outside of the annual open enrollment period.

"Look," I say, "if you can just push back my end date and keep me on for a few months, I'll at least be able to keep my health insurance, and I promise I'll get another job and get out of here."

But Abby, my old friend, a woman I've known since we were both in our twenties and starting out in the journalism business, says no, she can't do it. In two weeks I'm done, and that's that.

I hang up the phone, go downstairs, and tell Sasha what just happened. She's stunned. Wasn't I just telling her that it was safe for her to quit her job, because my *Newsweek* job was secure?

"I thought Abby was your friend," Sasha says.

"I thought so, too."

Sasha still has the vacation folder with the brochures and plane tickets and hotel and car rental confirmations out on the table.

"Maybe we should cancel the trip," she says.

There's no sense in that, I tell her. Some of the money has already been spent, in deposits that we can't get back. "We should go," I say. "We'll go, and we'll use the time to think about what we're going to do next. We can do anything, right? We can start over. We can move someplace new. It's a fresh start."

I talk about Vermont. We're always saying how cool it would be to live there. Our friends did that—one day they sold everything and moved to Vermont. They love it! Or there's Boulder. Or Bozeman. We could live in the Rocky Mountains! We should make a list of the best places to live, rent a Winnebago, visit each one, and then decide. We could spend the whole summer traveling around the country! We could see the Grand Canyon, and Zion, and Yellowstone, and Yosemite. In a way this whole thing is a gift. Because now we have all this free time! When are we ever going to have a chance like this again?

Sasha knows that I'm full of shit, and she also knows I'm panicking, because this is what I do when I'm panicking—I talk and talk and talk. But even as I'm reeling through my list of fantasy mountain towns where I can wear plaid shirts and drive a pickup truck and grow a beard, Sasha has arrived at the truth of our situation, which she feels the need to explain to me, as if by speaking the words out loud she might feel more in control of the situation.

"Let's just talk about where we are right now," she says. She's working hard to remain calm. "The reality is that I just quit my job, and I can't get that job back. They've already hired someone else. And now you've been fired."

"Laid off," I say, because that sounds better.

"Point is, we're both unemployed, and we have six-year-old twins, and no health insurance, and no income. And we're about to go on a really expensive vacation."

"Well," I say, "when you put it like that."

"How else would you put it?"

I launch back into my spiel about moving to the mountains, but she cuts me off. None of that is going to happen, and we both know it. We're not going to spend the summer cruising around the United States in a Winnebago like the Griswolds on some zany adventure.

"Look," I say, "I'll get another job. I'm going to start hitting the phone today. Right now. I'm going to email everyone I know. I've got a bunch of speeches booked, which should keep us going into the fall. And I can pick up some freelance work."

I'm trying to sound confident. But the truth is that I'm fifty-one years old and I have never gone looking for a job before. I've always had a job and then moved to a better one. I've never had to call my friends and ask them to keep me in mind if they hear of anything. I've always been the guy on the other end of that call, and I've always felt bad for those friends who were calling me. Sure, I told them, I'll pass the word around. I'll keep an eye open. I'm sure you'll find something.

But we all know the reality of our situation. Every year there are fewer jobs in journalism. It's a game of musical chairs, with a bunch of laid-off old hacks running around and fighting over the few remaining seats.

Things are even worse if you're over fifty. In what now seems like a cruel irony, I learned about this by reading my own magazine. In 2011, *Newsweek* published a cover story with the attention-grabbing headline THE BEACHED WHITE MALE. The cover depicted a middle-aged white guy in a suit, soaking wet, facedown on a beach at the water's edge—maybe not dead, but definitely *washed up*.

The article described a whole generation of once-successful men who, having been laid off during the recession, or "Mancession," as the magazine dubbed it, were now shuffling around in their bathrobes, stunned, emasculated, psychologically destroyed, humiliated in front of their wives and children, drifting through life like castrated zombies. In the new economy, age fifty was the new sixty-five. Hit fifty, and your company would find an excuse to fire you, and good luck trying to find another job. As for filing an age discrimination suit:

Forget about it. You wouldn't stand a chance. Even if you won your lawsuit, you'd never work again.

I'd read the article when it came out, but it hadn't bothered me too much. I figured that somehow I was immune to this. *Newsweek* wasn't doing well, but as long as the magazine remained in business, surely they would need a technology reporter?

Apparently not. Because suddenly, on this lovely sunny day in June, as I sit in my kitchen waiting for my kids to come home from school, wondering if I should tell them what happened and, if so, how best to present the news—right now I am no longer the technology editor of *Newsweek*. Instead, I am that guy on the cover of *Newsweek*: facedown on a beach, soaking wet, possibly dead. I am a Beached White Male.

I started working in newspapers in 1983, while I was still in college. After graduation I didn't know what else to do, so I just kept working at newspapers. I thought about law school and business school, but didn't have the heart for either. Originally I had been headed toward medicine, but I had fallen off the track and it seemed too late to start over. Newspapering didn't seem like much of a career. It seemed like something to do until you discovered a career, or, as one of my reporter friends, a Brit with a background on Fleet Street, once told me: "It beats working for a living." At some point I realized that I been working as a reporter long enough that journalism had become my career. It felt almost accidental.

In 1987, a friend of mine talked me into joining him at a newspaper aimed at the computer industry called *PC Week*, which was based in Boston. In those days Boston still had a lot of high-tech companies. I didn't know anything about computers, but nobody else did, either. The personal computer was still a relatively new thing. We were getting in on the ground floor of what would become a huge new market.

In the 1980s Silicon Valley technology companies were boring places where engineers worked in drab office parks writing software or designing semiconductors and circuit boards and network routers. There weren't any celebrities, other than Steve Jobs at Apple, and even he wasn't such a big deal back then. In the early 1990s the Internet era began, and Silicon Valley changed. The new companies were flimsy, based on hype and grandiose rhetoric and the promise of making a fortune overnight. The dotcom boom of the late 1990s was followed by the dotcom bust, and then came a period when Silicon Valley felt like a ghost town. Slowly, a new generation of Internet-related companies arose, and while this second boom wasn't a direct copy of the first one, there were some worrisome similarities, chief among them the fact that none of these companies seemed to be generating a profit. They were all losing money, and some were losing shocking amounts—billions of dollars, in some cases—and nobody seemed to mind.

I covered the first dotcom bubble and crash as a reporter at *Forbes*. Those years have turned out in retrospect to have been a kind of golden age not just for *Forbes* but for magazines in general. Magazine writers didn't get rich, but we made a good living, and the perks were amazing. We traveled the world, stayed in first-class hotels, and partied on the *Highlander*, Malcolm Forbes's superyacht, with rock stars and heads of state. During my years at *Forbes* I met my wife, Sasha, and in 2005 we had twins, a boy and a girl. After spending my twenties and thirties bouncing around like a nomad, I settled down in my forties, with a good job and a new family.

In 2006 I created a blog called The Secret Diary of Steve Jobs, where I wrote in a persona called Fake Steve Jobs. The idea was to satirize not just Jobs himself but all of Silicon Valley. I wrote the blog anonymously, and the mystery added to its appeal. Pretty soon it was attracting 1.5 million readers a month.

The blog depicted Jobs as an insufferable, insecure megalomaniac who had turned himself into the leader of a weird cult based around electronics. Jobs ranted and cursed at the people around him; he went drunk-driving with Bono and smashed into other drivers; he threw scalding tea on his long-suffering assistant; he got into trouble with the Securities and Exchange Commission and lied to investigators; he visited sweatshops in China where children made iPhones and came away feeling that *he* was the victim. With Sting, he traveled to the Peruvian rain forest, where they tripped on ayahuasca and ended up hugging and sobbing on a mud floor. He and his best friend, Oracle CEO Larry Ellison, drove to the Tenderloin in San Francisco and fired water cannons at transvestite hookers. They made prank phone calls, dialing a local Thai restaurants to order "penis sauce" or calling a hardware store in the Castro section of San Francisco to inquire about black caulk.

Eventually I got caught. A reporter at the *New York Times* figured out who was writing the Fake Steve blog and confronted me, and I came clean. There were profiles about me all over the place, from the *New York Times* to *Der Spiegel* in Germany and *El Mundo* in Spain. Conferences started inviting me to give speeches. Then I got hired at *Newsweek*, which led to even more speaking engagements, and I was on TV all the time, opining on Fox Business or CNBC or Al Jazeera. I published a Fake Steve novel, sold the rights to a Hollywood production company, and found myself in Los Angeles, developing a cable TV comedy while still working at *Newsweek*.

Then things went south. My cable TV show got killed before it even got off the ground. The *Washington Post*, which had owned *Newsweek* since 1961, sold the magazine to a new owner. The new owner merged *Newsweek* with a website called the Daily Beast, whose brilliant but crazy editor, Tina Brown, became the editor of *Newsweek*. Most of my colleagues left or got booted out. I hung on, but things were chaotic. People came and went. During the next two years I had a half dozen editors. Sometimes I had no editor at all and just floated around, trying to place stories into the magazine. It was not a happy time, but I kept hoping that things would turn around.

In March 2012, that seemed to happen. My old pal Abby was hired back and installed as the executive editor, and I was reporting to her. My job, which had felt precarious under the new ownership, began to feel secure. Finally, I had an ally, a friend in New York who would look out for me. That was a foolish thing to believe.

Two

When the Ducks Quack

Losing my job sends me into a tailspin. On the surface I'm okay, or at least I am trying very hard to pretend to be okay. Inside I feel like I'm barely holding it together, even with daily doses of Ativan. "You'll land on your feet," people keep telling me, and I want to believe them, but as time goes by I'm not sure. So far I've had a disastrous interview at a big PR firm, with a vice president who invited me down to New York, kept me waiting for an hour, then told me that he didn't like to hire journalists. At *Forbes*, an editor who less than a year ago was trying to poach me away from *Newsweek* now offers me a contract job that pays $32,000 a year and carries no health benefits. At night I lie awake in bed, unable to sleep, secretly afraid that I might never get hired again.

That *Newsweek* story about "beached white males" wasn't a work of fiction. I know guys my age whose careers are over. They're in their early fifties and once held senior-level positions, and then got downsized only to discover that no one wants them. Those guys have all been where I am now—freshly out of work, still hopeful, going on interviews. But six months goes by, and then a year, and at some point people stop taking your calls. I'm not there yet. I've landed some free-lance work, I'm still making money doing speaking gigs, and my lecture agent has promised that he will try to keep me working, but he also has warned me that without the word *Newsweek* in front of my name those speaking gigs are probably going to dry up. What happens then? Sure, we have savings. But those won't last forever. For now we're doing our best to economize.

The kids know what's going on. We don't talk about it a lot around them, but I have to say something. I don't know if talking makes things better or worse. I get the sense that they are a bit freaked out, especially my son. He's a sensitive kid. One night when I'm putting him to bed I recognize something in his eyes that I've never seen before—it's not that he's scared, it's that he knows what I'm going through and he feels sorry for me. It's almost too much to take. "Come here, dude," I say, and I give him a hug and try to make him laugh, and he does laugh, and I laugh, too, but I'm also trying not to cry. I realize that the way he sees me now is different from the way he saw me before. For the rest of my life I'm going to remember that flash of pity in his eyes. That look is going to haunt me. I need a job. Any job.

Soon enough, I get one. This happens in September 2012. It's not a great job. It's not even a good one. There are a lot of drawbacks, chief among them that the job will take me away from home, but I don't hesitate. I jump on it. Suddenly I am the editor-in-chief of a struggling technology news website called ReadWrite, a tiny blog with three full-time employees and a half-dozen woefully underpaid freelancers. ReadWrite is based in San Francisco, which means I fly out on Monday and take a redeye back to Boston on Thursday or Friday. On weeks when I'm not in San Francisco I'm either in New York, where ReadWrite's parent company is based, or in some other city, making sales calls, trying to get tech companies to buy ads from us. It's not a lot of fun, but I'm making a paycheck and keeping my eyes open for something better.

ReadWrite's offices are on Townsend Street, in the South of Market neighborhood, where all of the hot tech start-ups are located—Twitter, Uber, Dropbox, Airbnb. While the rest of the country is still licking its wounds from the worst recession in nearly a century, things here are buzzing. Start-ups are everywhere, and they're all raising money.

For a few years after the stock market crash in 2008, it was impossible for companies to pull off initial public offerings of stock. Without IPOs, the venture capital firms that put money into start-ups could not get a return on their investments, so venture funding fell off. But now things are loosening up. In May 2011, LinkedIn, a social network, went public and saw its shares more than double in their first day of trading. Later in 2011 Groupon and Zynga floated the biggest IPOs since Google in 2004. In May 2012 Facebook went public, in the biggest IPO in the history of the tech industry, one that placed a value of more than $100 billion on the social network that Mark Zuckerberg had started on a lark in his Harvard dorm room eight years before.

Now everyone is trying to spot the next Facebook, and a new tech frenzy is taking shape. Back on the East Coast, where I spend my weekends, there is a vague sense that maybe things are getting a little bit frothy out in the Bay Area. Here in San Francisco there is no doubt. There's money everywhere. Any college dropout with a hoodie and a half-baked idea can raise venture funding. Scooter rentals, grilled cheese sandwiches, a company that sends subscribers a box of random dog-related stuff every month—they're all getting checks. Blue Bottle Coffee, popular among the cool kids in San Francisco, has raised $20 million (and over the next two years will raise $100 million more) and brews coffee using Japanese machines that cost $20,000 each. A cup of joe costs seven bucks. There is always a line.

Thanks to all this new disposable income, San Francisco is bubbling with weirdo delights, like twee little shops selling liquid nitrogen ice cream and trendy bakeries making artisanal toast. Every morning, walking to work, I dodge a river of hipsters in skinny jeans and chunky eyewear riding skateboards—grown men! riding skateboards!—while carrying five-dollar cups of coffee to their jobs at companies with names that sound like characters from a TV show for little kids: Kaggle and Clinkle, Vungle and Gangaroo.

The place feels a bit too much like it did back in the late 1990s, during the first dotcom bubble. I have the eerie sense that we are about to live through that nightmare all over again. Back then I was a technology reporter at *Forbes*. I had spent years writing about business and learning the traditional methods by which companies are valued. During the bubble I felt like a sane person who had been thrown into an asylum. The economics of these companies made no sense. Their valuations were completely irrational. I wasn't the only one pounding the table about this. Yet the stock market kept going up and up. Scammers were getting rich, and I was missing out. It's a tough thing to be a tech journalist during a tech boom. You spend your days talking to people who don't seem any smarter than you—some don't seem very bright at all—and yet they are gazillionaires, while you're an underpaid hack who can barely pay his bills. I wasn't sure whether to resent them or envy them. In the end I felt a bit of both.

Of course the dotcom bubble finally blew up, and I felt a little bit vindicated and even a bit relieved. Now everything could go back to normal. I figured the dotcom bubble had been a historical anomaly akin to the Dutch tulip mania of the seventeenth century, something we would never see again in our lifetime.

Instead another one is taking shape. People my age, who remember the first dotcom bubble, are walking around San Francisco feeling like the character played by Bill Murray in *Groundhog Day*. We've lived through this before. We reckon it will all end in tears, just like the first one did. The young kids running these new companies, however, have almost no memory of the first crash. They were in junior high school when it happened. One day, Aaron Levie, the twenty-six-year-old CEO of Box, a well-funded new tech company, tells me it's really important to learn from what happened in the 1990s—which is why he has read a bunch of books about that era.

To be sure, this bubble is different from the first one. The first bubble was a mania driven by a new technology that captured the imagination of mom-and-pop investors. This new bubble contains the same kind of magical thinking, but with an added twist, courtesy of the Federal

Reserve. This time around the problem isn't just that investors have gone a little bit crazy, but also that money is cheap.

That at least is what one venture capital expert tells me. He theorizes that the policy of "quantitative easing" instituted by the Federal Reserve and other central banks after the financial meltdown of 2007 and 2008 is contributing to the stock market boom. By printing more money, the central banks are inflating stock prices. That in turn drives up the value of big pension funds and college endowments. Those organizations thus have more money to put into venture capital funds. As more money flows into venture capital, it becomes easier for start-ups to raise money. The surge of money also causes the valuation of some privately held tech companies to soar. This is an oversimplification, but basically the Federal Reserve is printing money, and a lot of that money is making its way to venture funds and from there into the pockets of a bunch of kids who are building start-ups in San Francisco. As long as the Fed keeps printing money and the stock market keeps going up, the party will continue.

There is more money than there are places to put it, so much that instead of entrepreneurs competing to get funded, the venture funds are competing to get into deals—fighting for the chance to give someone their money. There's more competition than ever before, not just from venture funds but also from start-up "incubators" and "angel investors" who are popping up all over the place.

Soon even more money will surge into the Valley from mom-and-pop investors, people who previously were prohibited from investing in start-ups because such investing was deemed too risky. In 2012 Congress passed the JOBS (Jumpstart Our Business Startups) Act, which relaxes the rules on private company investing and allows regular folks to pour money into start-ups, usually by pooling their money into syndicates on websites like AngelList. Silicon Valley companies lobbied for the JOBS Act, arguing it would give ordinary people—doctors, lawyers, retirees—the chance to catch the next Facebook or Google. But some Wall Street veterans are worried: "We are talking about companies that in all likelihood are not going to be winners, being invested in by people who clearly don't have the expertise and financial smarts of venture capitalists," former SEC chief accountant Lynn Turner tells *Bloomberg*, adding that the rule change creates "a real opportunity for scams and fraud and significant losses." The denizens of Silicon Valley see no such problem. "People are gambling in Vegas and blowing their money. They should have the freedom to angel invest with their money," is how Jason Calacanis, a Valley entrepreneur and investor who is leading a start-up investment syndicate, puts it.

The ranks of new Silicon Valley investors also include Hollywood celebrities and pop stars, the kind of people that Wall Street calls "dumb money." But in a way it's all dumb money. Nobody really knows what's going to work, or which companies are going to succeed. Some investors are just spreading money around everywhere—"spray and pray," they call it—hoping that somehow, if only through dumb luck, some of their money will land on the next Facebook, and the payoff from that one hit will more than make up for the duds. The biggest risk for venture capitalists is not that they will make a bad bet but that they will miss out on one of the good ones.

A lot of the entrepreneurs are just as inexperienced as the investors. Some raise money without even knowing what product or service they will build. Many have never run companies before. Some have never even had jobs before. On top of that, a lot of these new start-up founders are somewhat unsavory people. The old tech industry was run by engineers and MBAs; the new tech industry is populated by young, amoral hustlers, the kind of young guys (and they are almost all guys) who watched *The Social Network* and its depiction of Mark Zuckerberg as a lying, thieving, backstabbing prick—and left the theater wanting to be just like that guy.

Many are fresh out of college, or haven't even bothered to graduate. Their companies look and feel a lot like frat houses. Twitter, at one point, will literally hold a frat-themed party. In 2012 a new word has entered the Silicon Valley lexicon: *brogrammer*, which refers to a kind of macho dickhead who chugs from a beer bong and harasses women. Soon come the scandals and lawsuits and criminal cases, with tales of sleazy founders sexually harassing female employees or, in one extreme case, allegedly beating up a girlfriend. These are the people who now run tech companies, who have been entrusted with huge sums of other people's money. It would be nice to think that when everything falls apart, the only ones who get hurt will be venture capitalists on Sand Hill Road in Menlo Park. But a lot of the money being thrown at these kids originally came from pension funds. The pain, when it comes, will not be confined to Sand Hill Road.

Walking around San Francisco, it strikes me that this cannot end well, that the combination of magical thinking, easy money, greedy investors, and amoral founders represents a recipe for disaster. My first response is to feel the same kind of righteous indignation that I felt back in the late 1990s. (Journalists are really good at righteous indignation. It comes naturally to us.) But this time I also feel something else— maybe because I'm older and more pragmatic, or maybe because I now have kids to support, or maybe because I'm still stung by the loss of my *Newsweek* job and fearful that there is no future in the media business. Maybe it's because I hate my new boss at ReadWrite, and every day I slog into the office and bang out blog posts only to have her call me from New York and tell me the site isn't getting enough traffic. I feel like a hamster in a wheel, running and running, getting nowhere. I'm never going to make any money doing this, and meanwhile all around me there are kids in skinny jeans making millions, tens of millions, hundreds of millions of dollars—money for nothing, as Mark Knopfler sang in that old Dire Straits song.

This time I start thinking that I should get in on that. I should go get a job at one of these start-ups. Tech companies and VC firms are all poaching journalists to pump out blogs and get them some attention. They're flush with cash and hiring like crazy. Two of my journalist friends have already made the leap. One is working at Evernote, the other at Flipboard. They both live in San Francisco. I see them all the time. These guys aren't naïve. They just want to cash in on the madness. Out here, making money is the only thing anyone talks about. Funding rounds, valuations, deal terms, equity percentages, who made what—these are the topics of conversations when I visit friends for dinner in Marin County. The coffee shops are filled with techies who are hunched over laptops and frantically dashing out code, or pitching ideas to investors. Every morning when I'm waiting in line for my five-dollar caffè latte I see these meetings taking place.

Sure, this bubble will pop one day, but before that happens a bunch of people are going to make a lot of money. That's what happened last time—Netscape, which made the first web browser, never really succeeded as a company, yet its co-founder, Jim Clark, reportedly managed to put $2 billion into his pocket—and the same thing is happening now. Zynga and Groupon are losing hundreds of millions of dollars, yet their founders have become billionaires.

Finally I have a sort of epiphany. This takes place on a rainy Friday evening in November 2012, in Anchor & Hope, a fancy restaurant on Minna Street, a block away from Market Street, in the part of San Francisco where the financial district and start-up land converge—a spot that is, quite literally, ground zero for the revolution.

I'm on my way to the airport. Tonight I'll be taking a redeye back to Boston, but before I do I'm meeting a friend for a drink. Anchor & Hope is packed with techies and bankers who are spending some of their easily raised money on $200 bottles of Napa Valley Cabernet Sauvignon and oysters sold at $50 per dozen.

Tad is an investment banker. He's sitting at the bar, way in back. He wears black glasses and a gray bespoke suit that probably costs more than I make in a week. Back in the 1990s he made a fortune managing IPOs for tech companies. For the past decade he's been on the beach, but now he's back, because the opportunity is so huge that he can't ignore it.

"Do you have any idea how big this is going to be?" he says. "This is going to be huge. It's going to be way bigger than the last bubble."

Imagine there's a giant tsunami, way out at sea, he says. Right now you can barely see it, but soon that wave is going to arrive. Some people are going to get wiped out, but some are going to ride the wave and get rich.

I ask him if he thinks that start-up valuations are too high. Based on traditional metrics, it seems to me that some of these companies seem way too expensive.

"You think these valuations are high today? Wait until you see them a year from now, or two years, or three years. We're not even near the peak. Before this is over there's going to be a trillion-dollar transfer of wealth in Silicon Valley."

His bank will make money by helping people move that money around and carving off a little slice as it flows through the pipe. Tad will arrange mergers and acquisitions. He'll advise start-ups that are raising money, either from private investors or through IPOs.

Once again I bring up the issue of valuations and my fear that this can't be sustained, that we're going to have another crash.

"There's an old expression on Wall Street," Tad tells me. " 'When the ducks quack, feed them.' Have you heard that? Back in the nineties investors wanted to buy anything with the word *dotcom* at the end of its name. So that's what we gave them. Our job isn't to talk people out of buying. Our job is to make what people want. Our job is to feed the ducks. And right now, the ducks are hungry."

Nearby, a cheer goes up as a waiter delivers an enormous, two-tiered tower of seafood, a few hundred dollars' worth of lobster, oysters, and other shellfish, to a table of twenty-something techies wearing jeans and sneakers and Warby Parker glasses.

Tad tells me again about the trillion dollars that is going to change hands. A trillion dollars! It's the biggest transfer of wealth that has ever occurred.

"And I'm here writing about it, instead of getting in on it."

He sips his cabernet sauvignon, and shrugs. "Right."

"I'm in the wrong business," I say.

"That's true," he says, in a matter-of-fact voice.

It's time for me to go. There's an Uber outside, waiting to take me to the airport. We say our goodbyes. Out in the car, driving to the airport, gazing into the dark and watching rain lashing against the windshield, I keep thinking about that trillion dollars. That joke I made about being in the wrong business wasn't really a joke. It's the truth. I'm in the wrong business. I'm working in a bad industry where things are only going to get worse. But why? What law says that I have to keep doing what I'm doing, just because this is the only job I've ever done?

By the time I get to the airport I have made up my mind. The tech market is going crazy again, and this time I'm not going to sit on the sidelines and write about it. I'm going to work at a start-up. I am going to feed the ducks, or surf the tsunami, and maybe I will fall off my surfboard and drown, or maybe, I don't know, I'll get eaten by ducks, but to hell with it—I'm going to try.

As I see it I have nothing to lose. I hate my job at ReadWrite anyway. Sure, I am fifty-two years old and past the age when you're supposed to start a new career or go on any adventures. But if I don't do this now, I might never have the chance again. I might always wonder how things would have turned out if I had just sucked up the courage to make the leap.

The trick is to find the right company. Ideally I'd like to join the next Google or Facebook—a rocket ship. Realistically, I just hope to find a company that won't fizzle out, one that is likely to pull off a successfull initial public stock offering and put a few bucks in my pocket. Pretty soon, I find one.

Three

What's a HubSpot?

There's a post on LinkedIn—a software start-up in Cambridge is looking for a "content creator." The company is called HubSpot. Its offices are six miles from my house in Winchester, Massachusetts, yet I have never heard of the company and have no idea what they make. I pore through their website, which talks about something called inbound marketing, which I've also never heard of. All I can tell is that they make software used by marketing departments.

I call around to friends who work in venture capital, who tell me that HubSpot is the real deal. The company is a bit of a sleeper. It's not as well known as companies like Snapchat or Instagram, but it is run by a bunch of guys from MIT and headed for an IPO. Over the past seven years HubSpot has raised $100 million in venture capital, and its investors include some of the best firms in the business. Its business is booming. "Those guys," one of my VC buddies says, "are going to make a shit ton of money."

I write to the woman who posted the content creator job opening on LinkedIn. She's anxious to meet. Her name is Sharon. She's married, in her forties, and has two kids. In January 2013 we meet for lunch at a Thai restaurant in Cambridge, and she brings along Wingman, who runs the company's content group. Wingman is about thirty years old, has been at HubSpot for just over two years, and before that worked at public relations agencies. He says the job I applied for isn't right for me, but he has something bigger and more interesting in mind. He's also concerned about culture fit, which he says is a big deal at HubSpot. They like people who can get along well with others, "the kind of people that I'd like to go have a beer with after work." I'm not sure I'd want to hang out with Wingman after work, but he seems nice enough. Apparently he feels the same way about me, because a few weeks later they invite me back to meet Cranium, HubSpot's chief marketing officer.

Cranium is a big, affable guy in his late thirties. We meet at HubSpot's offices and talk over coffee. He has an MBA from the MIT Sloan school and uses the word *awesome* a lot. We talk about HubSpot's business model, its path to profitability, and the "stickiness" of its product, meaning how well HubSpot is able to keep customers from switching to a rival software product. Right away, I like Cranium. I can imagine myself working for him and learning from him. The position he has in mind for me, he says, is something called a marketing fellow, which seems to imply that I'm being brought in as a kind of special adviser to the company. The bad part is that it's not an actual title, like director or vice president, which are the titles you get if you are actually part of the management team. In fact the title marketing fellow implies that you are not really a part of the company; you're a visitor, a temporary hire, someone who is being kept at arm's length. I'm too clueless about corporate life to understand that. In my mind, marketing fellow sounds like a cool title. I like it.

In the days leading up to this interview with Cranium I have started thinking that HubSpot could be a really good fit for me. I'd be working in the marketing department of a company that makes software for marketing people. Where better to learn about marketing? And marketing seems like a natural next step for me. I could spend two or three years here, become a marketing expert, and then go work for a smaller start-up in a bigger role. HubSpot is small enough that I'll probably get to wear a lot of different hats. Who knows what I might end up doing? In the next year or two HubSpot will probably have a really hot IPO, and while I won't get rich on that, I will at least get a little something, and it will be cool to be on the inside of one of those events.

Cranium apparently likes me too, so next I get passed up the ladder. Toward the end of February 2012 I go back again and meet HubSpot's co-founders, Brian Halligan, the CEO, and Dharmesh Shah, the chief technology officer, or CTO. Before the meeting I watch some of their keynote speeches from HubSpot's annual customer conference, called Inbound. I read *Inbound Marketing*, the book they co-authored a few years ago, and pore through Shah's blog and the articles he has published on LinkedIn.

We meet in a conference room at HubSpot. They're both in their forties, which is a relief to me. I don't want to work at some company run by a twenty-five-year-old boy-king brogrammer and his frat brothers from college. Halligan and Shah met while they were both in grad school at MIT, but I cannot understand how they ever became a team. They could not be more different. Halligan is an extreme extrovert, a classic sales guy. He once sold software for a company in Boston and later worked as a venture capitalist. He is in his late forties and still single, a blustery, hard-partying Boston Irish guy who lives in a luxury condo in the South End, drives a BMW, and has a reputation as a ladies' man. Shah is married, has kids, and is an extreme introvert who claims he can go weeks without talking to anyone on the phone. He begins his speeches by saying how much he dreads giving speeches, and how he'd much rather stay home and write code. But once on stage he seems to enjoy playing the role of inspirational speaker—a kind of nerd Tony Robbins, overly fond of touchy-feely rhetoric and vapid aphorisms. "Success," Shah says, striding back and forth across a stage, with his head down, stroking his beard, as if impersonating a professor, "is making those who believed in you look brilliant." Then he will pause, as if he has just said something incredibly profound and wants to give you a moment to let it sink in. Then he repeats the line, and a ballroom full of marketing people cheer.

But when I meet them together it occurs to me that their different personalities are probably why their partnership works. There's a yin-and-yang quality, like the one between Steve Jobs and Steve Wozniak, the co-founders of Apple. Halligan is the Jobs figure, the corporate visionary, the guy who thinks about sales and marketing. Shah is like Woz, the nerdy software programmer. Shah is wearing scruffy jeans and a rumpled T-shirt, his usual attire. He has dark hair and a dark beard, flecked with gray. Halligan wears jeans, and a sports jacket over a button-down oxford shirt. His hair is gray, as gray as my own, in fact, and he wears the same kind of chunky horn-rimmed glasses that I do. I take this as a good sign.

As with Cranium, I like these guys right away. They're easy to talk to. It doesn't feel like an interview. It feels like we're just having a conversation. Shah, as it turns out, saw me give a speech at a conference a few months ago and really liked it. He says he'd like me to give the same talk at HubSpot's Inbound conference this year. I tell him I'd be glad to do that. We talk about some of the things that Shah has been writing about on his blog. They ask me about ReadWrite, and I tell them how we are struggling to sell advertising, and how I've come to believe that the problem is not our content—the problem is advertising itself. Ads no longer work. But this means the business model upon which the media business is built—create content, put ads next to it—no longer makes sense. The media business now needs to figure out a new way to produce journalism and make money from it, but so far nobody has any good ideas.

I mention a new documentary, *The Naked Brand*, made by a renegade advertising guy in New York, Jeff Rosenblum, who believes the entire advertising business is about to get blown to hell. Halligan's jaw drops. He just saw the movie and loved it. Everything the guy says in that movie is what he's been saying for years. It's why HubSpot exists, he tells me. In their book, *Inbound Marketing*, Halligan and Shah argue that instead of spending money on traditional marketing, things like buying advertising and cold-calling customers, companies should publish blogs and websites and videos, and use online content to draw customers toward them. The old marketing was *outbound*, meaning it involved sending messages *out* into the world. The new marketing is *inbound*.

It's less expensive and more effective. That's what HubSpot's software does. That's its sales pitch, in a nutshell.

Halligan turns to Shah. "Have you seen this movie we're talking about?"

Shah says he hasn't heard of it.

"You gotta see it," Halligan says.

That's when I play my ace. "You know, I know Jeff Rosenblum. I wrote a story about him for *Newsweek*. I went to the premiere of that movie in New York. We got to be friends. I can introduce you to him. I think you guys would love each other."

Rosenblum is a hard-partying wild man who went to University of Vermont, the same college that Halligan attended, and competes in Tough Mudder events, the nutso races where people charge through ten-mile obstacle courses straight out of Navy SEAL basic training. Halligan says he'd love the introduction and that maybe we could get Rosenblum to come up to Boston and give a HubTalk, which is what HubSpot calls its speaker series, where interesting people come in and give a quick talk at lunchtime in the big conference room downstairs. I tell Halligan I'm sure that Rosenblum would give a talk. We could probably even set up a showing of *The Naked Brand* for everyone at HubSpot. Or better yet, we could arrange a big showing in Boston, at a theater, with HubSpot as a sponsor.

The ideas are flying. We're hitting it off! This is going great. Then Halligan says he has another mission for me.

"It's our blog," he says. "It sucks."

I've looked at the blog, and he's right; it's awful. But I figure it's best to be diplomatic. I tell him that I think the blog is pretty good, as corporate blogs go—but Halligan cuts me off.

"No, it's terrible. It used to be better. There were other people running it. But lately, I don't know. It's kind of embarrassing." He turns to Shah. "Do you agree?"

Shah agrees. We talk about how a lot of companies, especially tech companies, are hiring journalists and actually producing high-quality news sites. Some of them are doing a really good job, better than what we can do at a place like ReadWrite, if only because they have more resources.

Halligan says he wants to produce material that raises awareness of HubSpot and establishes HubSpot as a "thought leader" in the world of marketing. I mention the idea of creating an independent site, sponsored by HubSpot but kept separate from the company. That's what Adobe, a big software company in California, has done as a way to promote its marketing software. I know the guys who run the Adobe-sponsored site and have talked to them about how they launched it. Halligan and Shah are non-committal. For now the deal is that I will come on board and find a way to produce better, smarter content that can be put out with the HubSpot brand attached to it. The work I'm doing will exist in a gray area—a mix of journalism, marketing, and propaganda. Halligan and Shah don't know what this will look like, and neither do I. But it could be an interesting experiment. We shake hands, and I leave the meeting feeling pretty good. Two weeks later, in the middle of March, they make me an offer.

The problem is that by the time this happens I also have two other offers, because even while I've been talking to HubSpot, I've also been interviewing at other places. One offer comes from a media company in New York; I can stay in Boston and write a blog about technology. The other job involves working in the public relations department of a huge Internet company, which wants me to move to Silicon Valley and will pay me more money than I've ever imagined I would make.

Nevertheless, I'm still leaning toward HubSpot. The media job could be fun at first, but I won't get to write interesting articles. I'll be grinding out blog posts and trying to get traffic, just like at Read-Write and at the Daily Beast, and I've had enough of that. The big company in Silicon Valley is tempting, but Sasha isn't thrilled about moving to California, and a friend of mine who has worked at the company, and knows the people I would work with, has told me she had a less-than-great experience, and doesn't recommend going there.

Then there's HubSpot. It's in Boston, so we don't have to move, which makes Sasha happy. We don't have to sell our house and buy a new one, or find a new school for the kids, or make new friends. I like that HubSpot is still a small company. I reckon that at HubSpot I'll end up doing lots of different jobs. I'll be more likely to have some influence than I would at some huge corporation with thousands of employees. Also, I like Halligan. He seems smart. I want to work with him.

HubSpot also potentially represents more upside, financially. The big company in Silicon Valley is already big. The people who got rich there were the ones who joined fifteen years ago. HubSpot is just starting out. If HubSpot goes public, and if its stock really takes off—if HubSpot becomes the next Microsoft, or Google—I might make some serious money, something I've managed to avoid doing over the course of my career as a journalist.

"Basically I'm making a bet," I say to Sasha, after we've put the kids to bed and we're talking about which job I should take. "The only way the HubSpot job is worth taking is if they're going to go public and have a big IPO."

The deal at a start-up is that you get a lower salary, but you also get a pile of options, which vest over four years. The strike price on my HubSpot options is set at a level that reflects the valuation put on the company's last private round of funding. If HubSpot goes public at a valuation higher than that, my options will be worth money. If the IPO is a dud, or if the market crashes and HubSpot can't go public, or if HubSpot fizzles out altogether, then my options will be worthless.

To pull off a successful IPO, HubSpot needs to reach $100 million in annual sales. That's about double what the company did in 2012. What are the odds that they can do it? How savvy are Halligan and Shah? What will investors on Wall Street think of these guys? My sense is that things will go well. Halligan used to work as a venture capitalist, so he thinks like an investor. Shah, before going to grad school at MIT, built a different software company and sold it.

Also, from the perspective of Wall Street, HubSpot ticks all the right boxes. It sells to businesses, rather than to consumers. It's a cloud computing company and uses a business model called software as a service, or SaaS, which means customers don't install the software on their own computers but instead connect to it over the Internet and pay a monthly subscription fee. Cloud computing is hot right now. The whole tech industry is moving to this model. Investors love it.

Over the years Halligan and Shah have come up with a creation myth about the company, which is that while they were in grad school they had a vision for how companies could transform their marketing departments. They came up with the concept that they call inbound marketing, then Dharmesh and a team of engineers wrote a set of software programs based on that concept. Companies that use HubSpot software are able to find new customers, boost their sales, and save money. That's the pitch.

In fact the early days were not quite so tidy. People who were around in those days later tell me that Halligan and Shah considered other things before deciding to make marketing automation software. What's more, I've been told, for the first five years, HubSpot's product wasn't very good. It was so bad, in fact, that according to one former engineer HubSpot's own marketing department couldn't depend on it and instead used marketing software made by one of HubSpot's rivals. "The fucking product was a disaster," the engineer recalls. "You'd try to do something, like run a query, and the system would just blow to shit. Every day there was an outage."

But Halligan knew how to sell. Among his first hires were a head of marketing and a head of sales. Those guys assembled an old-fashioned phone sales operation, with an army of low-paid telemarketers who would badger companies into signing up for a one-year subscription. The salespeople targeted small business owners, whose needs were relatively simple and who were, typically, not very tech savvy. Eventually some customers would become disenchanted with the software and refuse to renew for a second year. By then HubSpot's telemarketers would have found new customers to replace the ones who were leaving. By 2011, HubSpot had about five thousand customers.

That year, the company raised a new round of funding and used the money to acquire a company with good engineers. The new team threw out the old coders and began rewriting the software from scratch.

By 2013, when I arrive, HubSpot is selling a much better product.

The software is still not perfect, and one program in particular, the content management system, needs a lot of improvement. The code is not based on cutting-edge computer science or sophisticated artificial intelligence algorithms. These are just fairly simple programs that automate basic marketing chores, like sending email to a list of contacts. But friends of mine who use HubSpot tell me the software can more than hold its own against other marketing software products. One market research website, which rates software based on customer reviews, ranks HubSpot in first place among marketing automation programs.

Better yet, all those years of selling a weak product have forced HubSpot to get really good at generating hype. The vast majority of HubSpot's employees work not in engineering or software development, but in sales and marketing. They spend their days cold-calling customers, cranking out blog posts, posting automated email campaigns, flooding Twitter and Facebook with promotional messages, running webinars and podcasts, talking to user groups, and preparing for HubSpot's big annual customer conference, an extravaganza with musical acts, comedians, and inspirational speakers. Over the course of seven years, Halligan and Shah have built a hype machine that goes beyond anything I've ever encountered.

There seems to be nothing HubSpot will not do to get publicity. In 2011, the company took advantage of a service that Guinness World Records offers in which anyone can suggest a new category, set a record, and get an official Guinness World Records title. A spokesperson for Guinness says HubSpot came to Guinness with an idea to hold the "world's largest webinar," and then won the honor by holding a webinar that drew 10,899 participants. The spokesperson says HubSpot paid Guinness $8,700 for the service. HubSpot's record still stands, though more than a dozen others have tried and failed to do better, according to Guinness.

So far, HubSpot has devoted all of its energy to selling software. But in 2013 Halligan and Shah are getting ready to point their hype cannon at a new customer, with a new product. The product they will sell is HubSpot's stock, and the customers will be investors on Wall Street. Wall Street, I'm pretty sure, is going to eat this up.

I take the job.

Four

The Happy!! Awesome!! Start-Up Cult

One month later I'm driving home from my first day on the new job and telling myself that everything will be okay. Sure, my boss is half my age. Sure, I have no idea what I'm supposed to do. But it's only been one day.

"It's great," I say, when I get home and find Sasha and the kids waiting for me, anxious to hear about Dad's big new job. I tell the kids about the beanbag chairs and the Nerf gun fights and the kitchen with the giant wall of candy dispensers, with every kind of candy you can possibly imagine. The kids are seven years old now, and of course this sounds exciting to them. They can't wait to come to the office with me. They're going to bring their Nerf guns.

"I'm sure we can do that," I tell them.

After dinner I pull Sasha out onto the porch and tell her what I'm really thinking.

"This might be a mistake," I say.

"That's what you said last time."

"Yeah, and last time I was right."

It's galling to think that I may have leapt from one bad situation to another that's even worse. What the hell is happening to me? After years of steadily climbing up some imaginary corporate ladder, I'm now turning into a serial screw-up.

I glance through the window of the sliding doors. The kids are in the living room, fighting. They fight all the time, and with such passion that sometimes I think we should find an exorcist. They have been through a lot over the past couple of years. They've seen Sasha going in and out of the hospital, and then leaving her job. They've seen me lose my job at *Newsweek*, then take a new job in San Francisco and disappear for weeks at a time. They've seen me exhausted, burnt out, and depressed. They've heard us talking about moving to California. They're frazzled. We all are. Whatever happens at HubSpot, the best course of action is to hunker down, pretend to be happy, and let our lives regain some stability.

That doesn't mean I can't bitch to my wife about it. I tell Sasha about Cranium and Wingman not being there. I tell her about the guy who I thought was someone's administrative assistant and who turned out to be my boss, and how I'm sitting in a room called the content factory, crammed in with two dozen people.

Inside, something has happened. My daughter is screaming. She sounds like she has been set on fire.

"Want a paper bag to breathe into?" Sasha says.

"No, I want a plastic bag, and you can put it over my head and tie it around my neck."

"That's the spirit," Sasha says, and we open the door and head inside to face the mayhem.

Every new HubSpot employee has to go through training to learn how to use the software. That's a good idea, and it also keeps me from having to worry about what I'm supposed to be doing here, or why Cranium, who hired me, still has never come by to say hello or talk about what he wants me to work on.

Training takes place in a tiny room, where for two weeks I sit shoulder to shoulder with twenty other new recruits, listening to pep talks that start to sound like the brainwashing you get when you join a cult.

It's amazing, and hilarious. It's everything I ever imagined might take place inside a tech company, only even better.

Our head trainer is Dave, a wiry, energetic guy in his forties with a shaved head and a gray goatee. On the first day we all go around and introduce ourselves, and tell everyone about something that makes us special. Dave's thing is that he plays in a heavy metal cover band on weekends.

Dave is part teacher and part preacher. Every two weeks he gets a batch of new recruits, and he goes through the same spiel, showing the same slides, telling the same jokes. He's good at it. He loves HubSpot, he tells us, unabashedly. He's had lots of jobs, and this is by far the best place he's ever worked. This company has changed his life. He hopes it will change ours as well.

"We're not just selling a product here," Dave tells us. "HubSpot is leading a *revolution*. A *movement*. HubSpot is *changing the world*. This software doesn't just help companies sell products. This product changes people's lives. *We* are changing people's lives."

He tells a story about a guy named Brandon, a pool installer in Virginia. His business was struggling. He could barely get by. But then he started using HubSpot software, and his business took off. Soon, his company was installing pools all around the country. He was rich! Eventually he was doing so well that he hired someone else to run his pool company so that he could become a motivational speaker. He travels the world spreading the gospel of inbound marketing, transforming the lives of thousands of other people.

"This guy has become a *superstar*," Dave says. "He's a *rock star*. And it all started with HubSpot. *That's* what we're doing here. That's what *you* are part of."

The truth is that we're selling software that lets companies, most of them small businesses, sell more stuff. The world of online marketing, where HubSpot operates, has a reputation for being kind of grubby. In addition to pool installers and flower shops, our customers include people who make a living bombarding people with email offers, or gaming Google's search algorithm, or figuring out which kind of misleading subject line is most likely to trick someone into opening a message. Online marketing is not quite as sleazy as Internet porn, but it's not much better, either.

Nevertheless, Dave is laying it on thick, and the new recruits are nodding their heads and seem to be eating it up. Most of them are right out of college, clean-cut and well scrubbed. The guys wear khakis and button-down shirts. The women wear jeans and boots, and lots of makeup, and they have paid attention to their hair. The guy next to me has a buzz cut and just graduated from some college in New Hampshire. He tells me that he lives with his parents and commutes an hour to get here, but he's thinking about moving closer to Boston and getting his own place.

I feel ridiculous. I definitely don't belong here. When it's my turn to tell a little something about myself, I make a joke about how I'm friends with all of their parents, who have sent me here to keep an eye on them. The joke falls flat, which it should, because it's a shit joke. I'm nervous. I have to come up with something. What makes me a special snowflake? How am I different from everyone else here, other than the fact that my hair is gray, my cholesterol is too high, and I'm probably the only person in this room who has had a colonoscopy? I say something about being the parent of twins. The other recruits just look at me.

Dave ushers in a parade of executives who give us inspiring talks about what a great company we've joined. I'm not only older than all of the other trainees, I'm also older than all of the executives.

Assistant trainers lead various courses during the day and give us homework assignments. A woman named Patty does most of the training on how to use HubSpot's software. What we're selling is not one single product but actually a handful of separate programs that can be purchased individually or as a bundle.

The bad news is that some of the programs aren't especially good. I've already been using the content management system, or CMS, which is software for writing and editing blog posts, and it's awful— buggy, slow, prone to crashing, incredibly limited in its functionality. HubSpot's CMS is a tinker toy compared to WordPress, the most popular blogging software, which also costs nothing to use. I can't believe HubSpot charges people money to use its CMS, or that anyone is gullible enough to pay them. Then again, a lot of HubSpot's customers are small-business owners, so maybe they don't know any better. Or maybe they think using WordPress would be too much of a hassle. Maybe they would rather pay for HubSpot because then they can call a tech support line and get answers to their questions about how to use the software. They probably also figure that over time HubSpot will improve the software and add more features.

There's a program for sending out email. It automates the process, so you can blast thousands of people with a sequence of email messages that will be sent out on a schedule. Another program lets you store a database of customer contacts. There are tools that analyze the traffic to your website, to see which pages are attracting the most visitors and how much time people spend on a particular page. There is a search engine optimization feature that helps you load up blog posts with keywords so that people are more likely to find your page when they do a search on Google.

One of our assignments involves inventing a fake company and fake product and then crafting an email campaign to sell the product. HubSpot's software lets you set up a series of emails in a tree structure. You write one first-round email that goes out to everybody on the list. For the second-round email, you might create three versions—one for the people who deleted the first email without opening it, another for people who opened the email and looked at it before deleting it, and a third for people who went one step further, who clicked through on the link in the first email and looked at your website, but then left without buying anything. Then you create a third round of email messages based on the possible responses to the second email, and so on and so on. The goal is to keep pushing people toward your website until they buy something. Once they buy something, you set up a new campaign and try to get them to buy something else. You can set up a campaign with multiple steps, aim it at a list that contains thousands of names, then press SEND and let the software go to work.

At HubSpot this happens on an incredible scale. Every month,

HubSpot's customers send out, in aggregate, more than a billion email messages. And we're just one of dozens of companies selling tools to automate the work of sending junk around the Internet. Now I'm a part of this. I'm working for the people who fill your email inbox with junk mail, the online equivalent of those pesky telemarketers who call you at dinnertime to sell you new windows or a set of solar panels for your roof.

I rationalize this by telling myself that while the work might be ignoble, it's not necessarily evil. We're not *Hitler*. We're just annoying people. Sure, arguably we are making the world a little bit worse—but only a little bit. That's what I tell myself.

Online marketers have invented euphemisms to make the work they do sound less awful. For example, we're told that our email campaigns do not involve badgering people, or pestering them—rather, we're "nurturing" them. "Lead nurturing" is a big thing in the world of online marketing. If someone doesn't open our first email, we'll nurture them again, and we'll keep on nurturing them until they finally cave in and buy something.

HubSpot doesn't just sell this software—it also teaches people how to use it and in general how to be more effective at selling stuff online. At the annual customer conference, Inbound, thousands of online marketers flock to Boston to learn new tricks. One involves using a misleading subject line in an email—something like, *fwd: your holiday plans*—to dupe people into opening the message. "Boosting your open rate," they call it. At the conference HubSpot also shows off new features and products, like one that puts a tracking cookie on the computer of everyone who visits your website and keeps track of every page they visit. The software can even send you an alert when someone comes back to your website for a second visit—so you can call that person immediately and say, "Hey, I see you're on our website! Is there something I can help you with?"

That's the business we're in: Buy our software, sell more stuff, make more money. There's nothing wrong with that, but that's not exactly how HubSpot bills itself or describes what it does. The motto of the

Inbound conference is this: "Come together. Get inspired. Be remarkable." In training we're taught that the billions of emails that we blast into the world do not constitute email *spam*. Instead, those emails are what we call "lovable marketing content." That is really what our trainers call it. That is the exact term they use. The convoluted logic behind this is that "spam" means unsolicited email, and we only send email to people who have handed over their contact information by filling out a form and giving us their permission to be contacted. Our emails might be unwanted, but they're not, strictly speaking, unsolicited, and therefore they are not spam. And even though we and our customers send out literally *billions* of email messages, we're not trying to annoy people—in fact we are trying to help them. Sending one message after another, each time with a different subject line, is how we discover what someone wants. We're learning about them. We're *listening* to them.

Thus, what we're creating is not spam. In fact, the official line is that HubSpot hates spam, and wants to stamp out spam. We want to protect people from spam. Spam is what the bad guys send, but we are the good guys. HubSpot has even created a promotional campaign, with T-shirts that say MAKE LOVE NOT SPAM. This is breathtaking and brazen. This is pure Orwellian doublespeak. Night is day, black is white, bad is good. Our spam is not spam. In fact it is the opposite of spam. It's anti-spam. It's a shield against spam—a spam condom.

To me this seems like complete bullshit. Of course we're creating spam. What else can you call it when you blast out email messages to millions of people? For years after I leave HubSpot I will continue to receive "lovable marketing content" from HubSpot marketing people. The messages are addressed "Dear Marketing Fellow" and offer a free software download or invite me to check out an e-book. Some are addressed to Heinz Doofensmirtz, the CEO of Doofensmirtz Evil, Inc., because I once filled out a form using that name, too. "Hi Heinz," says a note from my good friend and former manager, Wingman. "Do you know the ROI on Doofensmirtz Evil, Inc.'s marketing efforts?"

In December 2015, as I write this, I am still receiving them. Just this morning I got one from a "senior growth marketing manager," offering me a six-hour course about inbound marketing and a certification. Once I pass an exam, I will get a "personalized badge and certificate." I can add this to my LinkedIn profile, or even "proudly hang it on your desk," my friend from HubSpot writes.

I get loads of these emails, all sent under the names of real people at HubSpot, often from people I know and worked with, including Wingman. The emails are set up to look like actual personal email messages. Instead of coming from a generic address like offers@hubspot.com, they come from an individual's HubSpot email address and include a sign-off with that person's name and title and Twitter handle at the bottom, under a closing like, "All the best," or "For the love of marketing."

This is what we learn in our training sessions. This is what we're taught how to do. I can't tell if the people around me actually believe this rubbish we're being fed. They seem to, but maybe they're just playing along. As for me, I am completely transfixed. I've never seen or heard anything like this. Have you ever received a call from one of those annoying telemarketers and wondered what it must be like on his end of the phone? How many people are in the room where he is sitting? How does he talk people into buying whatever he's selling? How did he learn how to do this? How does he rationalize what he does? The online version of that telemarketer's world is the one that I've now entered. I'm in the Land of Spam, learning how to send email to lists of names in the hope that some teeny tiny percentage of the recipients will open my message and buy something. It's appalling, but also fascinating. I have to learn more.

"You all must be pretty special to be here," Dave, our trainer, tells us. "HubSpot gets thousands and thousands of applications. Just to be sitting here in this room means you've climbed past a lot of other really exceptional people. Did you know that it's harder to get hired at HubSpot than it is to get accepted at Harvard?"

That line about Harvard is one that gets tossed around a lot. I hear it over and over again. Halligan likes to tout it. I have no idea how they came up with the claim, but Harvard has a 6 percent acceptance rate, so I suppose they just figured out that in a certain year HubSpot had hired fewer than 6 percent of people whose resumes they had seen, so that makes HubSpot more exclusive than Harvard. This is ridiculous, and oddly enough not that big of a deal: McDonald's and Walmart have at times also hired fewer than 6 percent of job applicants. Nevertheless, people at HubSpot take it seriously. I suppose it makes the new hires feel special.

HubSpot seems to recruit a certain kind of person: young and easily influenced, kids who belonged to sororities and fraternities or played sports in college. Many are working in their first jobs. As far as I can tell there are no black people, not just among my recruiting class, but across the entire company. The HubSpotters are not just white but a certain kind of white: middle-class, suburban, mostly from the Boston area. They look the same, dress the same. The uniformity is amazing.

HubSpot prides itself on having numbers for everything—it's *a data-driven organization*—and for being radically transparent. Yet oddly enough, HR, or "people operations," as it is called, claims to have no statistics on diversity. One day, after sitting through a company meeting and noticing the bleachy-clean, driven-snow, Mormon-level whiteness of the crowd, I send an email to a woman in HR asking if we have any statistics about diversity. She sends back a terse response: *No. Why?*

Rounding up the right kind of eager-beaver young white people is just the first step. Next, HubSpot applies a two-part process of indoctrination. First the newcomers are reminded how lucky they are to be here. Then comes the threat, which is that HubSpot is so competitive, and so intense, that a lot of people simply can't make the grade.

"Look around the room," Dave says. "A year from now, a lot of the people around you aren't going to be here anymore."

At HubSpot only the best survive. Getting in is just the first step. Now we all have to earn our place on the team. For the people who are going to work in the sales department this process will be particularly brutal. The reps have high quotas, and if you fall short, you get cut. Most companies put sales reps on a quarterly or annual quota. At HubSpot the quotas are monthly, which means sales reps never come up for air. The sales department churns through these young hires. Bring them in, burn them out, toss them away, find new ones—that's the model.

In every aspect of life, we're told, there is a HubSpotty way of doing things. Nobody can really explain what *HubSpotty* means, but it is a real word that people use, all the time. Some people are more HubSpotty than others. Some are 100 percent HubSpotty, possessed of a HubSpottiness that is so complete as to be beyond reproach. Those people "bleed orange." Their ideas cannot be questioned. They can do pretty much anything they want. They are the HubSpot equivalent of a Level 8 Operating Thetan in Scientology.

Newcomers are by definition not HubSpotty yet. We have to earn that designation, and it takes time. Nobody just comes in and gets accepted. A big part of establishing your HubSpottiness involves being relentlessly upbeat and positive. HubSpot is like a corporate version of Up with People, the inspirational singing group from the 1970s, but with a touch of Scientology. It's a cult based around marketing. The Happy!! Awesome!! Start-up Cult, I began to call it. Instead of ID badges, the company gives out rubber ID bracelets with the HubSpot logo on them. The bracelets contain a transponder that unlocks doors into different parts of the office. It feels ridiculous and cultish to wear a special bracelet, but you can't get anywhere without one.

I've spent years writing incredibly over-the-top satire about the technology industry, inventing stories in which Steve Jobs possesses the power to hypnotize people just by staring at them, and depicting Apple's headquarters in Cupertino, California, as a crazy cult compound policed by rifle-toting public relations people and populated by brainwashed corporate zombies who speak their own private jargon and all truly believe they are doing incredibly important work, making the world a better place.

Now I am encountering a real-life version of this, at a company in Kendall Square. It's amazing. It's the craziest, best thing ever. I love this place the way I love movies like *Showgirls* and *Battlefield Earth* and anything with Nicolas Cage—movies that are so bad you can't believe they exist, yet you're glad they do, movies that are so bad that they're good.

Five

HubSpeak

S o I can be the DRI on this, or Jan and I can be DRIs together, and we'll coordinate with Courtney to work up some potential KPIs, and then we can all meet again in like a week or two and we'll present some ideas and then we can develop an SLA. Does that sound good?"

This is Marcia, the senior member of the blog team, talking to the content team, of which I am now a member. I'm about one month into my time at the company. I've finished my training program. I've still never heard anything from Cranium about what he wants me to do. So every day I just show up and say yes to every meeting that I'm invited to attend. There are lots of meetings. Endless meetings. Entire days book up with meetings.

This meeting is taking place in a conference room on the second floor. We're sitting around a table, each of us with a laptop open. In attendance are the three women from the blog team—Marcia, Jan, and Ashley—and three women who write e-books, plus Paige, who has been hired to do market research.

Zack is nominally in charge. He has called the meeting because he wants the blog team to start coordinating its efforts with the e-book writers. The truth is that Zack is new and he's young, and two of the women on the blog team have been here for years and they can't stand the women who write the e-books and they have no intention of doing anything that Zack says. So Marcia is just yessing him to death, and filling the air with gibberish and jargon, things like KPI, DRI, SLA, TOFU, MOFU, SFTC, and SMB.

I have no idea what any of this mean. Afterward I pull Zack aside and ask him for a translation.

"TOFU and MOFU refer to the sales funnel—top of funnel and middle of funnel," he says. "SFTC means solve for the customer. SMB is small and medium-size business. SLA means a service-level agreement. DRI means directly responsible individual—it means the person who will be in charge of this task. KPI means key performance indicator, or what are the goals of this project."

Put them all together, and what Marcia was saying was that she and Jan would be in charge of the project—they'll be the DRIs—and they would try to figure out some suggested goals for the project, meaning the KPIs, and once they had those in place then the two teams, blog and e-book, could go over the goals and revise them, and finally agree on which things each side needs to do for the other on a monthly basis. That agreement will form the SLA, or service-level agreement.

Both teams need to bear in mind that they need to create some content for new prospects—the TOFU people—and different content for leads that are already in our system, or MOFU. All of the content should be aimed at SMBs, and all of the ideas should be based on what customers need, rather than what the writers think is interesting, because at HubSpot we're supposed to always solve for the customer, or SFTC.

I want to tell Zack that they all need to STFU because WTF does any of this have to do with how ordinary human beings actually speak to one another. Instead, I try a more diplomatic approach.

"Why don't we just say, 'Who's going to be in charge of this?' And instead of asking about KPIs, we could say, 'What are the goals?' That would be like speaking English. You know what I mean?"

Zack says he does know what I mean. He majored in English at college. But these are the terms people use here.

HubSpot has its own language, with so many terms and acronyms that they've created a special page on the corporate wiki where new people, like me, can look things up. *HubSpeak* is what I start calling it, but only to myself.

Arriving here feels like landing on some remote island where a bunch of people have been living for years, in isolation, making up their own rules and rituals and religion and language—even, to some extent, inventing their own reality. This happens at all organizations, but for some reason tech start-ups seem to be especially prone to group-think. *Drinking the Kool-Aid* is a phrase everyone in Silicon Valley uses to describe the process by which ordinary people get sucked into an organization and converted into true believers. Apple and Google are famous for being filled with Kool-Aid drinkers. But every tech start-up seems to be like this. Believing that your company is not just about making money, that there is a meaning and a purpose to what you do, that your company has a mission, and that you want to be part of that mission—that is a big prerequisite for working at one of these places.

How that differs from joining what might otherwise be called a cult is not entirely clear. What is the difference between a loyal employee and a brainwashed cultist? At what point does a person go from being the former to the latter? The lines are fuzzy. Perhaps by accident, or perhaps not, tech companies seem to employ techniques similar to those used by cults, the creation of special language being one example.

At HubSpot, employees abide by precepts outlined in the company's culture code, a document that codifies HubSpot's unusual language and sets forth a set of shared values and beliefs. The culture code is a manifesto of sorts, a 128-slide PowerPoint deck titled "The HubSpot Culture Code: Creating a Company We Love."

The code's creator is Dharmesh Shah, HubSpot's co-founder. Inside the company he is always referred to simply by his first name, Dharmesh, and some people seem to view him as a kind of spiritual leader. Dharmesh claims it took him one hundred hours to make the slides. He sent me a link to the slide deck a few days after I interviewed with him and Halligan, I suppose as an inducement to join the company. He said it was a slide deck that "describes HubSpot's culture."

The code depicts a kind of corporate utopia where the needs of the individual become secondary to the needs of the group—"team > individual," one slide says—and where people don't worry about work-life balance because their work *is* their life.

In creating this manifesto Dharmesh is actually conducting an interesting experiment. Corporate cultures usually evolve organically, but Dharmesh is trying to create a culture artificially and impose it on his organization. The use of the word *we* in the subtitle of the code—"Creating a company *we* love"—implies a sort of consensus. In reality, Dharmesh is a creating a company that *he* loves and hoping to persuade his employees to love it along with him.

The culture code asks, "What does it mean to be HubSpotty?" and then defines the meaning of that term explaining a concept that Dharmesh called HEART, an acronym that stands for humble, effective, adaptable, remarkable, and transparent. These are the traits that HubSpotters must possess in order to be successful. The ultimate HubSpotter is someone who can "make magic" while embodying all five traits of HEART.

Much of the code is "aspirational," as Dharmesh concedes, meaning that some of these values are ones that HubSpot doesn't actually put into practice yet, but hopes to someday. One of HubSpot's values involves being transparent, and not just transparent but "radically and remarkably transparent."

The culture code has been an enormous PR coup for the company and a model that a lot of other start-ups have emulated. When Dharmesh posted his slides online they received more than one million views. This inspired him so much that now he is setting out to write a book about corporate culture.

Dharmesh fancies himself a kind of New Age management guru, a person who can teach other people how to run companies—which is odd because, as I will discover after a few months at the company, Dharmesh doesn't run the engineering department and as far as I can tell he doesn't seem to have any day-to-day role at HubSpot. He is, however, an important investor. He put up $500,000 in seed money to start

HubSpot, and he owns nearly 9 percent of the company, more than any other individual. The only entities that own more are HubSpot's venture capital investors. If Dharmesh wants to use HubSpot as his testing lab for a corporate culture experiment, he can tinker all he wants.

Dharmesh's culture project is unusual enough that a sociology professor at the MIT Sloan School of Management in 2012 spent several months embedded at HubSpot, studying its culture. Unfortunately, when I write to the professor and ask to interview her for an article, she tells me she has promised HubSpot that she will not mention them by name unless they give her permission, and they won't do that until they see what she's going to publish. So much for HubSpot's commitment to "radical transparency." The MIT professor is so careful about her relationship with HubSpot that when she writes back to me, she makes a point of copying HubSpot's VP operations and people ops, who is also known as our "culture tsar," on the email. I let it go.

Dharmesh's culture code incorporates elements of HubSpeak. For example, it instructs that when someone quits or gets fired, the event will be referred to as "graduation." This really happens, over and over again. In my first month at HubSpot I've witnessed several graduations, just in the marketing department. We'll get an email from Cranium saying, "Team, Just letting you know that Derek has graduated from HubSpot, and we're excited to see how he uses his superpowers in his next big adventure!" Only then do you notice that Derek is gone, that his desk has been cleared out. Somehow Derek's boss will have arranged his disappearance without anyone knowing about it. People just go up in smoke, like Spinal Tap drummers.

Nobody ever talks about the people who graduate, and nobody ever mentions how weird it is to call it "graduation." For that matter I never hear anyone laugh about HEART or make jokes about the culture code. Everyone acts as if all of these things are perfectly normal.

HubSpotters talk about "inspiring people," "being remarkable," "conquering fear," and being "rock stars" and "superstars with super powers" whose mission is to "inspire people" and "be leaders." They talk about engaging in *delightion*, which is a made-up word, invented by Dharmesh, that means delighting our customers. They say all of these things without a hint of irony. This is really how people talk, every day. They use these exact words, all the time.

The ideal HubSpotter is someone who exhibits a quality known as GSD, which stands for "get shit done." This is used as an adjective, as in "Courtney is always in super GSD mode." The people who lead customer training seminars are called inbound marketing *professors*, and belong to the *faculty* at HubSpot *Academy*. Our software is *magical*, such that when people use it—wait for it—one plus one equals three. Halligan and Shah first introduced this alchemical concept at HubSpot's annual customer conference, with a huge slide behind them that said "1 + 1 = 3." Since then it has become an actual slogan at the company. People use the concept of one plus one equals three as a prism through which to evaluate new ideas. One day Spinner, the woman who runs PR tells me, "I like that idea, but I'm not sure that it's one-plus-one-equals-three enough."

What does any of this nutty horseshit actually mean? I have no idea. I'm just amazed that hundreds of people can gobble up this malarkey and repeat it, with straight faces. I'm equally amazed by the high regard in which HubSpot people hold themselves. They use the word *awesome* incessantly, usually to describe themselves or each other. *That's awesome! You're awesome! No, you're awesome for saying that I'm awesome!*

They pepper their communication with exclamation points, often in clusters, like this!!! They are constantly sending around emails praising someone who is *totally crushing it* and doing something *awesome* and being a total team player!!! These emails are cc'd to everyone in the department. The protocol seems to be for every recipient to issue his or her own reply-to-all email joining in on the cheer, writing things like "You go, girl!!" and "Go, HubSpot, go!!!!" and "Ashley for president!!!"

Every day my inbox fills up with these little orgasmic spasms of praise. At first I ignore them, but then I feel like a grump and decide I should join in the fun. I start writing things like, "Jan is the best!!! Her can-do attitude and big smile cheer me up every morning!!!!!!!"

(Jan is the grumpy woman who runs the blog; she scowls a lot.) Sometimes I just write something with lots of exclamation points, like, "Woo-hoo!!!!!!! Congratulations!!!!!!! You totally rock!!!!!!!!!!!!!"

Eventually someone suspects that I am taking the piss, and I am told to cut that shit out.

The cheerleading and delusions of grandeur are staggering. At one point HubSpot posts a job listing on LinkedIn, searching for a new PR flack. But because this is HubSpot, the advertisement says we are looking for a "Media Relations *Superstar*." The implication is that the person conducting the job search, our head of public relations, is herself a superstar and thus needs someone who can keep up with her. What she is actually looking for is an entry-level person, probably someone right out of college or with a couple years of experience, who will work for low pay, believing that time spent at HubSpot will look good on a resume.

The advertisement challenges potential candidates: "Think you can get HubSpot on the cover of *Time* magazine or featured on 60 Minutes?" Take it from someone who worked at *Time*'s primary competitor—the only way a company like HubSpot will ever merit that kind of coverage is if an employee brings in a bag of guns and shoots the place up. The question is nuts, and any experienced PR person—any actual "media relations superstar"—would know that. The only person who could answer yes to that question and then apply for the job is by definition someone with very little experience. Like the person who posted the advertisement.

This is the peppy, effervescent, relentlessly positive, incredibly hubristic and overconfident attitude that everyone in the HubSpot marketing department exudes from Cranium on down. These people are super cheery cheerleaders. The whole world of online sales and marketing is filled with people who listen to Tony Robbins audiobooks on their way to work and dream of unleashing the power within themselves, people who love schmaltzy, smarmy motivational-speaker guff about being passionate, following your dreams, and conquering fear.

Conquering fear! I have no idea what all of these people are afraid of, but to marketers, the world is filled with fears that must be conquered. Maybe they like this rhetoric because it makes online sales and marketing seem like some kind of epic adventure rather than the drab, soul-destroying job that it actually is. Marketing conferences are filled with wannabe gurus and thought leaders work themselves up into a revival-show lather about connecting with customers and engaging in holistic, heart-based marketing, which sounds like something I made up but is actually a real thing that really exists and is taken seriously by actual adult human beings, which makes me want to cry.

Except I'm also fascinated by this world. Part of me fantasizes about becoming one of these phony gurus. Some of these people make a lot of money, and all they do is fly around the world giving speeches. Part of me figures that if Brandon the pool installer can become Brandon the multimillionaire author and motivational marketing speaker, why can't I?

To become a marketing wizard, I will first have to survive here for a few years, and that means finding a way to fit in, which won't be easy, not only because I'm fifty-two years old, which is exactly twice the age of the average HubSpot employee, but also because the atmosphere is so different from that of a newsroom. I had expected the transition might be rough, but even so, I'm taken aback by how much I'm struggling. The weird language and the relentlessly chipper attitudes are both the polar opposite of the world I know. Reporters are trained to hate corporate jargon and to eliminate it, not to engage in it. We're expected to be cynical and skeptical, not to be cheerleaders.

Another challenge is that HubSpot has so many meetings. Like most journalists—and, I would argue, most sane people—I detest meetings. At HubSpot they have meetings all the time, even for little things. Instead of just pulling up a chair and talking for five minutes, at HubSpot people will scan your calendar—everyone keeps their calendars online—and send you an invitation for a meeting in a block of time that you've left open. Anyone can call a meeting for pretty much any reason. I don't want to look like a grumpy old man, so I just click *yes* on every invitation. Some mornings I come to work and find my calendar packed with back-to-back meetings for random things that have nothing to do with my job: brainstorm with the funnel team; learn what the e-book team has planned for next quarter; listen in on a conference call with our "social media scientist," a competitive weight-lifter who lives in Las Vegas and basically does nothing; talk to a sales-person who thinks she can sell our software to a newspaper in Orange County, California. I attend everything. I'm here to learn. I want to be a team player.

At HubSpot people use Gmail calendar invites for everything, even for making lunch plans. One Monday morning, Zack, who sits facing me, asks me if I've been to the burrito place on First Street. I tell him I haven't. He says maybe we can go there tomorrow, on Tuesday. Sure, I say.

"Great, I'll send you a calendar invite," he says.

"No need," I say. "We can just go. I'll be free."

"But this will remind you."

"I won't forget. It's tomorrow. I can just put in my calendar myself. See? I just did it. It's now on my calendar."

"I'll send you one anyway."

He does, and a few seconds later the email arrives, and I click *yes*, and now the appointment is on my calendar twice.

This is fine. I don't make a fuss about stuff like this. The one thing I don't want to be is the curmudgeon who goes around saying, "Back in my day, we did things this way." I've been warned that at a place like HubSpot the worst thing you can say is that anything that was done at your last company is something we should think about doing here. Even if your last company was Google or Apple, nobody at HubSpot wants to be told, especially by some newcomer—some *outsider*—that there might be a better way. HubSpot is HubSpot. It's unique. It's dif-ferent. HubSpot has its own way of doing things. We're rethinking everything. We're challenging all the assumptions. We're not just making software, we're reinventing the way companies do business.

Maybe that sounds arrogant, but who knows? Maybe the people at HubSpot have figured something out. Maybe the best way to do something really innovative is to hire a bunch of young people who have no experience and therefore no preconceived notions about how to run a company. Larry Page and Sergey Brin were twenty-five years old when they founded Google. Mark Zuckerberg was twenty when he founded Facebook, and once famously said, "Young people are just smarter."

Maybe Zuckerberg was right. Sure, experience is valuable, but I'm willing to accept the idea that experience can also be an impediment. *Forbes* and *Newsweek* were filled with old-timers who scoffed at the Internet, didn't understand it, and didn't want to understand it. They pined for the good old days. I couldn't stand them. I was on the side of change. Those people had lots of experience, but their experience kept them from being able to adapt.

I'm not here at HubSpot to fight these guys; I'm here to learn from them. If they think it's better to book lunch by using Gmail calendar invitations, then that's what we'll do.

But then, about two months into the job, there comes an experience where the cultural gap between me and the people I'm working with opens up like a yawning chasm, and I begin to doubt whether I will be able to make my way across.

This happens during our personality assessments. A lot of tech companies do these now. The idea is to figure out what kind of person you are, and what kind of people your co-workers are. Somehow by knowing these things about each other we will be able to work together more effectively.

Companies use various tests and methodologies. One popular test is called the Myers-Briggs Type Indicator. HubSpot uses a methodology called DISC, which stands for four basic personality types: dominant, influential, steady, and conscientious. You can be a mix of more than one trait—a D with a little bit of C mixed in, for example.

The basic idea on all of these things is that you answer a zillion random questions, and a piece of software analyzes your answers to determine what kind of person you are. You do the test online. In the DISC assessment, you're presented with statements to which you must answer yes or no. *I am a neat and orderly person. I like peace and quiet. I am very persuasive. I am a very modest type.*

A week or so after filling out my questionnaire I am sent to a meeting where I will find out my results. It's a group encounter, with about twenty people. I'm the only person from my department. The others seem to be mostly from sales. I don't know any of them.

DISC is based on concepts created in 1928 by a psychologist named William Marston, who also created the comic book character Wonder Woman. That tells you pretty much all you need to know about DISC. Other people picked up Marston's concepts in the 1950s and 1970s, and used them to create personality assessment tests.

The ideas are pretty much hogwash, and to make things worse, they are put into practice by people with no psychological training or expertise. At HubSpot, the assessment program is overseen by Dave, the energetic goateed heavy-metal guitarist who runs the company training program. Dave is assisted by a middle-aged woman named Deb, who sports dramatic eyewear.

The day begins with Dave and Deb explaining the four traits to us. No trait is better than any of the others. There are no bad traits and no good traits. They are all just different. We do an exercise where we all have to guess which type we think we are. Then we open our packets and find out the truth. It turns out I'm a D, which means the kind of person who hates sitting through personality assessment encounter groups and team-building exercises. I guessed right.

I'm hoping that the meeting is over, but in fact we're booked to be in this room for half a day, and, sure enough, now that we've all opened our packets, it's time for the dreaded role-playing games.

The big theory behind DISC is that if you know what kind of person you're dealing with, you can understand how to interact with them. Someone like me, with a D personality, is probably going to have trouble working with a C personality, because my personality type tends to be impatient, overbearing, and judgmental, and C personalities tend to be lazy nitwits.

Managers, people like Zack, get the same training that I'm getting, but then they go to an extra class where they learn how to use DISC when they are managing people. Try to imagine the calamity of that: Zack, age twenty-eight, with no management experience, gets training from Dave, a weekend rock guitarist, on how to apply a set of fundamentally unsound psychological principles as a way to manipulate the people who report to him.

If you put a room full of journalists into this situation they would immediately begin ripping on each other, taking the piss out of the instructors, asking intentionally stupid questions. If the boss wants us to waste half a day on *Romper Room* bullshit, we could at least have some fun. My HubSpot colleagues, however, seem to take the DISC personality assessment seriously. The scene feels like something out of *Office Space*, the Mike Judge movie about life as a corporate drone at a company called Initech. Dave and Deb keep asking for volunteers to engage in role-playing games. I keep my head down and avoid making eye contact. Luckily, I'm spared.

We watch an unintentionally funny training video that seems like a parody of a training video. A smarmy host introduces four actors who represent the four basic personality traits. The actors are the kind of actors who get hired to appear in corporate training videos, reading scripts written by the kind of people who write scripts for corporate training videos. After the video, Deb asks us to think about which person we liked the most and which one we liked the least. Then she starts calling on us.

"Who here is a D?" she says.

I raise my hand, but limply. I'm at the far end of the table, hoping she won't see me. She does.

"Dan," she says, "which of those people did you like the best?"

I choose the young African-American woman who was playing the role of the S personality. Deb says that's interesting, because D people and S people often don't get along.

"What did you like about her?" she says.

The truth is, I'm not sure.

"She seems pleasant," I say. "I think we'd get along."

"Fair enough," Deb says. "And which person would you least want to work with?"

That one is easy. There's a guy who plays the role of a corporate robot. He does exactly what he's asked to do, but nothing more. Basically this is a version of Milton, the character in *Office Space* who loves his red Swing-line stapler. When his boss asks the guy in the video why he hasn't sent over a certain report, the robot guy says it's because the boss didn't tell him to *send* the report, simply to *print out* the report. Robot Man says he always finishes his work on time, and he will never be late, but he will never finish early. He does exactly what he is told, no more and no less.

"I couldn't stand that guy," I explained to Deb. "I think it was just something about his face, just the way he looked. He's got that mustache, you know?"

Deb looks at me.

"And why is a guy like that working here, in a start-up? Why is he here? Who hired him? If I had to work with that guy, I'd want to smack him."

Nobody laughs. They all just sit there.

"Well," Deb says, in a patronizing voice, "I can hear your frustration. I think we all can agree that it can be hard to work with people who are different from us. I think what you're trying to say is that you might have a hard time interacting with that person."

"Definitely," I say.

She smiles. "And you would probably have to come up with a strategy for how to deal with him, right?"

"I suppose. But really I'd just want to strangle the guy."

If this were a room full of journalists, people would now be joining in, talking about various ways to kill the guy without getting caught.

Could you make it look like an accident? Could you lure him onto the roof by telling him the boss says he has to go there right away, and then push him off? Could you invite him to lunch, and arrange to have him hit by a car while crossing the street?

In a room full of journalists someone would already be doing an impersonation of the Robot Man. We'd also make fun of the smarmy host, who is a bit like Tom Bergeron, host of *Hollywood Squares, America's Funniest Home Videos*, and *Dancing with the Stars*, only cheesier, which is remarkable because Tom Bergeron is already the gold standard of cheesiness, and yet here is this total amateur, this *complete unknown*, blowing Bergeron away. Maybe the host of this training video should have his own game show. Maybe you could have a game show based on DISC, and pit the four personality types against each other. Put them into a cage and make it a fight to the death: Four drones go into the box, but only one comes out! Who will survive?

But these aren't journalists. An awkward silence has fallen over the conference room. In a gentle voice, the voice you might use to persuade a lunatic to put down the gun and step away from the schoolchildren, Deb says, "You know, Dan, some of the people here in our group today belong to that personality type. Surely you're not going to strangle any of the people in this room, are you?"

I try to backpedal and explain that I was making a joke, but it's too late. They're all staring at me. They don't look afraid; they look appalled.

Later, after the meeting breaks up, I pull Dave aside and apologize for my outburst. "No, that was great," he says, with a tight smile, quickly turning away. "Thank you for being honest."

Which I think means, *Thanks for ruining my training session, asshole.*

It occurs to me that spending twenty-five years surrounded by journalists has not prepared me for life in the outside world. *Civilians* is one term journalists use to describe non-journalists. Another is *laypeople*. Or *normals*.

As I'm now finding out, it's one thing to write about the normal, and quite another to work among them. This business of personal reinvention is going to be more difficult than I thought.

Six

Our Cult Leader Has a Really Awesome Teddy Bear

One morning in early July, about ten weeks after I've arrived at HubSpot, everyone in the marketing department receives word from Spinner, our peppy, ponytailed PR person, that Dharmesh has just posted an *awesome* article on LinkedIn, and it would be *awesome* if we could all use our Twitter and Facebook accounts to promote the article and drive lots of traffic to it so that it can *go viral* and *blow up the Internet*.

Spinner is in her early thirties and has never worked at a tech company before. She's married, and has an MBA from Sloan (that's the MIT business school), and was captain of her college volleyball team. Spinner has a *GSD* attitude and is a *total team player*. She is filled with school spirit! "Go HubSpot Go!" she exclaims in emails addressed to the marketing department.

Promoting a new article by our company co-founder by blasting links onto dozens of social media feeds is the kind of thing that HubSpot's marketing people do all the time. Recently we were all encouraged to vote for HubSpot in some local contest aimed at choosing the best place to work in Boston, and by "encouraged" I mean that HubSpot has been bombarding us with email messages reminding us that if we haven't voted, we need to go do that right now, because HubSpot really wants to win this thing. If we do, Halligan and Dharmesh will put out a press release saying how grateful and humbled they are to have had this honor bestowed upon them.

To make it easier for us to promote Dharmesh's LinkedIn post, Spinner has created some "lazy tweets," Twitter messages that she has written and that we can send out from our personal Twitter accounts, as if we have written them ourselves. All we have to do is click on a link and a tweet will go out from our account, urging our followers to check out this amazing new article about a brilliant management technique. Our tweets will contain a link to Dharmesh's post on LinkedIn.

The lazy tweets make life easier for us, but having a bunch of people from HubSpot suddenly flood Twitter with exactly the same messages at exactly the same time doesn't strike me as the smartest way to promote an article. On the Internet, ginning up fake grassroots support is called astroturfing, and the tactic is generally frowned upon. I'm surprised to see HubSpot doing it, because the company touts its expertise at social media marketing and claims it can teach small business owners how to attract attention online by creating unique, "lovable" content and being "remarkable." But here we are, bludgeoning social media with a barrage of identical tweets, all telling everyone we know to go read this great new article by our boss.

I'm willing to help, but before I post any tweets I take a few minutes to read the article—and what Dharmesh has written nearly knocks me off my chair. The title of the article is "Your Customers Are Not Ignorant, Selfish Control Freaks." Our company's "thought leader" claims he has made an innovative breakthrough in management science: He now brings a teddy bear to meetings, and he recommends that everyone else do the same.

That's right. A teddy bear.

Dharmesh argues that a company should always be "solving for the customer," or SFTC as people call it at HubSpot. This means that in everything you do, you should be putting the needs of your customers ahead of everything else. To remind his HubSpot colleagues of that, Dharmesh has acquired a teddy bear, and he sits her at the table during meetings as a stand-in for the customer. Her name is Molly.

Dharmesh goes on to say that he started out just placing an empty chair at the conference table and pretending that the chair was a customer. But the empty chair wasn't enough, he decided. So now he has taken his *innovation* to the next level and brought in Molly.

Dharmesh's LinkedIn article even includes a photograph of Molly sitting at a meeting, next to Cranium. In the photo, Cranium is the big guy in the white shirt at the right side, and Molly is the little one next to him, drinking what appears to be a Red Bull and looking like she's ready to carve someone a new asshole.

I cannot believe this. Here are grown men and women, who I presume are fully sentient adult human beings, and they are sitting in meetings, *talking to a teddy bear.* And I am working with these people. No: worse! I am working *for* them. At *Newsweek* I worked for Jon Meacham, who won a Pulitzer Prize for his biography of Andrew Jackson. Here I work for a guy who brings a teddy bear to work and considers it a management innovation.

How do people sit in a meeting and not make fun of this? Who can read this bullshit on LinkedIn about a teddy bear and not burst out laughing? Who could respond to this kind of inanity with anything other than complete and total derision?

Does the teddy bear have a mind of its own? Does she ever disagree with Dharmesh, and if so, what happens then? Does she ever contradict the other members of the management team? How, exactly, does Molly lobby on behalf of customers? If you really want actual customer feedback, you could create a customer advisory panel and ask for their input, which is something that other companies actually do.

People on LinkedIn can post comments under the articles, and I figure that Dharmesh will get savaged. But I'm wrong. In fact people seem to think that Molly the teddy bear is a fantastic idea. People post glowing comments saying what a brilliant idea this is, and vowing that they, too, will start bringing teddy bears, or perhaps different stuffed animals, to their meetings.

I feel like Mugatu, Will Ferrell's character in the movie *Zoolander*, when he finally loses his patience and screams out: "Doesn't anyone notice this? I feel like I'm taking crazy pills!"

My colleagues see nothing ridiculous about the teddy bear. Even Zack will not joke about it. This surprises me, because Zack is still sort of new here, and he has worked at other companies, including Google.

I lean around the side of my monitor to get his attention.

"Hey," I say, in a quiet voice, looking around to make sure no one is listening. "Did you read this essay that Dharmesh just published on LinkedIn?"

"I did," he says.

"What'd you think?"

"He's a good writer."

"But the teddy bear," I say. "What'd you think of that?"

"I think it's cool that he's so serious about solving for the customer. A lot of companies lose sight of that."

"Okay," I say. "All right. But the teddy bear. You really think that's a good idea? That's a big breakthrough in management? When you were at Google, if you found out that Larry Page was carrying a teddy bear to meetings, would people think that was okay? Because I think people would be afraid that Larry had lost his mind."

Zack just shrugs. "Start-ups are eccentric," he says.

So that's that. Zack isn't going to dish on the boss. No one is. This in itself is amazing to me. In any place I've ever worked, if the boss started bringing a teddy bear to meetings, he would be a laughingstock, for-ever. There would be stuffed animals everywhere. Mean questions would be asked at all-hands meetings. The teddy bear would be kid-napped and hung from a noose, photographed in flagrante delicto with other stuffed animals, dressed in bondage gear and sodomized by a Smurf. You get the idea.

Here at HubSpot there is none of that. Dharmesh is our Dear Leader. A HubSpotter mocking his teddy bear would be akin to a Scientologist making fun of L. Ron Hubbard's cravat, or his kooky captain's hat.

But maybe I'm wrong. Maybe after spending all those years in the news business I have become overly cynical. Maybe bringing a teddy bear to meetings is the big new thing and everybody is going to do it. Maybe the world has changed, and I've been left behind, back in that outdated, old-fashioned era where people don't bring stuffed animals to meetings. I check with my friend Chuck, a guy who once worked in marketing at a really big tech company. I send him a link to the teddy bear article, asking him if this is really what life is like in the corporate world. "Are all companies like this?" I ask.

Chuck assures me they are not. "Any place with a founder who brings a teddy bear to meetings," he writes, "is a step away from Jonestown." He tells me to run out of this place as fast as I can.

Another friend, Mike, is a former Microsoft executive who now does some angel investing and works with start-ups. He agrees that the teddy bear is nuts, but he says that quitting would be a huge mistake.

"You've only been there for three months. If you leave now, it'll look like you got fired," he says. "And they'll do nothing to dispel that impression. In fact, they'll probably tell people they fired you. They'll do everything they can to make you look bad."

If I quit now, all the reporters and bloggers who wrote stories about me going to HubSpot are going to start asking questions. No way will HubSpot let the stink land on them when they're getting ready to do a billion-dollar stock offering.

"Stick around through the IPO," Mike says. "Even if you have nothing to do with the IPO, if you're working there when they go public, it will look good for you. Then once the offering is over you can get another job."

In fact, Mike says, once the IPO takes place I may have no choice but to find a new job—because I'll probably get fired. Mike's theory is that HubSpot hired me as a kind of publicity stunt. All they wanted was to get a little bit of good PR by bringing me on board. The downside of that is that once the IPO takes place they won't need me.

"Don't take it personally," he says. "This happens all the time. The company goes public and then they clean house. As soon as they register for an IPO, start looking for a new job."

Mike is a smart guy, and he spent years in the corporate world. I don't know if he's right about why HubSpot hired me, but in all the years I've known him, I can't remember a time when he has been wrong.

The funny thing is that I consider myself a pretty cynical person. But apparently there is a level of cynicism that I didn't even know existed, a world occupied by guys like Mike and the people who run HubSpot, where I might be way out of my depth.

Seven

We Need to Make the Blog a Lot More Dumberer

What exactly is my job? What am I supposed to do? After three months this remains unclear. I thought I would be working with Cranium, the CMO. But I rarely even see Cranium. I run into him in the hallway once in a while, and I see him at the weekly marketing department meeting, which he runs. One morning, when I get to work early, I sit with him in the kitchen, and we chat over a bowl of Cheerios. But that's it. He never sets a meeting with me, never sits down and tells me what my job is supposed to be. He's friendly, but he has no instructions or guidance. Just: *Hey, glad you're here.* I'm starting to think that Mike, my buddy the former Microsoftie, might be correct about my hiring.

It turns out that Cranium rarely speaks to any of the people in the sixty-person marketing department. He spends four days a week in the office. On Friday he works from home. He talks to Wingman and apparently to a few other people who are his direct reports, but that seems to be it. He never takes the gang to lunch, never pulls people aside to ask how they're doing, never sets up a one-on-one just to check in or give you feedback.

Instead, he conducts anonymous online surveys. Constantly. *Are you happy? How happy are you? On a scale of one to ten, with ten being the happiest day in your entire life, how happy are you? What if anything could make you happier? How could HubSpot be better?* "More surveys," I suggest once.

Since Cranium is not in contact with me, I am left to get direction from Wingman. But Wingman is equally tuned out. One day he sets a meeting with me to ask how things are going. I tell him I'm not sure what they want me to do. He says I should just write articles for the blog. "Just write about anything you want," he says.

I thought I had been hired to help make the blog better. Apparently not. All Wingman wants me to do is write two articles a week. So that's what I do. I write articles about anything I want, and I send them to Jan, the grumpy editor, and she publishes them.

Day to day, I deal with Zack. Zack has lots of energy. He loves to send out long memos bursting with enthusiasm and peppered with phrases in ALL CAPS about some half-formed idea that he believes will enable us to "conquer the world" and "blow up the Internet." People at HubSpot love that phrase about blowing up the Internet. They use it all the time.

The problem is that Zack changes his mind a lot. We're heading south! No, we're going north! We're taking a plane! No, a train! No, bicycles! One of my colleagues compares Zack to Dug, the peppy dog in the movie *Up*, who is constantly being distracted by squirrels.

Zack realizes that the blog sucks, and he wants to make it better. One day, he asks me to write up a memo explaining what changes we should make. He says he will send the memo to Wingman. Finally, I think, here's my chance to do something.

I write a long, detailed memo explaining all the problems with the blog. The memo isn't vicious, but it is pretty critical. This turns out to be a mistake, because in addition to showing the memo to Wingman, Zack shares it with Marcia, Jan, and Ashley, the three women who run the blog.

Now they hate me. Who am I to come in and criticize their work and tell them how to do their jobs? Marcia has been here for five years, which means she's one of the longest-serving employees in the entire company. Jan has been here for two years, which doesn't sound like much but at HubSpot this makes her a grizzled veteran. They're too smart to show their contempt openly, but it's real, and I can feel it. They're terse when they talk to me. My articles, which until now would just get published the way I wrote them, now get kicked back with suggested edits. Some articles get held for weeks, or rejected altogether because Jan doesn't think they're a good fit for the blog, or because someone at HubSpot already wrote something about the same subject a few years ago.

Marcia and Jan sit across the aisle from Zack and me, about three feet away. They sit facing each other, their monitors back to back, and they communicate by trading instant messages. Marcia types something— tap, tap, tap—and a second later, Jan giggles. Jan types something back—tap, tap, tap—and Marcia bursts out laughing. They're having a blast over there.

"You know," I tell Zack, "I think maybe it wasn't a good idea for you to share that memo with the women on the blog team."

"What do you mean?" he says.

I can't tell if he's playing dumb or if he is actually a simpleton.

"Well I thought the memo was only going to Wingman. If I'd known you were going to show it to them, I might have worded things differently."

Zack assures me that everything will be all right. I wonder if perhaps he has intentionally set a trap for me. There's also the possibility that I am not his intended victim. Maybe he showed the memo to the blog women because he wants to make them miserable and push them out. If they leave, we could hire some real journalists. A new guy in another department used this tactic on his boss, Joanna, whose qualifications and experience he deemed to be less than his own. He challenged the quality of her work; she complained to her boss; her boss refused to fire the new guy. Joanna threatened to quit, and they called her bluff. The new guy got her job.

If this is what Zack hopes to do with Marcia and Jan, it's not going to work. Marcia has been at HubSpot for five years. She was one of Cranium's earliest hires. She and Jan are deeply entrenched. The blog is their fiefdom. And now I've pissed them off with my memo critiquing their work.

There's nothing to do but soldier on and act like that memo never happened. I put my head down and write my two articles a week. But everything I write has to pass muster with Marcia and Jan as well as other people in the marketing department, and soon I start running into roadblocks. Kim, a 25-year-old who buys ads on Facebook and Twitter, spikes stories that she fears might upset those companies. Spinner, the PR woman, kills posts that she considers controversial.

I argue that a little bit of controversy is good, especially for a small company that nobody has heard of. Isn't that partly why Halligan hired me—to stir things up, and get HubSpot some attention? It turns out I have failed to understand the mission of the blog. The blog as it turns out has nothing to do with the things Halligan talked to me about. The blog, as Zack explains to me, has one main goal, which is to generate leads for the sales department.

Just like a salesperson, Jan has a monthly quota to hit, a certain number of leads that she is required to produce. Her quota is insane. The blog is supposed to generate 14,000 new leads every month. Leads are defined as people who fill out a form and hand over their name and email address. The blog gets leads by putting a little box at the end of every blog post inviting the reader to download a free e-book and "learn more." To get the e-book, people need to fill out a form. Hardly anyone goes to all that trouble. For Jan to generate 14,000 leads, the blog has to attract about 1 million visitors a month.

At the end of the month the blog team sends the fresh leads to the sales department, where telemarketers start "nurturing" them, asking them to try a demo of the product. The prospects who look at a demo are handed off to other sales reps who try to get them to buy a subscription. This process is what's known as the funnel. The blog team sits at the top of the funnel, drawing in new visitors, generating new leads, and starting people off on their "buyer's journey"—the lovable, nurturing trip down the funnel that we hope will end with them becoming paying customers.

Our ideal reader is a small-business owner who is trying to learn about marketing, or a low-level person inside a marketing department. "Mary the Marketer" is the "buyer persona" HubSpot uses to describe this bread-and-butter target customer. We also have Ollie the Owner, who operates a small business, and Enterprise Erin, a marketing person in a big company, but Mary is our main customer. (The name of Shah's teddy bear, Molly, is a blend of Mary and Ollie.)

We have conversations about Mary all the time. People talk about her as if she really exists. "Mary is busy," Wingman will say. "She's overworked, and stressed out. There are new social media tools coming out all the time. She needs to stay on top of the latest trends. She's looking for information that can help her get her job done in less time. That's what we're trying to give her." People also use Mary as an adjective, as in, "That's really good Mary content," or "That's an extremely Mary idea."

Who is Mary? HubSpot has created a slide that describes her. She has a bachelor's degree in communications from Boston University, and an MBA from Babson. She's 42 years old and has two kids, ages 10 and 6. According to the women on the blog team, Mary responds best to articles like "How to Create a Facebook Brand Page," "Here Are 15 Free Stock Photos You Can Use," and "Five Tips for Effective Email Marketing." Mary also loves pictures of cute baby animals.

Marcia, Jan and Ashley are great at writing for Mary. They understand Mary, because they are a lot like Mary. Me? Not so much. I am trying to write articles for venture capitalists and CEOs. My articles are of no interest to Mary. Much to my chagrin, Marcia, Jan, and Ashley are way better at this than I am. Despite all my experience as a journalist, maybe because of it, I'm lousy at writing lead-gen blog posts. I have no aptitude for it.

My articles might be interesting, and some generate a lot of traffic, but we don't get many leads from them. My readers are not shopping for marketing software. They don't want an e-book, and won't fill out any forms. In marketing lingo, my stuff does not "convert well." Thus every time Jan publishes one of my articles, she's using up a slot that could have been given to a lead-generation post. As a result, the blog has been falling short of its lead-generation goal. The guys in the sales department are yelling at Wingman. Wingman is yelling at Jan.

No wonder Jan is always walking around looking as if someone just left a turd in her backpack. Her job is tough enough already, and I'm making it harder. On top of that I've had the temerity to write a memo insulting her work. As far as Jan is concerned, I am not an asset. I'm a detriment. I'm the reason Jan is missing her quota. Clearly, this is a problem.

One day a few weeks after my memo critiquing the blog I get a calendar request from Wingman, via email. He wants to have lunch. We go to the California Pizza Kitchen at the Galleria mall, across the street from HubSpot's building. Over lunch, Wingman tells me that our little experiment with producing smarter content—meaning, the stuff I've been writing—is not working.

Wingman has decided that we need to end this kooky experiment with smart content and go back to what works: really basic stuff, the kind of thing that people who know almost nothing about the Internet would be likely to search for on Google. That's what Mary wants to read, and that's what we are going to give her. HubSpot's blog is already packed with low-end content, like "12 Tips for Doing Awesome Email Marketing" and "How to Make Chrome Your Default Web Browser." Wingman says we need to ratchet things down even further. There is an even lower level whose depths we have not yet plumbed.

Basically Wingman is arguing in favor of making the blog dumber. It's fascinating, in a perverse way. Wingman has one goal: to get leads. If our software analytics were to indicate that our best conversion rate comes from publishing a blog post that just says the word *dogshit* over and over again, like this:

dogshit dogshit dogshit dogshit dogshit dogshit
dogshit dogshit dogshit dogshit dogshit dogshit
dogshit dogshit dogshit dogshit dogshit dogshit
dogshit dogshit dogshit dogshit dogshit dogshit

then Wingman would publish that post. Every day. Three times a day. Twelve times a day, if the software said twelve works better than three. It simply, truly, does not matter to him. Wingman isn't a bad guy. He's just a guy who has a number to hit.

My heart sinks. I'm not angry. I'm disappointed. I realize that there probably is a legitimate business to be made from churning out crappy content. But that is not something you hire the former technology editor of *Newsweek* to write for you.

What Wingman is really telling me is that whatever Halligan promised me, it isn't going to happen. Part of me just wants to quit. Instead, I decide to be a good soldier and go along with Wingman's directive. Soon I am writing articles like "What Is CRM?" and "What Is CSS?" aimed at the reading level of Marketing Mary. It's a long way from writing features on supercomputing and artificial intelligence, or interviewing Bill Gates for *Newsweek*. In a way it's humiliating. I hate to think that people who knew me will see these articles with my name on them.

I came to HubSpot with grandiose ideas about creating a new kind of corporate journalism. I was going to give speeches and write books and become a big-shot brand evangelist marketing guru. Instead, at the age of fifty-two, I'm writing lead-generation copy. In the world of publishing, lead-gen is about as low as you can go, a step down from writing copy for clothing catalogs. It's hack work. It's worse than what I was doing twenty-five years ago when I was toiling away in a computer industry trade magazine.

I wrack my brain trying to figure out how this has happened. Why did Halligan hire me, if they were just going to stick me over here, doing this? My theory is that Halligan wanted to hire me but he didn't want to manage me, so he passed me off to Cranium, but Cranium wanted nothing to do with me, so he handed me off to Wingman, and Wingman realized that Cranium didn't consider me important, so he stuck me in the content factory working under Zack and hoped I would just go away.

Wingman doesn't want to hear my ideas about how to improve the blog by producing higher-quality articles written by real journalists. The only improvement Wingman cares about is our lead-generation number. That's what Wingman gets paid to do. That's how he gets measured and how he gets rewarded. He has zero incentive to change anything.

After mulling things over a bit I come up with a solution that will let us attract the audience that Halligan wants to reach without interfering with the marketing blog and Jan's lead-generation goals. My idea is that HubSpot should create a separate, high-end publication, a new website with beautiful graphics and video elements—an online magazine— and put me in charge of it.

I write Wingman a long memo pitching him the idea. I suggest we call the magazine *Inbound*. I mention the idea to Tracy, the vice president who runs the brand and buzz department and organizes the annual Inbound conference. My online magazine dovetails perfectly with the conference. Tracy says she loves the idea.

Wingman waits a week and writes back saying no.

I think this is the wrong decision for the company, but it's even worse for me. I suppose I could appeal to Cranium, but I'm pretty sure Cranium is the one who made this call. Wingman doesn't really have a lot of autonomy. He does what Cranium tells him to do. Even if Wingman did make the decision, I doubt Cranium will overrule him.

One thing I've started to figure out is that the top guys, like Halligan, might really want to change things, but below them there are middle managers like Cranium and Wingman, and entrenched veterans like Marcia and Jan, and these people want nothing to do with newcomers and new ideas. They don't want change. They like things the way things are. After all, they're the ones who made things that way. Some of them have been here since the very early days. In their mind, HubSpot belongs to them, not to these interlopers and outsiders who are now storming into the place and writing memos and telling everybody how they should be doing their jobs. Many of these people have never worked anywhere else. A lot of them aren't very good. But here, they're in charge. And I'm stuck working under them.

Eight

The Bozo Explosion

Apple CEO Steve Jobs used to talk about a phenomenon called a "bozo explosion," by which a company's mediocre early hires rise up through the ranks and end up running departments. The bozos now must hire other people, and of course they prefer to hire bozos. As Guy Kawasaki, who worked with Jobs at Apple, puts it: "B players hire C players, so they can feel superior to them, and C players hire D players." That's the bozo explosion, and that's what I believe has happened at HubSpot in the course of the last seven years.

"How weird are you, on a scale from one to ten?" is an actual question that HubSpot's twenty-something managers ask job candidates during interviews, according to reviews posted on Glassdoor, a website for job seekers. Also: "What does your desk look like? What would you put on it?"

The thing about bozos is that bozos don't know that they're bozos. Bozos think they're the *shit*, which makes them really annoying but also incredibly entertaining, depending on your point of view. Shrinks call this the Dunning-Kruger effect, named after two researchers from Cornell University whose studies found that incompetent people fail to recognize their own lack of skill, grossly overestimate their abilities, and are unable to recognize talent in other people who actually are competent.

Cranium is a classic example. He was one of the first five employees at HubSpot, and in his mind, HubSpot is a huge, important company. He sends us emails telling us that HubSpot has the best marketing team in the world, and claiming that the biggest companies in Silicon Valley are jealous of us. This is insane. I've spent years covering Silicon Valley, and before coming to HubSpot I'd never heard of the company.

The thing is, Cranium isn't lying. He's brainwashed. Better yet, he has brainwashed himself. He has mixed his own Kool-Aid and drunk too much of it. Cranium joined in 2007 and is considered almost a co-founder of the company. It turns out that Cranium's father is a Boston venture capitalist and was once a top sales executive at a software company called Parametric Technology Corp., or PTC. Parametric is where Halligan cut his teeth as a sales guy when he first got out of college. Basically, Halligan worked with Cranium Senior, and later, when Halligan started HubSpot, he hired Cranium Junior to run marketing. Cranium didn't have a lot of experience at the time, but he came with a bonus: money to invest. Crunchbase, a website that tracks venture capital investments, lists Cranium as one of three participants in HubSpot's Series A round of funding in 2007, the year he joined the company.

Cranium believes he is a marketing genius. He has people surrounding him who believe that, too. But sometimes I wonder if Cranium knows what he's doing. One of his ploys to get attention involves publishing an article on Mashable, a technology news site, with the provocative headline 10 REASONS WHY I IGNORED YOUR RESUME. In the article Cranium makes fun of the awful resumes he fields in his position as a world-famous marketing superstar. Cranium says people need to proofread their resumes, catch typos, and spell things correctly—but his article contains typos, and includes a reference to the actor Will Ferrell, but misspells his name as Will *Farrell*.

Some readers post comments praising the article, but others savage Cranium, not only for the Will Ferrell mistake and typos, but for his snooty tone. "Would anyone want to work for HubSpot after the CMO writes something like this?" one person writes. "All the money in the world as payment would not be enough to work for this moron," another commenter writes. "Someone has a power/ego problem," says a third.

Cranium perceives himself as being skilled at recruiting and hiring, yet turnover in his department is so high that people in other parts of HubSpot refer to the marketing department as "the French Revolution." People are constantly being hired and fired, or "graduated," as Cranium says in his emails to the group. I keep making friends, only to have them disappear.

These "graduations" sometimes happen suddenly, with no warning. In my second week at HubSpot I have lunch with a woman named Bettina. She's right out of college, working in her first job, and wants to write a book about marketing to Millennials. That night everyone in the department gets an email saying Bettina has "graduated" and will not be back in the morning. I email Bettina and ask why she never mentioned this at lunch. She tells me she didn't know. Her boss just fired her, out of the blue, and told her to never come back. Usually, Cranium has other people do the firing for him, and he typically does not speak to the "graduates," even in cases where the person being fired has spent years working in his department.

Before my time, Cranium created a weekly video podcast called HubSpot TV, starring himself and a co-host. The show streamed live, every Friday afternoon. I can't imagine many people outside HubSpot actually watched it. Cranium didn't care! He and his co-host kept doing the podcast for *four years* and recorded 225 episodes. Those videos still exist online someplace. They are like a real-life version of the comedy done by Ricky Gervais in the British version of *The Office*, where the goal is not so much to make you laugh as to make you feel uncomfortable. You wish it would stop, but you can't look away.

Wingman is Cranium's right-hand man, his trusty sidekick, the Robin to his Batman. Wingman's experience before coming to HubSpot consists of a few years doing low-level jobs in PR agencies. In 2010, while working at one of those jobs, he co-authored a book called *The B2B Social Media Book: Become a Marketing Superstar.* The implication was that Wingman, then age twenty-six, had achieved marketing superstardom himself and wanted to help others emulate his success. He now bills himself as a "marketing author and speaker."

Like Cranium, Wingman believes HubSpot is an extraordinary place. One month when the blog team almost but not quite hits its lat insane lead-generation goal, Wingman sends around this email: "You all are amazing. I know the work you do is extremely hard, but we are on the verge of doing something legendary. Take a step back and look at what you are building [sic] is a rare thing."

Twice during my time at HubSpot I try to bring in job candidates. Both are in their fifties. One was the founding editor of one of the biggest business news websites in the world and then became a vice president of global digital marketing for a multinational computer firm that did tens of billions of dollars in annual sales. The other is a woman who has spent eighteen years at Time Inc., working on both the editorial and the business sides of the organization. She managed hundreds of people and was responsible for a multimillion-dollar budget.

The woman from Time takes the train up from New York to Boston and spends a day being interviewed by various people on the content team, including one woman who is less than a year out of college. The content factory workers come back saying they are not impressed. The veteran marketing guy meets Wingman for lunch and follows up by sending a detailed plan for how HubSpot can expand its business. Wingman never even acknowledges the email. The marketing guy gets hired as VP of marketing at a different software company. The Time Inc. woman becomes a producer for a major cable news network.

So it goes. Cranium and Wingman have surrounded themselves with people who are younger than they are and have even less experience, but who are loyal. Jordan and Holly are two of Cranium's favorites and were among his first hires. They are Level 8 Operating Thetans, and can do whatever they want.

Jordan is twenty-eight years old, was hired in 2007, straight out of college, and now manages a dozen direct reports. Holly was hired in 2008, also directly from college, and has a small team under her. In addition, Holly has put herself in charge of making parody videos that are meant to promote the HubSpot brand but don't always help the company. "Watching this video gave me cancer" is how one commenter reviews one of Holly's productions, a parody of "What Does the Fox Say?" called "What Does the Web Say?" Says another: "After watching this video I gouged out my eyes and shoved knitting needles in my ears so I would never have to endure it again." The video is so bad that one of HubSpot's engineers posts a question on the corporate wiki asking why the video was even created in the first place. Cranium defends Holly, and insists the video was a brilliant piece of marketing. A few months later, Holly strikes again, recording a video that takes "All I Want for Christmas Is You" and changes it to "All I Want for Christmas Is *Leads*," with lyrics about sales and marketing. Everyone tells her it's great.

Beneath these people lies another layer of fortified bozofication, which consists of people like Sharon, a forty-something woman who describes herself on Twitter as a "manic pixie dream girl" and calls herself a member of the management team even though she has no one reporting to her. "I manage a team of one," she tells us one day in a department meeting, and by *one* she is referring to herself. She runs "influencer relations," which means she's supposed to identify people who influence corporate software buying decisions, and become friendly with them. One year at Halloween she gives a speech at a marketing conference while wearing a witch costume, with sparkly shoes, a broom and a big pointy black hat. She posts pictures of herself doing this on Twitter.

Marcia from the blog team, who has been at HubSpot since 2008, discovers that by changing the date or byline or some of the information in an old blog post she can trick Google into thinking the post is new, which boosts its rank in search results so it gets more traffic. She starts changing the dates on old blog posts, and writes a blog post teaching Marketing Mary how to do the same. "Historical Blog Search Engine Optimization," she calls it.

Ashley, the youngest blogger, publishes a post titled, "Fifteen Common Grammar Mistakes We All Need to Stop Making," in which she (a) suggests the passive voice is grammatically incorrect, and (b) claims that "e.g." stands for "example given." Ashley also dreams up a solution to one of Marketing Mary's problems, which is how to come up with ideas for new blog posts. Ashley's solution is a sort of Mad Libs generator, which she calls the Blog Topic Generator. Type in three keywords, and the BTG will spit out three headlines. The problem is that the headline ideas come from Ashley, whose preferences lean toward BuzzFeed-style lists ("15 Reasons," "7 Ways") and Miley Cyrus.

The idea is obviously cockeyed. A child could see that. Nevertheless, Zack allows Ashley to proceed. Zack believes that computers one day will do the work of content generation instead of humans. The BTG is just a first step, ushering in this brave new world. Ashley schedules countless meetings to "brainstorm" ideas and give us progress reports. At last, with great fanfare, Marcia, Jan, and Ashley launch the BTG. The project immediately blows up in their faces, because the BTG produces ridiculous, pointless results. A woman who runs a blog for a hospital complains in the comment section that she tried to use the BTG to generate ideas for Cervical Cancer Awareness Month and received the following:

WHY WE LOVE CERVICAL CANCER
(AND YOU SHOULD TOO!)

and

MILEY CYRUS AND CERVICAL CANCER:
10 THINGS THEY HAVE IN COMMON

Those headlines are so good that I want to print them out in seventy-two-point headline typeface and paste them on the wall. The BTG is never spoken of again. But it remains online, because, as one manager tells me, if they take it down that might hurt Ashley's feelings. Six months later, Ashley gets a promotion.

These are the bozos. They are graspers and self-promoters, shameless resume padders, people who describe themselves as "product marketing professionals," "growth hackers," "creative rockstar interns," and "public speakers." They create websites to build their "personal brands," with huge photos of themselves and lists of their accomplishments. They have a Toastmasters club, where they take turns giving presentations and sharing tips on the art of making PowerPoint slide decks. They dream up ridiculous activities, like having a scavenger hunt in Kendall Square or going kayaking on the Charles River.

Marcia and Jan, who run the blog, decide to have a "content hackathon," where they will round up a bunch of people and work late into the evening, brainstorming ideas for blog posts. On the day of the hackathon I'm packing my bag to go home when Olivia, an intern, asks why I'm leaving. I tell her I have two kids at home and dinner waiting for me, but in addition to that, I don't see the point of pulling an all-nighter just to write some blog posts.

She looks at me as if I'm an imbecile. "It's a *hackathon*," she says.

"I know," I say, "but why have a hackathon? If we need more blog posts, why can't we just write a few extra posts over the next few weeks and bank them up?"

She pauses. She really is a very nice young woman, and I like her a lot. "There's food," she says.

I go home.

The greatest of all bozo events is Fearless Friday. This is organized by Jordan, the twenty-something manager who has read Facebook COO Sheryl Sandberg's book *Lean In* and been inspired by Sandberg's admonition that women should "do what you would do if you weren't afraid." Jordan seems to believe that Sandberg's admonition can be used as the basis of a one-day exercise, which she dubs Fearless Friday.

She sends us this email:

```
We've got a brilliant team and, at times, it can
be hard to innovate due to fear of failure and
the pressure of our day-to-day goals. That's why
we're creating this day to exist in total isola-
tion to work on ANY project that you're passionate
about. The only goal: Be Fearless.
```

I read the email and forget about it. A couple weeks later, on a Thursday afternoon, I'm sitting at my desk when Ashley from the blog team suddenly asks me, "So what are you going to do for Fearless Friday?"

"Oh," I say, "when is that?"

"It's tomorrow!" Her big eyes widen with alarm. "Did you not sign up? You were supposed to sign up! Each team is doing a different project."

"I think I'm going to skip it."

"You can't skip it! You have to pick one of the activities."

"What are the choices?" I say, filled with dread.

"It's all on the wiki," she said. "I'll send you a link."

"No, look, you can just tell me."

She is, after all, sitting right next to me.

"No, I'll send it to you," she says. I guess she thinks it will be good for me to learn how to do these things by myself.

I pull up the link. The idea of Fearless Friday is that we will break into small teams and spend the day doing something *fearless*. That can be anything we want, but there is one thing we cannot do, which is our actual job. No matter how busy you are, the prime directive is this: *No working on your actual job.*

There's no getting out of this. There are no exceptions. I have no idea by whose authority we are commanded to do these things. Jordan is not my boss, but here she is, making us all stop work for a day. After doing some research, I discover that Jordan was one of Cranium's first hires, and that in fact he knew her before he came to HubSpot. They worked together at a software company where Cranium was a marketing manager and Jordan was a college intern. At that company, Jordan's uncle was the VP of marketing. He was the one who hired Cranium. He's also a longtime HubSpot customer.

In other words, at HubSpot Jordan can do anything she wants. In this case, I believe Jordan wants to demonstrate her leadership abilities by appointing herself the leader of our whole group for a whole day. Marketing people are obsessed with leadership. Attend any marketing conference and you will find someone giving a speech to an auditorium full of glassy-eyed marketing drones, telling them that they are *all* leaders.

Jordan has added a clever twist by attaching her exercise to Sandberg's feminist manifesto. Tech companies like HubSpot are sensitive, and rightfully so, about having so few women in top positions. Connecting Fearless Friday to the cause of female empowerment pretty much forces the company to go along with it, although I doubt that anyone in management is paying enough attention to know that Fearless Friday is even taking place. The linkage to feminism also makes it impossible for me to skip, because if I do I will risk looking like a classic middle-aged male chauvinist, the old guy who won't take part in an exercise just because it's being led by a woman.

According to the wiki page, other people in the department have already appointed themselves team leaders and decided what their teams will do. I don't want to think about what kind of *fearless* things these people have come up with. I have visions of things like jumping out of airplanes, wrestling bears, or seeing who can stand on the subway tracks for the longest time. Luckily it's nothing that extreme. One group, under the direction of team leader Jan, will create personal accounts on BuzzFeed and each write one post for that site. Another team will make paintings to decorate our offices. A third will do something that involves sending thank-you notes to customers. Those are the choices.

The next morning we all gather in the big conference room on the first floor, where Jordan stands at the podium, grinning like an activity director at summer camp. "How will we know that this day has been a success?" she asks rhetorically. "Well, just by doing this, just by being here, right now, we've already succeeded!"

Well then, I think, if that's the case, then let's declare victory and go home. It's a nice day. I could play some golf. I don't actually play golf. I don't even like golf. But I would rather play golf than do this.

Unfortunately, going home is not an option.

I join Jan's group and settle down to write my BuzzFeed post. After a grueling hour, I'm done. I spend the rest of the day wandering around, checking out the other teams. The best by far are the women who are making paintings. Their team leader is Olivia, who a few months ago was an intern but now seems to have become a full-time employee. They have big pieces of poster board and jars of paint from an art supply store, all spread out on the carpet in the main conference room. The paintings are ghastly. I pretend to love them. I ask if I can take photographs. The painters proudly hold up their work, beaming with pride. One of them has created a painting of the HubSpot sprocket logo. Another has just used a paintbrush to write words: "Marketing is not (just) arts and crafts," her poster says.

At the end of the day we regroup in the first-floor conference room to discuss our results. What have we learned? What bold new outside-the-box ideas can we take away from this day and apply to HubSpot's marketing plans? The team leaders give presentations.

At home that night, I tell my kids about this and show them the photos of the paintings. They think this is hilarious. They are now eight years old, in the third grade. They claim their classmates could make better paintings than what the grown-ups at HubSpot have produced. Even preschoolers could do better, they say.

The following Monday, when I leave for work, they taunt me: "Have a good day at kindergarten, Daddy! Have fun making your paintings!" At the office I find that everyone is talking about Fearless Friday and what an *awesome* success it was. Emails are whizzing around, with everyone praising Jordan for doing such an *awesome* job.

A few weeks later Jordan announces that Fearless Friday was such a huge success that we're going to be doing it again.

"Welcome to the world of start-ups," my friend Harvey says when I tell him about Fearless Friday. Harvey is about my age, maybe a little older. He lives in San Francisco. He spent years working at big tech companies, but a few years ago he left a very cushy gig and took a job as a vice president at a start-up, a tiny place that had less than one hundred employees. Eleven months after he joined, the company was acquired for more than $1 billion. Harvey won't tell me how much he made, but I'm guessing it's more than $10 million. Now he has joined another start-up, this time with a C-level title, and is hoping to do it all over again.

Harvey is one of the people who encouraged me to bail out of journalism and take the job at HubSpot. He's calling to check in and see how things are going. I tell him I'm frustrated. It's not just batshit crazy stuff like Fearless Friday. It's everything. Decisions get made but no one knows who made them. Who's in charge? Nobody. Everybody. One day we are told the company will focus on big enterprise customers and that this decision has been etched in stone and will not change. Two weeks later, we're going back to selling to small businesses.

"I'm worried," I tell him. "This place seems out of control."

Harvey says everything I'm describing about HubSpot is absolutely normal. "You know what the big secret of all these start-ups is?" he tells me. "The big secret is that nobody knows what they're doing. When it comes to management, it's amateur hour. They just make it up as they go along."

Examples abound of tech start-ups trying to bring in more experienced people who end up leaving, sometimes citing a lack of "culture fit." Evan Spiegel, the twenty-five-year-old founder of Snapchat, a photo sharing application, raised $1 billion in venture funding and realized, or was told by his investors, that he needed to hire people who could run a business and make money. Spiegel brought in veterans from Facebook and Google, then lost eight top executives in less than a year, with some people lasting only six months, according to Business Insider. Then there is twenty-two-year-old Lucas Duplan, whose wildly overhyped start-up, Clinkle, hired a well-known VP of engineering only to have the guy quit *after one day*. Soon after that, five other executives also abandoned ship.

Even some of the biggest and best-known new tech companies are totally dysfunctional. Twitter, for example, seems to have survived in spite of its management rather than because of it. The company is valued at $13 billion and not long ago was valued at more than $30 billion. Yet Twitter has never reported an annual profit, and has lost billions of dollars. For nine years Twitter has undergone wave after wave of management upheaval, hiring and firing CEOs, reshuffling, reorganizing, announcing new business plans, making acquisitions. The people responsible for this mess have become incredibly wealthy. Two of Twitter's co-founders, Evan Williams and Jack Dorsey, are billionaires.

Dorsey once had blue hair and played music in the street. For a while he went around dressing like Steve Jobs. Then he was obsessed with Japanese culture. Then he was going to become a fashion designer. Then he reportedly wanted to be mayor of New York. After being pushed out of Twitter he started a payment company called Square, which raised $590 million in venture funding and in November 2015 successfully sold shares to the public, despite having lost nearly $500 million—half a billion dollars!—in just four years. In 2005, Dorsey became CEO of Twitter again, so he now runs *two* companies.

Williams left Twitter and founded Medium, but by 2015, after three years in business, he still was not sure what he wanted that company to be, and he started firing people he had just hired. Williams also runs a venture capital firm, Obvious Ventures, which in 2015 raised $123,456,789—get it?—from limited partners such as noted technologist Leonardo DiCaprio.

A third Twitter co-founder, Biz Stone, has a net worth of $200 million and since leaving Twitter has launched two companies, Jelly and Super. Nobody, including Stone himself, seems to understand what these companies do. In one interview, trying to explain Super, Stone said: "I know this is eye-rollingly, hallucinogenically optimistic . . . but our mission is to build software that fosters empathy."

Now *that* is some pure, unadulterated bozo talk. Unfortunately, such rhetoric has become the rule rather than the exception inside tech start-ups.

By the occasion of the inaugural Fearless Friday I've come to realize that HubSpot is just as crazy as the rest of them. But all of HubSpot's lofty bullshit about inspiring people and being remarkable and creating lovable content might actually be part of a cynical, and almost brilliant, strategy. HubSpot is playing the game, saying the kind of ridiculous things that investors now expect to hear from start-ups. HubSpot is feeding the ducks.

The *happy!! awesome!!* rhetoric masks the fact that beneath the covers, there is chaos.

"HubSpot was the first software company I worked for, and it was extremely eye-opening," says a salesperson who joined the company during its early days and has since worked for other early-stage tech companies, which were equally clueless and out of control. "People in these companies live day-to-day. They don't know how to run a sales team. They don't have a sales process. They don't even know what the product itself is going to be. The product itself keeps changing. It's mind-boggling, the amount of time and money that gets wasted."

Nine

In Which I Make a Very Big Mistake

By August, four months into my tenure at HubSpot, I am ready to give up. I'm stuck in the content factory writing articles for imbeciles. I cannot do this for a living. I've already appealed to Wingman and pitched him on a project that would be a better use of my time—the one where we launch an online magazine called *Inbound*, with me in charge—and he has rejected it outright. As I see it, there is only one way out at this point. I can leap over Wingman and go straight to the top. I will pitch my idea directly to Halligan and Shah. They're the guys who run the company. And they are the ones who hired me.

To be sure, Wingman isn't going to appreciate me doing an end run around him. On the other hand, what do I have to lose? I'm not going to stay in the content factory, banging out listicles and how-to articles for Marketing Mary. If Halligan and Shah don't put me in charge of something worthwhile, I will put in my year and leave anyway.

I find a day and time when Halligan and Shah will both be in the office and send them a calendar invite, asking for a meeting. They accept. We meet in one of the tiny conference rooms on the second floor. It's just the three of us. I explain to them that I've now been working here for four months, and that I've been stuck in the content factory, where I'm cranking out articles like "What Is HTML?"

"There's no point in having me here if that's what I'm going to do," I say. "And that's not what you hired me to do."

It seems to me that these guys are exactly the kind of rule-breaking iconoclasts who will appreciate my chutzpah. These are start-up guys. Isn't this the HubSpotty thing to do? I'm showing initiative! I'm being remarkable! One of the famous stories at HubSpot is about a young sales guy who had a huge argument with Halligan about creating a new division in sales. The sales guy turned out to be right, and he now runs that division.

"Here's what I think we should do," I say. "I think we should create a really great publication, separate from the blog, where we can publish articles aimed at the kind of people you want to reach. We can't do this on the blog. It gets in the way of the lead generation, and then the sales guys start screaming, and Wingman comes in and tells us to start writing more dumb shit to attract more Mary leads. But a new publication, separate from the blog, could do everything you want to do. We'd have great art, nice layouts, smart writing, interviews with really interesting people. We have really talented designers in our art department, and they'd love to work on something like this."

We could call the publication *Inbound* and tie it in with the Inbound conference, I tell them. I could coordinate with Tracy, who runs brand and buzz, and we could draw on the people who speak at the Inbound conference. We could either get them to write for us or run interviews with them. We could incorporate video. I show them a few sites like this that other companies are producing. Microsoft has one called Stories, run by a friend of mine whose official title is chief storyteller. Qualcomm has a publication called *Spark*, run by a former *USA Today* journalist, that is doing beautiful work.

They love the idea. Dharmesh is particularly enthusiastic. He leaps up and goes to the whiteboard and starts sketching out ideas for a social network that he wants to develop. He thinks we could combine our ideas. We could blend content and social media, and create something that works a bit like LinkedIn.

The thing Dharmesh is describing is far beyond what I imagined. I'd just been thinking of creating an online magazine to promote the HubSpot brand. But Dharmesh wants to take this to a different level. What he has in mind would be something entirely new in the world of media. With the right resources, we might do something amazing. I'm thrilled. I desperately want to work on this.

"You have our blessing," Halligan says. "Go tell Cranium that we said yes. We want you to do this."

That night I go home feeling like a conquering hero. "I did it!" I tell Sasha. "I pitched my idea to Halligan and Dharmesh, and they loved it! Not only that, but they're making it even better than what I pitched them. They're going to put me in charge of my own publication. It's perfect!"

From now on I won't have to deal with Marcia, Jan, and Ashley. I will have my own staff. I've already talked to Atticus, the creative director. He loves the idea and already has ideas for the design. One of his guys will make up some wire frames. Finally, I will be turned loose to do what I was supposed to be doing all along.

The next day, however, when I mention all this to Spinner, she doesn't seem excited. In fact, she looks concerned.

"Who else was in the meeting?" she asks.

"What? It was just me and Brian and Dharmesh."

"Well, that was a mistake. You should have had a witness."

"A witness? What do you mean? Why would I need a witness?"

"You need someone who can back you up, who can vouch for the fact that Halligan really said that."

Spinner explains that just because Halligan and Dharmesh are the co-founders, and just because they approve something, that doesn't mean it will happen. Halligan probably forgot everything we said as soon as he walked out of the room, and he will never think of it again, she tells me. Nobody will feel any obligation to do what Halligan said in some meeting that none of them attended. As for Dharmesh, he's hardly ever here at all.

I can't believe this. I've never worked in a place, or even heard of a place, where the CEO can give an order and the people below him just ignore it.

I send an email to Cranium and tell him about my big meeting with Halligan and Dharmesh. I explain to him that they have approved my idea to launch a new publication.

Cranium writes back and says that this sounds great. He just needs some time to get the pieces in place. The Inbound conference is right around the corner, and everybody in the marketing department is going to be overwhelmed until the conference is over. Let's just get through Inbound, he says, and then we can circle back on this.

The conference takes place over the course of four days in August, at the Hynes Convention Center in Boston. Five thousand people are here to come together, get inspired, and be remarkable. They want to learn how to *crush* it, how to be *awesome*, how to make one plus one equal three. Arianna Huffington gives a keynote speech. Dharmesh talks about being lovable. Halligan rambles on about the Grateful Dead—he's a huge fan—and then starts playing air guitar and doing a weird hippie dance, unaccompanied by music. The dance goes on for too long. It's painful to watch. The crowd eats it up.

After the conference Sasha and I take the kids on a rafting trip in Maine, in a place so remote that there's no cell service. We will be gone until Labor Day. I figure that in September, when everyone returns from the holiday, I will sit down with Cranium and start scoping out my project. Up in Maine we have no Internet connection, thus no tablets or laptops. We play cards and board games, cook on a fire outside the cabin, and hang our wet clothes up on the rafters to dry. The kids make new friends and go swimming and fishing. For the first time in months, Sasha is free of pain; she goes five days without having a migraine, a new record. We're all together and enjoying one another. The kids aren't fighting. It's bliss.

For the first time since joining HubSpot, I feel happy about my work. At the Inbound conference I gave a speech about storytelling and it went over well. Though things were rocky for the first four months, it seems that now I have figured out how to navigate the company and get what I want. Maybe I'm not so bad at this corporate stuff after all!

But when I return to work after Labor Day, I get no word from Cranium. Before I can set a meeting to discuss our next steps, Zack pulls me aside. Some decisions have been made, he says. We are going to redesign the blog. Grumpy Jan is getting a promotion. Zack says maybe I can be an adviser to her.

"Sure," I say. "Sounds good. I'm going to be working on the new thing anyway. But I'm glad to help her out."

"Yeah, see, that's the thing," he says. "You're still going to be working on the blog. They're giving you your own separate section. It's part of the redesign."

From now on, Zack says, the blog will have several sub-blogs. I will be writing one of those sub-blogs, all by myself. That way I can write my articles without interfering with Jan's lead-generation goals.

"But I'm supposed to be launching a whole new site," I tell him. "*Inbound*. The online magazine."

Zack knows about my project. He knows that I pitched the idea to Halligan and Dharmesh, and that they approved it. Nevertheless he says he doesn't know what happened to that idea, but for now it isn't going to happen.

"Zack," I say, "my idea was approved by the two guys who run the company. How can people just ignore what those guys tell them?"

Zack says he doesn't know how people can do that.

"And I talked to Cranium, and he signed off on it too," I say. "This was weeks ago. He told me to wait until after the Inbound conference and then we'd do it."

Zack knows this, too, but again he pleads ignorance. This wasn't his decision. He's just telling me what's been decided. When I ask who made the decision, he says he doesn't know.

I'm trying not to sound pissed, because nobody ever raises their voice around here, but in a newsroom if this happened people would be slamming doors and turning the air blue with profanity. We're out in a public space, a sort of lobby with couches and chairs, with lots of people streaming by.

"Zack." I'm working very hard to keep my voice down. I glance around to see if anyone is nearby. "Zack, what kind of place is this? You're telling me that things just happen, and nobody knows why? Decisions get made, but nobody knows who made them? Does nobody make the decisions? Do the decisions make themselves?"

"Well I think what they want is just—"

"Who's *they*?" I say, cutting him off. "You see what I mean? Who's *they*? All I know is that someone just fucked me, and I don't know who. There's a dick in my ass, but it's a mystery dick. Did *you* make the decision, and you just don't want to tell me? Did Wingman make the decision? Did Cranium? Did Halligan change his mind? You keep saying *they* did this, and *they* want that, but who are we talking about? And why did *they* make this decision? What were *their* reasons? Why didn't I get a chance to argue my case? It's like a voice just comes out of a burning bush and tells us what to do. There's a man behind the curtain, like in *The Wizard of Oz*. Is that where we are, Zack? Are we in the merry old land of Oz?"

Zack remains calm. He has no doubt anticipated that I would be pissed. He says that who knows, maybe someday they will let me launch the online magazine, but for now this is what the team needs. At a place like HubSpot it's important to be a team player.

Zack tries to spin it. He says that in a way I'm getting what I asked for. I'm going to have my own project. Along those lines, I now will have my own monthly traffic goal, a number that I have to hit. Wingman will set the number.

There's not much I can do here. I could confront Wingman and Cranium, and demand to know why they're ignoring a direct order from their bosses. I could go back to Halligan and Dharmesh and ask them to intercede on my behalf. But I'm starting to think that Halligan and Dharmesh don't really have much juice around here. And they have bigger things to worry about. As Spinner told me, Halligan probably forgot everything we talked about the minute he walked out of our meeting.

Spinner was right. I played it wrong. I thought I could jump over Cranium and Wingman, but they have leapt up and blocked my shot. I tell myself that at least I tried, and now I know that I'll just have to wait out a year and then leave. It's over. I'm done.

I force a smile. I tell Zack thanks for the update. I tell him I'm sorry about my outburst, and I can't wait to get started on this new project.

"Oh," Zack says, "there's one more thing."

The content factory has been getting overcrowded, he tells me. So in addition to getting my own little blog, I am going to be moving to a new location, away from the blog team, in the telemarketing call center. It's the loudest room in the building. People call it the spider monkey room. Zack assures me that this move will only be temporary. HubSpot is renovating space on the fourth floor, and eventually our team will move up there.

Once again I give him my best "team player" smile and tell him this all sounds great.

"You know," I say, "I could really use your advice on how to set up this new blog. Do you think you could help me out? I love your writing. Would you be willing to maybe write some articles for the blog? I think we can do something really great with this."

Zack says sure, he'd love to do that. I tell him I'll get on his calendar and set a meeting so we can discuss some ideas.

A few days later, I arrive at the office and find that my desk is empty. The blog girls, smirking, say they don't know what happened to my stuff. I go to the telemarketing center and wander around. There, on a desk against a wall, piled in a sad heap, I find my belongings: my laptop, my monitor, my books, pictures of my kids. Someone has just tossed my things into a cardboard box, carried them here, and plunked them on a desk.

Ten

Life in the Boiler Room

Hi, is that Jeff?...Hey Jeff, this is Pete from HubSpot up in Boston. How's the weather down there in Tampa?...I bet it is! Hey, I wish we'd get some of that sunshine up here, right?...So Jeff, I saw that you downloaded one of our e-books, so I thought I would follow up to see if I could answer any questions you might have...Right. Sure. Okay. Well when would be a good time?...Jeff, what's your marketing plan this year? What are your goals? Have you thought about what you need to do to hit those goals?...Okay, sure. So when would be a good time for us to have a talk?

Pete is a big ginger-haired guy who moonlights as a cheerleader for the Boston Celtics. Loud Pete, I call him. He stands ten feet away from me, wearing a headset and reciting variations of that script, again and again, all day long, in a booming voice. He laughs, he roars, he cracks himself up. He asks questions, gets hung up on, dials again. All. Day. Long. There are dozens more like him in this room.

This is the telemarketing center, and it reminds me of the boiler-room operations you see in the movies, with people arranged in rows, some standing, some sitting, packed in close to each other, barking into headsets. Imagine *Glengarry Glen Ross*, but instead of four sales guys there are a hundred, and they are all in their early twenties, all talking at once, all saying the same things, over and over again. To be sure, the telemarketers at HubSpot are not selling penny stocks or fake real estate. They are selling a real product. I don't see anything fraudulent or illegal in what they are doing. It's just tacky and low-tech. At HubSpot these people are called business development representatives, or BDRs. They wear shorts and T-shirts, with baseball hats on backward, and drink beer at their desks.

Officially, HubSpot's products are supposed to be stamping out cold-calling, just like we're supposed to be stamping out spam. Our sales pitch is that if you buy our software you won't need to hire an army of *outbound* sales reps who spend their days blindly calling people, because our software will generate *inbound* leads and bring the customers to you.

Yet here we are, operating an old-fashioned call center, with a bunch of low-paid kids calling thousands of people, day after day. HubSpot doesn't keep this room a secret, but the company doesn't talk about it much, either. It's not exactly a lovable, magical, one-plus-one-equals-three kind of place. The truth is that most tech companies do some selling over the phone, and for a simple reason: It's cheap. Oracle, a $40 billion software company, has started hiring thousands of college students and cramming them into call centers, as a way to lower its selling costs.

Tech companies refer to these operations as "inside sales," which sounds more respectable than "telemarketing." While a lot of tech companies do some selling over the phone, from what I've been told HubSpot's operation is more aggressive than most. But it has to be. We're selling to small businesses, and our software isn't expensive. The basic version costs $200 a month, and the "pro" version cost $800 a month. Our average customer spends about $500 a month, or $6,000 a year. These are not big accounts. The only affordable way to sell to them is over the phone. As a CMO friend of mine puts it, "The lower end of the market is a dial-for-dollars segment."

HubSpot isn't the only software company using a low-cost sales model. Another friend of mine works at a software company that's about the same size as HubSpot and engages in the same kind of touchy-feely rhetoric while behind the scenes operating the same kind of call center. The company's investors are demanding astronomical growth rates, and while cold-calling thousands of leads may be a brute-force, blunt-instrument tactic, it's the only way they can hit their numbers.

"When you get a hard-charging sales culture in place, and you're trying to keep up insane growth rates, all that high-minded preaching about how the New Economy means not doing things like they used to do in the Bad Old Days—all that stuff goes out the window, and they bring in Alec Baldwin to give his steak knives speech," my friend says. "Our recruiters go out to college campuses and load up the slave ship with a shit ton of identical-looking lax bros. We put them in a frat house with a big brass bell to ring when they close a deal and a basketball hoop arcade game. They walk around shooting hoops while wearing wireless headsets and talking to their victims. We have an army of these people."

So does HubSpot, and the company also has created software that keeps the salespeople on their toes. Our website embeds a tracking code on the computers of people who visit the site. If someone comes back for another look, and if it's someone who has filled out a form and given us their email and phone number, a spider monkey will get an alert on his screen and call that person and launch into a spiel: "Hi, Cheryl? It's Eddie from HubSpot. I see you're looking at our website and I wonder if I can help you find something."

Maybe this tactic lands customers, though it seems more likely to annoy someone or scare them. The sales bros presumably know how creepy this must be for the people who receive these calls, but what can they do? They have a number to hit. Spider monkeys are paid $35,000 a year to smile and dial, with a bonus based on performance. This is the lowest rung on the sales ladder. It's almost a form of hazing. If you want to become a high-level (and better paid) salesperson, you first must make your bones in the telemarketing pit.

The call center is about the size of a football field, with redbrick walls, a high ceiling, exposed beams, and no sound dampening. The noise level is astounding. When I was nineteen years old I dropped out of college and spent a few years working in a textile mill. This room seems about as noisy as the mill.

HubSpot's offices are in an old furniture factory, built in the middle of the nineteenth century. Except for the free beer, the job of a HubSpot BDR doesn't seem much better than the job his great-grandfather might have had in this same room a hundred years ago. The old sweatshop has just been turned into a new sweatshop. In some ways the new one is worse. You spend your day tethered to a desk, with software programs tracking everything you do, counting how many calls you make, reminding you constantly that you're falling short of your quota and could be out of a job next month.

My noise-canceling headphones can't drown out the din. I try wearing foam earplugs under the headphones, and it's still not enough. Even after I plug the headphones into my computer and find some classical music, I can still hear Loud Pete and his comrades barking into their headsets, but at least the sound is muted.

The call center is like a scene from Dante's *Inferno*, a ring of hell. Have Wingman and Cranium sent me here as punishment for trying to go over their heads? Are they trying to make me miserable? If so, it's working.

On the other hand, my exile to the spider monkey room is a kind of gift, because now I am seeing another side of HubSpot and learning how the company really operates. It turns out that HubSpot has a split personality. On one side there is the touchy-feely stuff about the culture code and having HEART, which comes from Dharmesh. On the other side is Halligan's domain, which is this room, where the only thing that matters is making your numbers, and nobody gives a shit about having HEART.

The spider monkey room has one simple rule: Make your numbers, and you live. Fall short, and you get canned. Guys like Loud Pete operate under tremendous pressure and against long odds. They'll hit the phone all day. On average, one call out of eighty lands someone who agrees to look at a demonstration of the software.

That's all the spider monkeys have to do, just get someone to say yes to a demo. At that point the lead gets passed to someone else. Those people are paid better than the telemarketing people, but they too operate under insane pressure. Selling software is a grueling job, and it's especially rough at HubSpot, which imposes monthly quotas on its sales rep rather than quarterly or annual quotas that other companies use.

"Your life hits reset every month. It's a hamster wheel," one high-level sales rep says. "That's why the sales reps are so young. There's hardly anybody who has been here more than five years. People don't last. People who are forty years old, who are married and have kids, they don't want to live like this."

Halligan is a former sales guy. He knows the kind of pressure he is putting on his reps. He is aware that no one can do this job for long without burning out, and he is okay with that. The spider monkeys are not being hired with the expectation that they will spend their careers at HubSpot. They are being rounded up to work for a few years, then go somewhere else.

I don't doubt that Dharmesh really does care about creating a company that people can love, but I am equally sure that Halligan cares only about the numbers. While Dharmesh obsesses about the five principles that make up HEART, Halligan's big metric is something called VORP, or value over replacement player. The idea comes from Major League Baseball, where it is used to set prices on players. At HubSpot, VORP means evaluating the difference between what you are paid and the least amount the company could pay someone else to do your job. It's a vicious metric, with only one goal, which is to drive the price of labor as low as possible.

All that stuff from Dharmesh about being lovable, engaging in *delightion*, having HEART, and creating a culture code—that's great for the keynote speech at the Inbound conference. That's the face we show to the outside world. But there's not much *delightion* in this room.

Yet this canyon of desperation, packed with beer-drinking shitheads trying to hit their quotas—this, I realize, is the real heart and soul of HubSpot. This is where the money gets made. VORP may be heartless, but it works. Halligan never lets up the pressure.

Then again, Halligan is under pressure himself. He has taken $100 million from venture capital firms and is expected to deliver a return. His investors include Sequoia Capital, a firm with a reputation for throwing out founders who fail to meet expectations. HubSpot needs to pull off a big IPO, and to do that, the company must keep growing. By the strange rules of bubble economics, companies do not have to generate a profit before they can go public, but they do have to demonstrate revenue growth. Every month, every quarter, HubSpot's sales must keep rising. A start-up that stops growing is like a shark that stops swimming: dead in the water.

Unfortunately that is what has been happening at HubSpot in the autumn of 2013, when I arrive in the spider monkey room. Our growth rate has dropped. Nobody is panicking, but Halligan is concerned. One day in October he calls a come-to-Jesus meeting for everyone in sales and marketing, and he makes a big announcement—he's booting out Karl, the guy who runs sales, and has started searching for a replacement. Karl is not being fired; he is being moved onto a special project. Still, this is a huge deal. Karl was one of Halligan's first hires. He's practically a co-founder. He is also one of HubSpot's top executives.

Halligan runs through a litany of problems. The biggest one is growth. HubSpot's sales grew more than 80 percent in each of the past two years, but in 2013 the growth rate has slowed to about 50 percent. That's still a lot but apparently it's not enough. Our rivals are growing faster than we are, Halligan says. We've just hit the end of the third quarter, which means results are in for the first nine months of the year and management can estimate what full-year 2013 results will be. My guess is that Halligan and his board of directors have looked at the numbers and are not pleased—and the board has told Halligan to do something about it.

That's the second big piece of news: Halligan says that until he finds a new head of sales he is going to run the sales department himself. He makes it sound like he's coming back ready to kick ass and take names. "I don't want to get up in everyone's shorts, but I'm going to be taking the wheel here for a couple of months," he says. "The machine is just not working that well."

Slowing growth is only one problem. Our churn rate is too high, meaning too many customers fail to renew. Our close rate is too low, meaning we generate a lot of leads but don't turn enough of them into customers. Zendesk, a software company on the West Coast that HubSpot's executives recently visited, has a close rate that is far better than ours. Morale in HubSpot's sales department has plummeted.

"We're going to make some hard calls," Halligan says. "There are going to be winners and losers. People will just have to deal. We're going to make things as fair as we can. But if you're not performing, we're going to put you on a plan."

Being put on a plan is the first step toward getting fired. Most people who get put on a plan don't recover. It's really a way to give you a few weeks to find another job.

It seems to me that the problem is not that HubSpot's salespeople aren't working hard enough. The problem is that (a) HubSpot's software isn't that good and that (b) the way we sell it is inefficient. Despite all its rhetoric about reinventing how products are sold, HubSpot itself relies on an old-fashioned business model based on brute-force lead-generation tactics. We're working too hard and getting too little back for it.

Generating tens of thousands of new leads every month is ridiculous in and of itself; by definition most of those leads are shitty and worthless. The sales department tries to winnow out the best 20 percent and focus on those, but that still means the sales department is trying to chase ten thousand leads every month. "Boiling the ocean" is the business cliché for the way HubSpot hunts for new customers, and it's only one problem. Another is that our software isn't very intuitive, and people can't figure out how to use the programs on their own. So we have to assign consultants to teach new customers how to use the product.

This is all incredibly labor-intensive, and that effort is reflected in the amount we spend to acquire each new customer. This metric is called customer acquisition cost, or CAC, and HubSpot's is soaring. The numbers are going in the wrong direction.

The irony of this is that we tout our software as a modern miracle that lets companies attract new customers and grow faster, while spending less. Our sales pitch is basically *Jack and the Beanstalk*: Buy our magic software, and your business grows to the sky. You'll get more customers, and save money. That's what we tell people.

But *we* use our software. Our business is built on top of our software. We "eat our own dog food," as they say in the tech industry—or, as Cranium likes to put it, "We drink our own Champagne." If our software really does what we claim, why are we working so hard to find new customers? Why do we need an army of sales reps and an army of marketers and an army of consultants? For that matter, why, after seven years in business, does HubSpot still not make a profit? Why does it cost us more to make, sell, and deliver our software than customers will pay to use it? Isn't HubSpot itself the ultimate test case of how well its own software works, and doesn't our own financial performance raise questions about the efficacy of our software?

Halligan tells us that he plans to boost spending on research and development. He wants to invest in technology tools that will help the sales reps sell more stuff and make them more productive. But he's not going to create a new business model, not at this stage of the game. Yes, it costs a lot of money to sell our software, but this is the machine that Halligan has built. It seems to me that the only course of action is to crank the machine into higher gear. Get marketing to generate even more leads every month. Whip the sales department to work harder. Hire more spider monkeys, make more cold calls, chase down more prospects. Get to the IPO.

Halligan caps off the meeting by telling a story about the software company where he began his career, called Parametric Technology Corp., or PTC. When he joined PTC it was tiny, and by the time he left, a decade later, the company was doing $1 billion a year in sales. A lot of people got rich at PTC, and the same thing is going to happen here, he says. People right here in this room are going to make millions of dollars, enough money to change their lives. Halligan's personal goal, he tells us, is to have more money than anyone else who worked at PTC. He knows their net worth, and he's determined to beat them. He's pretty sure he's going to make it.

That's great for Halligan, but I'm not sure how this is supposed to pump us up. He is basically telling us that we should work hard so that he can have more money than his friends.

But Halligan knows his audience. Sales reps love this stuff. They're just like Halligan. They bounce from the meeting all pumped up. Back in the spider monkey room, the lax bros start drinking beer and hitting the phones.

As for me, I'm not feeling so enthusiastic. When I joined HubSpot, it seemed certain that the company would pull off a huge IPO. Today, after hearing the numbers that Halligan just divulged, the place seems a bit rickety.

Nevertheless, I'm hoping they can pull it off. After all, when I joined I was granted twenty thousand options. To get all of my options I need to stay for four years. I doubt I can survive here that long. But even if I stay only one year, I will get five thousand options, and if the IPO goes well, those options could be worth some money.

Ten feet away, Loud Pete is braying into his headset. For the first time ever, I don't mind the noise. Bark away, you male cheerleader madman. Make those calls. Sell that crappy software. Hit your numbers and get us all paid.

Eleven

OMG the Halloween Party!!!

There are two big party days at HubSpot. One is Cinco de Mayo, when the company ships in a truckload of tequila and Dos Equis beer and Mexican food, and five hundred twenty-something gringos go mental in the first-floor conference room drinking margaritas and chowing down on nachos, and Halligan roams around wearing a huge straw hat—the kind that people wear in Mexico, geddit?—like a real-life version of Frank the Tank, the beer-bong-hitting character played by Will Ferrell in *Old School*.

But Halloween is an even bigger deal, a sacred tradition in the cult of the orange people, a day when the entire company comes to work wearing costumes and spends the day running around behaving like idiots. In the afternoon the company brings in food and beer, and work grinds to a halt.

HubSpot people are incredibly proud of this tradition, which they view as part of their culture. Dharmesh even included a Halloween photo in his Culture Code, with this message: "We dare to be different."

Photos of the Halloween madness are also featured on the website, so that prospective customers can see what a cool, fun place HubSpot is. The idea seems to be that this will make people want to work at

We dare to be different.

HubSpot, and will make customers want to buy our software. I don't understand why prospective customers care whether HubSpotters have fun at work. If our software can't save customers money, or make them money, or both, all the kooky Halloween parties in the world won't matter. (As an aside: I urge you to count the non-white faces in that Halloween photo and consider the claim about "daring to be different.")

As it happens, on the day of the Halloween party I have a friend in town. Rose is a friend of mine who works in marketing. She lives in New York and has come to Boston for meetings. She is in her forties and is executive vice president of marketing for a big sports brand. We meet for breakfast at a hotel near the Charles River. Seeing Rose makes me remember my old life, when I wore a suit, moderated panels in Washington, DC, and participated in actual journalism.

I tell her what's happened to me at HubSpot, how I was promised one job but given another. Rose doesn't seem surprised—or sympathetic. Rose is British. She has no patience for complainers.

After breakfast she has some free time, so I offer to give her a tour around our offices. She's heard of HubSpot and is curious to see the software. She thinks her company might be able to use it. I set her up with a sales guy, who gives her a demo, and after she's seen enough I take her for a spin around the offices. I show her my sad little desk in the telemarketing room, which is a bit of a step down from the office I had in New York, which had a view out over Central Park. I show her the nap room and the shower rooms and the groovy kitchen with the candy wall and the little spot on the second floor where they keep the musical instruments for impromptu jam sessions.

I've heard that Halloween would be crazy, but even after six months at the company I am not prepared for what we're encountering. Everyone but me has come to work in a costume. All over the place, packs of actual adults are racing around, whooping and shrieking, posing for selfies. They're dressed up like Smurfs and witches, sexy pirates, sexy Snow Whites, naughty devils, characters from Harry Potter. They're all trying really hard to show everyone how much fun they are having at this totally rad company with all these totally cool people.

But it's not cool. It's sad. And weird.

"I must say," Rose says, "I don't think I've ever *heard* of a company where people come to work in costumes on Halloween."

She does not seem to mean this in a good way.

"Well," I say, "we dare to be different."

I bring her to the content factory, the room where the blog team works and where I used to work before I was banished. I introduce her around. Three women have come to work dressed as the mean girls in the movie *Mean Girls*. The HubSpot mean girls seem not to realize that in the movie the mean girls are the butt of the joke. Our mean girls seem to believe that the mean girls were the heroes.

"We even made a burn book," Fatima tells me. "Look, you're in it!"

Sure enough, they really have printed out an actual burn book, which in the movie is a book where the mean girls make fun of people they don't like or consider to be losers. Fatima flips to my page. "You see?" she says. Indeed, there I am. They have created a page about me, with a photo of me looking old and stupid. There are words, too. I don't read them.

I walk Rose outside and put her in a cab to the airport.

"You have to get out of here," she says. "This place will destroy your soul."

"I know. I figure I'll put in a year and then I'll—"

"No." She cuts me off. "Right away. Right now. Today. Get out."

She closes her door. The cab zooms off. She never becomes a HubSpot customer.

Rose is right: I really should find a new job. But it's November, and the holidays are arriving, and nobody will be hiring at this time of year. I figure I can ride things out for a few more months. I'll go into the office a couple of days a week, just enough to keep up appearances. Over the winter I'll do a lot of skiing. I'll take a trip to Utah and visit some friends. By the time ski season ends it will be April, and I'll have hit my one-year anniversary and can slip out quietly from HubSpot.

I remind myself that I have a lot to be thankful for—realizing, even as I do, that the only people who say this are people who are desperate and miserable. Nonetheless, my health is good. I'm employed. The family is happy. My son has been playing soccer, and this season I have seen all of his games. My daughter has a piano recital and will dance in the local *Nutcracker,* and this year I can attend both of them. Last year I was in San Francisco. Sasha's migraines are under control. She's happier and less stressed out. So what if my job sucks? I'm working. I'm getting paid. Things could be worse.

HubSpot has a policy that says anyone can work from home whenever they want. I now take full advantage of this. When I have to work in the office—usually because there's a meeting that I have to attend—I go in late and leave early. In meetings I say as little as possible. I stare at my laptop and pretend to take notes, when really I'm browsing the web and catching up on Facebook.

Between meetings I return to my desk in the cacophonous spider monkey room, put in my earplugs and headphones, listen to Mozart, and gaze around at the doomed souls. It's a lonely, isolated existence. Around noon I walk across First Street to the Galleria mall, eat sushi in the food court, then return to my desk and my headphones, burying myself in my cocoon. Sometimes I go for a walk around the offices. I visit different floors, just looking around. I'll find a kitchen and make a cup of coffee and sit by myself on a couch in a lounge area, reading news on my phone. By around four o'clock it's dark outside, so I put my laptop into my backpack and head home. Entire days go by when I do not speak a word to anyone. The whole thing feels surreal.

Gradually I slide into depression, swinging between a restless, herky-jerky anxiety and a mind-numbing lethargy. Some nights I lie awake, unable to sleep, my mind racing, until finally I take an Ambien to knock myself out. Other times I do nothing but sleep. I go to bed at eight, sleep until seven, and still have a hard time waking up.

Sasha and the kids can tell how miserable I am. Instead of regaling them with stories about the latest hijinks at HubSpot, as I used to do, now I arrive home and shuffle upstairs and put on my pajamas. There is no choice but to soldier on. Sasha is not working. The job of making money has fallen to me.

A friend of mine, a reporter with a plum job at the *New York Times* and a second plum job teaching at UC-Berkeley, tries to cheer me up: "Man's got to feed his kids," he writes to me one day when we are trading messages and I'm complaining about the horrible hack work I'm doing. "Makes you respect the average bus driver and cafeteria worker a little more," he writes.

I send back a one-word response: "Ouch."

In December a friend introduces me to the CEO of a technology company in Boston. Thomas is an engineer by training, a nerdy guy in his mid-forties. His company is publicly traded and turns a profit. He employs a lot of engineers and doesn't engage in much hype. In some ways his company is the antithesis of HubSpot. But he's friendly with Halligan and Shah, and knows a lot about HubSpot and its culture.

We meet at a Starbucks in the suburbs. It turns out we know a lot of the same people, and we have kids who are about the same age. Thomas tells me he was a fan of my Fake Steve Jobs blog, and he was surprised when he heard that I was going to work at HubSpot. "It seems like an odd fit," he says.

I confess that things aren't going so well, and that I didn't know enough about HubSpot before I joined. "I thought I was going to work at a software company run by a bunch of smart engineers from MIT," I say.

He finds this hysterical. Thomas seems to have little regard for HubSpot's culture, and even less for its software. He makes a joke about Dharmesh, the company's supposed chief technology officer, who doesn't seem to be around much. "I'm the CEO of my company, and I'm still working my ass off," he says. "Then there's Dharmesh. I want *his* job."

He's quick to add that he likes Dharmesh, and thinks Dharmesh is a nice guy. He says he admires Halligan and Shah, and that while they may not be the best software developers in the world, they're certainly good at sales and marketing.

"They've done an amazing job," he says. "I never thought they'd make it as far as they have."

I ask Thomas about something that puzzles me, which is that it seems pretty clear to me that HubSpot is losing a lot of money, and yet Halligan and Shah keep squandering money on ridiculous things—the parties, the beer, the nap room, the free massages, the fancy offices. HubSpot has an enormous kitchen on the first floor, and loads of little satellite kitchens all over the rest of the building, yet now Halligan is remodeling the second floor of the building and will install another kitchen, this one with taps for beer and hard cider. Just to be kooky, HubSpot is also building a replica of a bright red British telephone box, where people can have privacy for making phone calls.

I could see living large if you were running a company like Google, which throws off more than $1 billion in profit—not revenue, but profit—every month. But HubSpot is a relatively tiny company that's losing money. Shouldn't HubSpot be running lean, trying to make their VC money last as long as possible? Shouldn't they be spending their money on software development rather than beer blasts? Why aren't the VCs imposing any financial discipline?

"Do the investors ever visit and walk around? Do they know how out of control things are?"

"They may or they may not," Thomas says.

Board members don't always know everything about a company,

he says. They only know what the management team tells them, and sometimes that is not too much.

"I tell my board as little as possible," he says. "I treat them like mushrooms, I keep them in the dark and feed them shit. I don't want them meddling in my business and telling me what to do."

For that matter, the board members usually don't want to start getting involved in the day-to-day running of the company. Some have their own companies to run. Others are retired, and sit on boards as a kind of hobby. The VCs who sit on HubSpot's board have skin in the game, but it's not in their interest to interfere too much.

"You don't want to get into a battle with the founders. That's a last resort. If a founder leaves, or gets thrown out, investors get spooked. It sends a bad message," Thomas says.

Founders and investors need each other, but they're also wary of each other. It's an uneasy partnership. The founders see VCs as a necessary evil, tricksters who will try to cheat founders or even steal their companies away from them. VCs see founders the way music labels see bands, or the way Hollywood studios see movies—they're the talent, the way you make money. You bet on a bunch of them and hope that one or two hit it big.

As for the wasteful spending, the investors may not like it, but what they really care about is the end game. If Halligan and Shah deliver a big return for their investors, they can have all the free beer and British phone booths and Fearless Fridays they want.

What's more, whatever money they're spending on cool offices and the frat-house parties, it's peanuts compared to everything else. "And think what they're getting in return for that," he says. "They're getting all these young kids who work cheap and don't stick around long enough to vest, and even if they do vest, they don't have much equity to begin with. When you look at it that way, the perks seem pretty cheap."

You could argue that HubSpot would be better off investing in software development, rather than spending money to throw a big conference every year, and hiring Cyndi Lauper and Arianna Huffington to entertain people.

"On the other hand," Thomas says, "what they're doing seems to be working."

I'm a bit taken aback. Thomas is a hardcore engineer, and a frugal manager. His company is way bigger than HubSpot, but he's not throwing money around. Nevertheless, he admires them. The way he seems to think about business is the way I imagine political operatives think about candidates, where all that matters is whether they can say the right things and get themselves elected.

"You know," he says, "I have an idea for you."

He suggests I should forget about trying to become a marketer, but stay at HubSpot anyway. "Think of yourself as an anthropologist," he says. "Like you've been dropped into some strange culture, and you're studying their rituals. You could maybe write about it. It might be interesting."

We finish our coffees and say our goodbyes. When I get to my car, his comment about being an anthropologist stays with me. Wet snow is falling, fat flakes falling on my windshield. The stores are decorated for Christmas. People hurry past on the sidewalk, carrying shopping bags, bundled against the cold.

Thomas is right about the people at HubSpot. They really are like a strange tribe. What's more, tribes like this are popping up all over the place. A new kind of workplace has emerged, with culture codes and frat-house parties and rhetoric about making the world a better place.

But the real story is not just about the free beer and the foosball tables and the talk about being on an important mission—the real story is about why those things exist. The real story is about two founders and a handful of investors who are about to extract more than $1 billion from the public markets, and how they pulled it off.

It seems to me that HubSpot is not a software company so much as it is a financial instrument, a vehicle by which money can be moved from one set of hands to another. Halligan and Shah have assembled a low-cost workforce that can crank out hype and generate revenue. HubSpot doesn't turn a profit, but that's not necessary. All Halligan and Shah have to do is keep sales growing, and keep telling a good story, using words like *delightion*, *disruption*, and *transformation*, and stay in business long enough for their investors to cash out.

Twelve

The New Work: Employees as Widgets

It turns out I've been naïve. I've spent twenty-five years writing about technology companies, and I thought I understood this industry. But at HubSpot I'm discovering that a lot of what I believed was wrong.

I thought, for example, that tech companies began with great inventions—an amazing gadget, a brilliant piece of software. At Apple Steve Jobs and Steve Wozniak built a personal computer; at Microsoft Bill Gates and Paul Allen developed programming languages and then an operating system; Sergey Brin and Larry Page created the Google search engine. Engineering came first, and sales came later. That's how I thought things worked.

But HubSpot did the opposite. HubSpot's first hires included a head of sales and a head of marketing. Halligan and Dharmesh filled these positions even though they had no product to sell and didn't even know what product they were going to make. HubSpot started out as a sales operation in search of a product.

Another thing I'm learning in my new job is that while people still refer to this business as "the tech industry," in truth it is no longer really about technology at all. "You don't get rewarded for creating great technology, not anymore," says a friend of mine who has worked in tech since the 1980s, a former investment banker who now advises start-ups. "It's all about the business model. The market pays you to have a company that scales quickly. It's all about getting big fast. Don't be profitable, just get big."

That's what HubSpot is doing. Its technology isn't very impressive, but look at that revenue growth! That's why venture capitalists have sunk so much money into HubSpot, and why they believe HubSpot will have a successful IPO. That's also why HubSpot hires so many young people. That's what investors want to see: a bunch of young people, having a blast, talking about changing the world. It sells.

Another reason to hire young people is that they're cheap. HubSpot runs at a loss, but it is labor-intensive. How can you get hundreds of people to work in sales and marketing for the lowest possible wages? One way is to hire people who are right out of college and make work seem fun. You give them free beer and foosball tables. You decorate the place like a cross between a kindergarten and a frat house. You throw parties. Do that, and you can find an endless supply of bros who will toil away in the spider monkey room, under constant, tremendous psychological pressure, for $35,000 a year. You can save even more money by packing these people into cavernous rooms, shoulder to shoulder, as densely as you can. You tell them that you're doing this not because you want to save money on office space but because this is how their generation likes to work.

On top of the fun stuff you create a mythology that attempts to make the work seem meaningful. Supposedly, Millennials don't care so much about money, but they're very motivated by a sense of mission. So, you give them a mission. You tell your employees how special they are, and how lucky they are to be here. You tell them that it's harder to get a job here than to get into Harvard, and that because of their *superpowers* they have been selected to work on a very important mission to change the world. You make the company a *team*, with a team color and a team logo. You give everyone a hat and a T-shirt. You make up a culture code and talk about creating a company that everyone can love. You dangle the prospect that some might get rich.

But Silicon Valley has a dark side. To be sure, there are plenty of shiny, happy people working in tech. But this is also a world where wealth is distributed unevenly and benefits accrue mostly to investors and founders, who have rigged the game in their favor. It's a world where older workers are not wanted, where people get tossed aside when they turn forty. It's a world where employers discriminate on the basis of race and gender, where founders sometimes turn out to be sociopathic monsters, where poorly trained (or completely untrained) managers abuse employees and fire people with impunity, and where workers have little recourse and no job security.

In December 2014 Nicholas Lemann published an essay in the *New Yorker* contrasting the vision of work that Alfred P. Sloan, the legendary CEO of General Motors, described in his 1964 memoir, *My Years with General Motors*, with the vision laid out in a series of books published by executives from Google.

In the twentieth-century model under which Sloan's GM operated, companies "were heavily unionized, and offered their white-collar employees de-facto lifetime tenure. Employees got steady raises during their working years and pensions after retirement," Lemann writes. Things changed with the emergence of the Internet and in particular with Google, the first successful Internet company with a large workforce. Google succeeded, Lemann writes, by "breaking the rules about how to run a business."

The biggest rupture involves the social compact that once existed between companies and workers, and between companies and society at large. There was a time, not so long ago, when companies felt obliged to look after their employees and to be good corporate citizens. Today that social compact has been thrown out. In the New Work, employers may expect loyalty from workers but owe no loyalty to them in return. Instead of being offered secure jobs that can last a lifetime, people are treated as disposable widgets that can be plugged into a company for a year or two, then unplugged and sent packing. In this model, we are basically freelancers, selling our services in short-term engagements. We may have dozens of jobs over the course of our careers.

"Your company is not your family" is how LinkedIn's multibillionaire cofounder and chairman Reid Hoffman puts it in his book *The Alliance: Managing Talent in the Networked Age*. Hoffman says employees should think of a job as a "tour of duty" and not expect to stay for too long. In his view, a job is a transaction, one in which an employee provides a service, gets paid, and moves on. In addition to his duties at LinkedIn, Hoffman works as a partner at Greylock Capital, a top venture capital firm. Forbes calls him "the most connected man in Silicon Valley." He is widely respected, even revered, and his ideas about the relationship between employers and employees have influenced a generation of entrepreneurs, who take his word as gospel.

Hoffman's line about a company not being a family traces its roots to a "culture code" that Netflix, the Silicon Valley video-subscription company, published in 2009, and which famously declared, "We're a team, not a family." The Netflix code inspired a generation of tech start-ups and "may well be the most important document ever to come out of the Valley," Facebook COO Sheryl Sandberg once said. Shah used the Netflix code as the model for his HubSpot culture code and lifted the original Netflix line: "We're a team, not a family."

Netflix justified the "not a family" idea by arguing that like a pro sports team, tech companies need "stars in every position." That deal makes sense if you're a professional athlete who can earn millions of dollars a year and retire at age thirty or thirty-five, but seems a bit ruthless when applied to the rank-and-file worker. The result, according to countless articles in publications like *Fortune*, the *New Republic*, *Bloomberg*, and *New York Magazine*, is that Silicon Valley has become a place where people live in fear. As soon as someone better or cheaper comes along, your company will get rid of you. If you turn fifty, or forty, or thirty-five; if you demand a raise and become too expensive; if a new batch of workers comes out of college and will do your job for less than what you are paid—you're gone. So don't get too comfortable.

This new arrangement between workers and employers was invented by Silicon Valley companies and is considered an innovation as significant as the chips and software for which the Valley is better known. Now this ideology has spread beyond Silicon Valley. We are living in a period of huge economic transformation, in which entire industries—retail, banking, healthcare, media, manufacturing—are being reshaped by technology. As those industries change, so does their approach to treating workers.

But does anyone really want to have twenty to twenty-five different jobs over the course of a forty-year career? It's hard to see how this arrangement can be good for workers. Bouncing around when you're young is one thing, but at some point people want to get married, have kids, and settle down. Stability becomes important. In the World According to Hoffman, you will spend half of your life searching for a new job, going on job interviews, getting trained, settling in, signing up for the new insurance (that is, if you get insurance), filling out your tax paperwork, moving over your 401(k) plan. You'll barely figure out where the foosball tables are located before it's time to go find a new job.

Amazon, which has gained a reputation as an especially harsh place to work, adds a cruel twist to Hoffman's short-term "tour of duty" philosophy. The median Amazon worker lasts only one year at the company, according to a 2013 study by PayScale, a company that tracks compensation data. Amazon compensates workers in part with restricted stock units spread over four years—but, unlike most tech companies which distribute an equal number each year, Amazon backloads the grants so that the lion's share of the stock units arrive in years 3 and 4. Employees who leave after one year might reportedly get only 5 percent of their grant.

While many tech companies treat employees poorly, they also expect them to be loyal, to feel for their employer the kind of passion that a sports fan feels for a team. Employees at HubSpot are told that the needs of the company are more important than their own.

"Team > individual" is how Dharmesh expresses this in his culture code, whose subtitle is "Creating a company we love." Who falls in love with a company? Especially when that company tells you that *we're not a family*?

Yet those Millennials running around the HubSpot offices in their orange clothes and orange shoes don't just *like* HubSpot; they *love* HubSpot. It's their *team*. It doesn't bother them that their team feels no such loyalty to them.

One day in the content factory I have a kind of *Norma Rae* moment where I try to raise awareness among my fellow workers. Specifically, we're talking about the candy wall. People are saying how amazing it is to have so much candy available. I'm hoping to persuade them that the candy wall is a bit of a con.

"You know," I say, "you guys are the first generation that's willing to work for free candy. My generation would never have fallen for that. We wanted to get paid in actual money."

I'll admit this might not be the best way to open up this dialogue.

"We get paid," one says, sounding defensive.

"I know," I say. "I'm just trying to make a point about why companies do these things."

"It's because they want to create a cool culture. They want people to be happy."

I have no idea how much these people are paid, but most of them are right out of college, and I suspect Cranium has gulled them into taking small salaries in exchange for the great experience they will get at HubSpot, as well as all the fun stuff, like the parties and the outings and the free beer and the candy.

"We're not getting paid in candy," another one says.

"No, I know that."

The others join in. They love the candy. They eat candy every day. Now I'm backpedaling, trying to explain that what I really mean to say is that a big wall of candy dispensers is not an incentive for people like me.

"If it were up to me, if I had the choice, I would not have a candy wall and I would just get paid a little bit more money instead. You see what I mean?"

They don't.

"Because I have kids, right? I can't bring home a huge bag of candy every day and feed the candy to my kids for dinner. I can't sell the candy and use the money to buy food and clothes for my kids. That's what I'm saying."

They look at me like *Crazy Old Man Alert! Why is he angry about the candy? Don't make any sudden moves that might scare him! Back away slowly, and call for help!*

The woman who really loves the candy says that she doesn't think the company actually spends that much on candy. What's more, even if the company took away the candy that doesn't mean they would pay us more money.

"I know," I say.

"But that's what you said." She stares at me, triumphantly.

I'm not quite sure where to go with this. Did Norma Rae run up against this kind of thinking in her textile factory? Were there twenty-something people there who loved the coffee in the coffee machine and didn't want to form a union?

"You know, you're right," I say. "I'm sorry I brought it up. The candy is great."

If I were Halligan, or Dharmesh, or Cranium, I would do exactly what they've done: I would hire hundreds of people just like this, give them all the candy and beer they can stomach, and keep telling them what important, meaningful work they're doing.

I understand why people don't get my point about the candy wall. But I can't understand how they overlook the cruelty with which some of the people around them are treated. What kind of company just "graduates" employees, gives them no warning, makes them clean out their desk and disappear immediately, and never mentions them again? Despite all the talk about *delightion* and *creating a company we love*, HubSpot is by far the cruelest place I've ever worked.

Again and again I see smart, experienced, accomplished women in their mid-thirties (at HubSpot, these are the *old* people) get fired, with little or no warning, by their twenty-something managers. In each case the woman getting axed is stunned by the news, devastated, reduced to tears.

Isabel, thirty-four, has put in three and a half years at HubSpot, has a one-year-old baby at home, and has just returned from a month-long medical leave when her twenty-something boss tells her that she's not meeting expectations and she's done. Denise, thirty-five, has been with HubSpot for four and a half years but is told one day (by Jordan, age twenty-eight) that her job no longer exists, even though her department is actively hiring. Denise is allowed to put in two more weeks. During that time, Cranium ignores her. He never pulls her aside to thank her for her service or say that he's sorry about how things have worked out. He walks right past her desk. He can see her—*she's sitting right there*—and he says nothing. He acts like nothing is happening. Meanwhile, Denise can barely hold it together. She cries in her car. She has panic attacks about going to work. She feels humiliated. She has no idea what she did wrong or why she's being let go.

Paige, thirty-five, gets tossed on a Friday morning, a few weeks shy of her one-year anniversary, when her first batch of options would vest. Ironically, Zack fires her during Fearless Friday, our feminist empowerment team-building exercise. While a group of women just out of college are downstairs in a conference room making paintings on the floor, Paige, a former Wall Street analyst, is up on the second floor being sacked for an alleged lack of productivity. Zack tells her to clean out her desk and leave. She's done. Right now. She gets no severance pay. She walks out, fighting back tears, and texts me from her car in the parking garage: *You won't believe this. I just got fired.* When I call her, she's crying.

A colleague in the marketing department tells me that back in 2011, before my time, another thirty-something woman was fired after only four months on the job. She was pregnant with twins. "The company can do whatever it wants," one manager tells me, and my jaw drops.

This is the New Work, but really it is just a new twist on an old story, the one about labor being exploited by capital. The difference is that this time the exploitation is done with a big smiley face. Everything about this new workplace, from the crazy décor to the change-the-world rhetoric to the hero's journey mythology and the perks that are not really perks—all of these things exist for one reason, which is to drive down the cost of labor so that investors can maximize their return.

We're a team, not a family. Just like a Major League Baseball player, on any day, without warning, you might get cut. But hey, enjoy that candy.

The difference between this kind of capitalism and the kind that Norma Rae encountered is that tech companies know how to spin negatives and present them as positives. HubSpot offers unlimited vacation time and pitches this as a perk. The truth is that this policy saves money for HubSpot. When a company has a traditional vacation plan, it is required by law to set aside a cash reserve to cover the cost of all of the vacation days that it owes to its workers. When employees quit or get fired, the company must pay them for the vacation time they have accrued. But if a company has no vacation plan, it doesn't have to set aside the cash reserve. Better yet, the company can fire people without having to pay them for any accrued vacation time. Paige, who got canned after eleven months, had taken only five days of vacation. At a traditional company she would have been owed a week or two of vacation pay, but from HubSpot, she got nothing. Think about how many hundreds of people churn in and out of a place like HubSpot, and you can see how the savings add up.

Another way to drive down labor costs is to deny people employee status in the first place. Uber, the ride-sharing company, saves money by categorizing drivers as independent contractors rather than employees. Uber insists drivers prefer this because they enjoy more freedom. Uber and others in the "share economy" are creating a new form of serfdom, an underclass of quasi-employees who receive low pay and no benefits. As former secretary of labor Robert Reich put it in a June 2015 Facebook post: "The 'share economy' is bunk; it's becoming a 'share the scraps' economy."

Tech companies also are pushing the U.S. government to increase the number of skilled foreign workers who can enter the country on H-1B visas. Reich says that too is a way to drive down labor costs. In a 2015 Facebook post, Reich recalls that during his time in office in the 1990s Valley employers claimed they could not find skilled workers in the United States, "when in reality they just didn't want to pay higher wages to Americans." Foreign workers are "easy to intimidate because if they lose their jobs they have to leave the U.S.," Reich says.

Why are tech companies so obsessed with cutting costs? Look at their financial results. Many don't make a profit. The biggest difference between today's tech start-ups and those of the pre-Internet era is that the old guard companies, like Microsoft and Lotus Development, generated massive profits almost from the beginning, while today many tech companies lose enormous amounts of money for years on end, even after they go public. They need to constantly drive costs down, using things like Halligan's VORP metric.

A more interesting question is why there are so many companies that remain in business while losing money. This seems like a peculiar business model. The point of creating a company is to generate a profit—or that used to be the case, anyway. That changed in the 1990s, during the first dotcom bubble, when Silicon Valley created a new kind of company, one that can lose money for years, and in fact might never turn a profit, yet still can make its founders and investors incredibly rich.

A watershed moment occurred on August 9, 1995, when Netscape Communications, maker of the first web browser, pulled off a huge IPO and saw its shares nearly triple in their first day of trading. Until then, companies were typically expected to be profitable before they could sell shares to the public. Netscape was gushing red ink. Mary Meeker, an investment banker at Morgan Stanley, which underwrote the IPO, later recalled to *Fortune*:

Was it early for the company to go public? Sure. There has been a rule of thumb that a company should have three quarters of obviously robust revenue growth. And you also traditionally wanted to see three quarters of profitability—improving profitability, for newer companies. Netscape was not profitable at the time, so that was certainly a new idea. But the market was ready for a new set of technology innovations, and Netscape was the right company in the right place at the right time with the right team.

Over the course of its brief existence Netscape lost a lot of money, but nevertheless a few people got rich. In 1999, at the peak of the dotcom bubble, AOL acquired Netscape in a deal worth $10 billion when it closed. After that Netscape more or less disappeared. Yet one Netscape co-founder, Marc Andreessen, reportedly walked away with shares worth nearly $100 million. Another co-founder, Jim Clark, reportedly made $2 billion. "On the Internet, nobody knows you're a dog" is the famous line from a 1993 *New Yorker* cartoon. The tale of Netscape added a new twist: On the Internet, at least when it comes to investments, nobody cares if you're a dog.

The Netscape IPO set off the dotcom frenzy. In Silicon Valley it was as if someone had flipped a switch. Suddenly there was a new business model: Grow fast, lose money, go public. That model persists today. It's a simple racket. Venture capitalists pump millions of dollars into a company. The company spends some of that money coding up a "minimum viable product," or MVP, a term coined by Eric Ries, author of *The Lean Startup*, which has become a bible for new tech companies, and then pumps enormous sums into acquiring customers—by hiring sales reps, marketers, and public relations people who can get publicity, put on flashy conferences, and generate hype—*brand and buzz*, as HubSpot calls it. The losses pile up, but the revenue number rises. Basically the company is buying one-dollar bills and selling them for seventy-five cents, but it doesn't matter, because mom-and-pop investors are only looking at the revenue growth rate. They have been told that if a company can just grow big enough, fast enough, eventually profits will arrive. Only sometimes they don't. Zynga, Groupon, and Twitter are a few big examples. In the past five years, from 2010 through 2014, Zynga racked up annual losses totaling more than $800 million; Groupon lost nearly $1 billion; and Twitter reported annual net losses that added up to more than $1.5 billion, according to the 10-K forms they filed with the Securities and Exchange Commission.

Old-guard tech CEOs seem baffled by the phenomenon of companies that operate for years in the red. "They make no money! In my world you're not a real business until you make some money," Steve Ballmer, the former CEO of Microsoft, said about Amazon in 2014, a year when the company lost $241 million yet saw its market value climb to $160 billion. Oracle CEO Mark Hurd, another old-guard business guy, expressed similar astonishment about Salesforce.com. "There's no cash flow," he said about that company in April 2015. "What are they worth right now? $35 billion?... It's crazy, just crazy." That was nothing. A few months later Salesforce.com was worth more than $50 billion.

One consequence of not making profits is that companies don't last as long. In 1960, the average lifespan of a company on the S&P 500 index was just over sixty years, while today it is less than twenty years, according to Innosight, a research and consulting organization. Another consequence is that the spoils are distributed less evenly than in the past. The disparity between CEO pay and the pay of the average worker has been widening since 1965, but the huge leap occurred during the dotcom boom, according to the Economic Policy Institute. In 1965, the average CEO made 20 times as much as the average worker. By 1989 that ratio had edged upward to about 60. But in 1995 things went nuts. The average CEO was making 122 times as much as the average worker. By 2000, the CEO-to-worker compensation ratio reached 383, according to EPI. The ratio now stands at about 300.

People at the top are taking more of the pie. That's irksome enough, but even more so when you realize that some of the founders who are raking in so much money for themselves are doing so while running companies that don't make a profit and that treat employees in ways that would have been unthinkable only two decades ago.

"Our most important assets walk out the door every night," was the mantra I heard from tech CEOs when I covered technology companies in the 1980s and 1990s. At Microsoft, "everybody made money, including secretaries," my friend Mike, the former Microsoft employee, recalls. "Microsoft made tens of thousands of millionaires. The company was incredibly supportive of people facing personal issues. If you had cancer they would keep you on payroll and not expect you to ever come in, while still paying for all of your medical costs."

In that era the big obsession among tech CEOs was how to retain talent. No company told employees to think of their jobs as short-term "tour of duty" engagements, or informed them that "We're not your family."

It's no wonder Reid Hoffman, who is both a company founder and a venture capitalist, espouses the "we're not a family" approach. He has been one of the biggest beneficiaries of the grow-fast-lose-money-go-public business model. Hoffman's first big hit company, PayPal, went public while losing money. In 2002 Hoffman co-founded LinkedIn. In three of its thirteen years LinkedIn has reported an annual profit. In the other ten, it has posted losses. Recently the losses have been prodigious—LinkedIn lost $150 million in the first nine months of 2015. Yet Hoffman's net worth stands at nearly $5 billion. Amazon, the online retailer, is twenty-one years old and has never made huge profits, yet its founder, Jeff Bezos, is worth $60 billion. Salesforce.com, a software company, reported net losses totaling three-quarters of a billion dollars from 2011 through 2014, yet its founder, Marc Benioff, is worth $4 billion.

Someone has to get left holding the bag. In summer 2015 I speak with Pat, a well-known Silicon Valley serial entrepreneur who is both the CEO of a privately held company and an angel investor. We're talking about the soaring valuations being placed on privately held companies. Suddenly the Valley is filled with so-called unicorns, privately held corporations that supposedly are worth billions, even tens of billions, of dollars. *Fortune* says there are now 145 unicorns, nearly twice as many as existed only seven months before.

"You realize who's going to get hurt, right?" Pat says.

"I don't know. The VCs?" I ask.

"No! The investors are protected."

Pat explains: The funds investing in late-stage start-ups and paying ridiculous valuations are demanding, and receiving, a kind of guarantee called a ratchet. That is a promise that if the company goes public at a valuation lower than what the private investors have paid, the company will grant them enough extra shares to make them whole. Some investors are guaranteed to make at least 20 percent on their investment. Unless there's an apocalyptic meltdown, the investors cannot lose money on these deals. They are taking pretty much no risk.

Founders are cashing out too. Groupon raised $1.1 billion in its last private round of venture funding before its IPO, but relatively little of the money actually went to the company. Most of it—$946 million—reportedly went into the pockets of insiders who sold their personal shares to venture capital investors.

"So the founders are safe. They're selling their personal shares in these private rounds at these high valuations," Pat says. "They're taking money off the table now, instead of waiting for the IPO. So who does that leave to get hurt?"

I say I'm not sure.

"Jesus, dumbass. The employees!"

Pat explains: The employees are paid in part with stock options. The strike price on the options is calculated based on the valuation of the company at the time the options are granted. If you joined the company late, you probably have a high strike price. If the company goes public at a lower valuation—if it suffers a "cramdown," as it's called—then your options might be underwater.

This is definitely going to happen to a lot of the unicorns, Pat says. Every time another late-stage investor comes in and makes another investment at an even more insane valuation, a cramdown becomes more likely. "The probability that employees are going to get screwed," Pat says, "is very high."

The company will go public, and the VCs will make a killing, and the founders will have pocketed their millions. But employees will get little or nothing. By December 2015 *Bloomberg* will be writing about this phenomenon, in an article headlined, "Big IPO, Tiny Payout for Many Startup Workers."

It might be difficult to feel sympathy for tech workers whining that their company went public and they didn't become millionaires. It depends on your perspective, and whether you view options as a bonus—a potential windfall—or as part of your compensation. Start-up workers often forgo part of their salary in order to get options and view their options as part of their pay. Now some people are discovering that they have been paid with Monopoly money. A cynic might say it's their own fault; they took a risk on a start-up and it didn't work out. But the risk is not shared. The people at the top are profiting from this game, which they have rigged in their favor.

What's more, the VCs and the founders know what they're doing, and they don't care. "I don't think any founder is really sitting there thinking about how they can screw their employees," Pat says. "But on the other hand, your friends are doing this, and your peer CEOs are doing this, and so you do it, too."

"Don't these guys feel guilty?" I ask. "They have to go into the office and look their employees in the eye. Right? How do they do that?"

Pat takes a deep breath. "I've been in the Valley a long time. As far as I can tell, nobody here ever feels guilty about anything they do. What I have observed from these guys is that they have a strong sense that they are moral actors. They believe very strongly that they operate with high integrity. They believe they are the most moral folks on the planet. But they are not."

These are the people who claim they are making the world a better place. And they are. For themselves.

Thirteen

The Ron Burgundy of Tech

Imagine Joel Osteen pumped up on human growth hormone. Imagine there's a secret government lab where scientists have blended the DNA of Tony Robbins with the DNA of Harold Hill, the aw-shucks shifty salesman from *The Music Man*. Imagine a grizzly bear in a pinstriped suit, standing on his hind legs and talking about changing the world through *disruptive innovation and transformation*.

If you can imagine those things then you can almost imagine the horror of seeing Marc Benioff, the billionaire founder and CEO of Salesforce.com, on stage at his company's annual conference, Dreamforce.

It's November 2013, and that's where I am, along with Cranium and Spinner and a bunch of other HubSpotters, sitting through Benioff's three-hour keynote speech on the opening day of the conference. I was psyched when Cranium asked me to go to Dreamforce, if only for the chance to spend a few days in San Francisco. I haven't been back here since I left my job at ReadWrite. I have a list of people I want to see, restaurants I want to visit.

But San Francisco is a shitshow. One hundred forty thousand people have descended on a one-square-mile area of downtown. Dreamforce takes place over four days, with concerts and comedians and inspirational speakers. It's basically Woodstock for people who work in sales and marketing. Or, as Benioff has declared, "the largest and most trans-formational event in the history of enterprise technology."

Entire blocks have been shut down to traffic. All of downtown is gridlocked. Restaurants and hotels are booked solid. I'm staying at the Courtyard Marriott, which was my home away from home during my stint as editor of ReadWrite. Last year I spent so many months living in this hotel that when I walk into the lobby the woman at the front desk recognizes me and remembers my name. Last year I paid $129 a night. This week, because of Dreamforce, I'm paying close to $700 a night. As for getting around town, forget about finding a taxi. They're all booked. Oh, and the forecast calls for rain. It's a nightmare.

None of this is as awful as Benioff himself. He stands six-feet-five-inches tall and weighs three hundred pounds, with gleaming white teeth and curly black hair that glistens with hair gel. He is a former salesperson who now sells software that lets other salespeople sell more stuff. It's called customer relationship management, or CRM, software. Benioff is also one of the wealthiest people in the world, a member of the *Forbes* billionaire list. Here in the main auditorium of the Moscone Center, thousands of people who sell things over the Internet are stand-ing up and cheering for him as if he's some kind of superhero.

The whole thing makes me depressed, in part because Benioff is a buffoon, a bullshit artist, and such an out-of-control egomaniac that it is painful to listen to him talk. He lives in Hawaii and signs his emails "Aloha." He's a Buddhist and hangs out with Zen monks from Japan, and he gave his golden retriever the title "chief love officer" at his com-pany. He is the Ron Burgundy of tech. He and this conference are the essence of everything that has gone wrong in the industry. "Have you transformed the way you innovate?" was Benioff's big line at the 2012 Dreamforce show. Note that you can switch the two buzzwords in the sentence and it still sounds good and still means nothing. *Meaningful-lessness* is not a word, but should be. There's an art to this kind of horse-shit, and Benioff is its Michelangelo.

More depressing is that Benioff represents a threat to HubSpot, and while he may be ridiculous, he's not someone you want to have as an enemy. Salesforce used to be HubSpot's biggest ally, investing in HubSpot and even selling HubSpot software to its customers. Halligan loved Benioff so much that he named the company's biggest conference room after him. That happy relationship ended six months ago when Salesforce acquired one of HubSpot's rivals, ExactTarget. Supposedly Benioff first tried to buy HubSpot, but Halligan rejected his offer.

At the keynote I'm sitting next to one of our sales reps, who tells me that Salesforce.com has been calling our customers, urging them to dump HubSpot and switch to ExactTarget, which has been renamed Salesforce Marketing Cloud. Salesforce.com claims that its marketing software is better than HubSpot and works seamlessly with Salesforce .com's core CRM software.

These claims may or may not be true, but Salesforce.com makes a compelling sales pitch. A lot of our customers use Salesforce.com. They bought HubSpot as a kind of add-on to their CRM software. Why keep paying extra for HubSpot when they can buy their marketing software from the same company that makes their CRM software? No doubt Salesforce.com also offers an attractive price if you buy the bundle.

"So what do you say when your customers tell you that Salesforce .com is trying to poach them away?" I ask the sales rep. "What story can we tell our customers to counter the story they're getting from Salesforce?"

The sales rep just shrugs.

Halligan has decided that if Salesforce.com is going to enter our market space, then we will enter theirs. In secret, HubSpot's engineers have started developing a CRM program to compete against Sales- force.com, but we haven't announced it yet.

Cranium has become obsessed with Salesforce.com. He hates these guys! He wants to kill them! He's like Ahab stalking the whale. Before the ExactTarget deal, Cranium loved Salesforce.com. He used to spend a fortune buying booth space at Dreamforce. In 2011 he made forty HubSpot employees dress up in orange cheerleader tracksuits and run around handing out tiny stuffed unicorns. He still thinks this was a brilliant marketing scheme. I cringe when I look at the photos. I wonder if anyone refused to wear a tracksuit, and if so, what happened to that person. I'm relieved that this year we can all just wear regular clothes, so I don't have to find out.

We're here in part to steal ideas—we'll see what these guys do to create a spectacle and copy that for our Inbound conference in Boston. We're also here to gather competitive intelligence, to see how Benioff talks about his new marketing software and what the audience makes of his pitch. We want to find out what we're up against.

Based on what I'm seeing, we're in trouble. Sure, Benioff is full of shit, but so are we, and Benioff is way better at being full of shit than we are. Also, Salesforce.com's sales are about fifty times what ours are. In terms of hype, the disparity is even greater. Just two months before this, HubSpot's Inbound drew five thousand people, a tiny fraction of the Dreamforce audience—even after giving away or selling a lot of our tickets at a discount.

We're screwed, I keep thinking. We're totally, absolutely screwed. Not because the ExactTarget product is better than ours, because who even knows, and who even cares? Having the best product has nothing to do with who wins. What matters is who can put on a great show, who can create the biggest spectacle, who can look huge and unstoppable and invincible, and who is the best at bluster and hype.

When it comes to these things, nobody comes close to Benioff. Nobody has cashed in on the bubble as well as he has. In 2012, Salesforce.com lost more than a quarter of a billion dollars, and in 2013 it will lose almost as much. In 2013 the company is fourteen years old and not making a profit. But its revenues are growing more than 30 percent each year, and growth is what investors are looking for, so even though Salesforce.com is bleeding red ink, its stock has doubled over the past two years, and Benioff's personal net worth has soared to $2.6 billion.

Now, here in the Moscone Center, the P. T. Barnum of the tech industry is giving a master class in how the game is played. It's the Marc Benioff show, brought to you by Marc Benioff, with special guest Marc Benioff. Fifteen thousand people are packed into this hall. Thousands more are packed into spillover rooms. It feels like a rock concert. In fact it *is* a rock concert. Before Benioff appears, the lights go down and suddenly Huey Lewis and the News are performing "The Power of Love." It is nine in the morning. From our seats, way in back, we can barely see the band, but we watch on huge screens, the kind used at football stadiums.

Next comes Benioff, making a big high-energy entrance, like some kind of cheesy talk-show host, roaming up and down the aisles, a man of the people. He wears a blue suit and a pair of multitoned shoes, called Cloud Walkers, custom made by Christian Louboutin. He says he chose that Huey Lewis song because *the power of love* is what Salesforce.com is all about. He doesn't want to talk about business. He wants to talk about the hundreds of millions of dollars that he and Salesforce.com have donated to worthy causes. "The best drug I ever took," he says, "was philanthropy."

I suspect that opening with a big-name band is also a form of dick measuring. It's Benioff's way of saying, "I just spent three hundred thousand dollars to have a band play one song. You know why? *Because I can.*" The same goes for his philanthropy. Benioff says he's challenging other tech billionaires to give away as much money as he does. The thing is, a lot of rich tech people do give away a lot of money; they just don't go around bragging about it. Benioff's challenge is a form of self-aggrandizement, his way of saying that while others might give away money, *Mine is bigger.* He wields his philanthropy like a four-foot cock, slapping us all in the face with it.

Benioff talks about the UCSF *Benioff* Children's Hospital, which used to be called UCSF Children's Hospital until Benioff donated $100 million and got them to rename the place after him. Next he shows a movie about Haiti and earthquake victims, and talks about all the money Salesforce.com has sent there to help rebuild the country. When the movie ends, he introduces the prime minister of Haiti, Laurent Lamothe, along with supermodel-turned-philanthropist Petra Nemcova, and actor-slash-asshole Sean Penn. The crowd goes nuts. I'm feeling like I might be sick.

The idea is for Benioff to "interview" these people, but the "interview" consists of Lamothe saying how grateful he and his impoverished countrymen are to Benioff, and then Benioff talking over him. It's painful. Here is the prime minister of a sovereign nation, flown into a tech conference by a billionaire, *in those shoes*, just so that the prime minister can kiss the billionaire's ring in public. Everyone eats this up. They love Benioff! They stand and cheer. Benioff walks down off the stage into the aisles like a televangelist, bathing in the adoration, saying *awesome* and *phenomenal*, again and again. What, exactly, is *awesome*? This whole thing! All of us! Just for being here, just for caring, we're all awesome! It's phenomenal!

I glance over at Cranium. I wonder if he's thinking what I'm thinking, which is that we could purchase nuclear-powered orange tracksuits that shoot lasers from both sleeves and we would still be no match for this guy. Why would customers buy software from pikers like us when they can buy software from Benioff? I'm appalled by Benioff's performance, and I find him completely repellent, but even *I* want to buy his software. Cranium looks pissed off.

Finally the presentation shifts to product announcements. Huey Lewis returns to the stage and plays "Back in Time," and then there's a huge fake thunder explosion, dry ice machines blanket the stage in fog, and the co-founder of Salesforce.com, Parker Harris, drives onstage in a white Tesla and leaps out dressed as Emmett "Doc" Brown from the movie *Back to the Future*, in a white lab coat and a crazy snow-white wig.

Harris and Benioff perform a clumsy skit about how Harris has just returned from the year 2019 and brought back some software he found there, and that is what Salesforce.com will be announcing today. The truth is that Salesforce.com has little new to introduce. All of the stuff about hospitals and Haitians and Huey Lewis is meant to distract us from noticing that Benioff doesn't really have much to talk about other than warmed-over versions of old products. The misdirection works. People whoop and clap. They nod their heads as if they totally understand phrases like *the Internet of customers*, where people *make decisions at*

superhuman speeds, and companies operate at *the speed of now*, as well as
at *the speed of sales*. What sales and marketing people must do, someone
informs us with great urgency, is race into the future a little *faster* than
our customers, and *get to the future first, and be ready to greet them when they
arrive*.

Before you can try to figure out what that means, Dreamforce rolls
on. Over the next few days the show features some of the biggest names
in tech, like Dropbox CEO Drew Houston, HP CEO Meg Whitman,
Yahoo CEO Marissa Mayer, and Facebook COO Sheryl Sandberg.
Benioff has latched on to the "Women in Tech" crusade and made it
his cause célèbre. "Powerful women" is a theme of the conference—
yet oddly enough only four members of Benioff's twenty-two member
management team and only one member of his board of directors are
female. Salesforce.com is run almost entirely by white men. But look—
over there! It's the prime minister of Haiti! And wait, hold on—is that
thunder and lightning? *Indoors?* Is that a Tesla? From the future? *On
stage?*

Green Day plays a concert in AT&T Park, home of the San Francisco Giants. Alec Baldwin gives a talk. Tony Bennett and Jerry Seinfeld make appearances. It's all part of what Salesforce.com describes
as "dynamic programming to exhilarate the Dreamforce community."
Cavernous halls are lined with countless booths rented out by software makers hawking programs that work with Salesforce: add-ons,
plug-ins, mobile apps. There's a "connected devices playground" and
a "Dreamforce hackathon." There are more than a thousand break-
out sessions and "success clinics," where people can learn how to sell
stuff. Two people dressed up in foam balls—the Salesforce.com mas-
cots, SaaSy and Chatty—bounce around the conference, dancing awk-
wardly with legions of mostly white people.

The final day features a speech by Deepak Chopra, noted charla-
tan and quack. He and Benioff are friends. Chopra rambles on about
joy and meaning and interconnectedness and the importance of lov-
ing yourself. The old W. C. Fields line "If you can't dazzle them with
brilliance, baffle them with bullshit" seems like the motto not just for

Chopra but for the entire conference. Benioff and his philanthropy, the dry ice and fog machines, the concerts and comedians: None of this has anything to do with software or technology. It's a show, created to entertain people, boost sales, and fluff a stock price.

I roam the show floor, gazing at middle-aged salespeople in suits who sit on beanbag chairs staring at their phones, and tech bros in T-shirts and man buns playing Ping-Pong. I sit in the Tesla that's on display outside the auditorium, dreaming that my HubSpot options might someday be worth enough that I can buy a car like this.

I figured Cranium would be setting up dinners for the HubSpot gang. But…nothing. No email from Cranium, no invitations to get together. Just like with my first day at HubSpot, I've been flown out here to attend this show then left to myself, with no instructions, no socializing.

Cut loose, I spend my evenings catching up with friends in San Francisco. I do some shopping in Union Square. I have breakfast with a tech CMO from the East Coast and lunch with a PR exec from a company in the Valley. Torrential rains strike on the night of the Green Day concert, but thousands of people go anyway. Many of them stay even after the sound system blows out and Green Day's Billie Joe Armstrong tries to carry on as an acoustic show, with no microphone.

I stay in my hotel and gaze out my window at the rain-blurred lights down below, marveling at all the money and evil sloshing around down there. One hundred and forty thousand salespeople have hit San Francisco, armed with expense accounts and determined to have the time of their lives. They will sleep with their clients. They will sleep with their colleagues. Hookers have flown in from all over the country for this. Tinder and Grindr and the Craigslist "casual encounters" listings are packed with out-of-towners looking to hook up. The strip bars and S&M clubs are booming. Dreamforce turns out to be a four-day orgy worthy of Caligula, a triumph of vulgarity and wasteful spending, with free booze and endless shrimp cocktail and a rate of STD transmission that probably rivals Fleet Week.

Gazing down on this mess is like looking into the pit of Mordor.

So many lost souls! These glorified car salesmen, these people whose jobs involve coercion and manipulation, whose lives revolve around making their numbers. Every month, every quarter, every year: sell, sell, sell! These are the people who took the Internet, one of the most wonderful and profound inventions of all time, and polluted it with advertising and turned it into a way to sell stuff. No wonder these zombies need to take a week off in San Francisco once a year, with some Deepak Chopra and maybe an eight ball of coke and a Canadian hooker to make the whole thing seem worthwhile.

Dreamforce is only part of Benioff's mad campaign of megalomaniacal self-aggrandizement. Five months from now, in April 2014, Benioff will announce plans to make Salesforce.com the anchor tenant for a new skyscraper that is already under construction in San Francisco. Salesforce.com will commit $560 million to help finish work on the one-thousand-foot glass-and-steel skyscraper, which will become the company's headquarters and be named the Salesforce Tower. When it opens in 2018, it will be the tallest building in the city, dwarfing everything around it. Maybe Benioff is oblivious to the phallic symbolism, or maybe he doesn't care, or maybe—and this is my theory—he knows exactly what he's doing and he loves it. *Mine's bigger! It's the biggest!*

For P. T. Benioff there is no end to the extravagant spending. At the 2015 Dreamforce he docks a one-thousand-foot-long luxury ocean liner at pier 27 to serve as a hotel and party space—the Dreamboat, he calls it. Salesforce.com still isn't turning a profit, but thanks to Benioff's huffing and puffing Salesforce.com's market value has topped $50 billion and Benioff's own net worth has swollen to $4 billion. Benioff has invented a form of financial alchemy, one where he makes money by losing money. The more Benioff squanders on parties, the richer he gets.

Looking down from my hotel window in November 2013, I realize that things are playing out exactly the way Tad, my investment banker friend, told me they would when I met him for a drink just one year ago at Anchor & Hope. This is what a trillion-dollar wealth transfer looks like. Across the country, in New York, bonuses on Wall Street are going to be the highest they've been since 2007, before the crash. In 2013, there will be more IPOs than in any year since the dotcom bubble peaked in 2000, and in 2014 there will be even more, according to Renaissance Capital, a company that tracks the IPO market.

Surely it cannot end well when a bunch of money-losing companies go racing into the public markets, and when risk that previously was confined to private investors gets shifted onto the public. Nevertheless, the Fed keeps printing money, and the stock market keeps going up. The ducks are quacking, and the VCs are racing for the exits, launching IPOs as fast as they can.

Somehow I find myself sitting in the middle of the maelstrom. Part of me finds the whole thing appalling. But another part still hopes to profit from it.

Fourteen

Meet the New Boss

I'm still in San Francisco when I get an urgent message from Wingman asking me to call him. There's some big news, he tells me. The company is about to announce an important new hire—a guy named Trotsky. Trotsky will oversee HubSpot's content operations and thus will now be my boss, instead of Wingman.

On the phone, Wingman keeps talking about Trotsky as if he's a celebrity. Finally I confess to Wingman that I've never heard of Trotsky. I'm a little bit embarrassed to admit this, but who is this person and why is it a big deal that he's joining HubSpot?

Wingman seems taken aback.

"He was content marketer of the year in 2012," he says.

"Oh, right," I say, as if I've heard of that award. I feel a twinge of sadness that such a thing even exists.

"It's pretty huge for us to get him," Wingman says.

"I can imagine," I say. "That's great. I can't wait to meet him."

After we hang up I do a Google search about the Content Marketer of the Year award. It turns to be one of forty prizes given annually by a guy in Cleveland, Ohio, who runs an organization called the Content Marketing Institute. Trotsky did indeed win a coveted CMI award. Brandon the Sales Lion, the pool installer turned marketing superstar we learned about during our HubSpot training classes, also took home a trophy, in the Visionary category.

It seems to me that getting a new boss can only be a good thing. I've screwed things up pretty badly with Wingman and Cranium. But now maybe I have a chance to start over. I email Trotsky and congratulate him on the new job. I tell him how excited I am to be working for him. Trotsky lives in the suburbs, a couple towns away from me. He won't start working at HubSpot for a few more weeks, but I ask him if he wants to have dinner before then, because I can't wait to start brainstorming.

A week or so later we meet at a pub in Winchester. Much to my relief, we hit it off. Trotsky is in his early forties, with curly dark hair, a bushy lumberjack beard, and big weightlifter arms, both of them covered in full-sleeve tattoos, like a carny. He tells me that he used to box, and he has a dog—a Doberman. He's married and has a young kid. Like me, he once considered moving to Silicon Valley, but he chose to stay in Boston, because he thinks his family is happier here.

Trotsky has been around the industry for a while, and it turns out we have some mutual friends. He started his career in PR agencies and bounced through five shops in six years. Then he started working at software companies, hoping to hit it big on an IPO. So far he has struck out. At one company, Eloqua, he bailed out just after the company went public and just before it got acquired, in a deal that would have made him rich. His next employer, the place he's just leaving, is a tiny start-up in Boston that is fizzling out.

Now he's coming to HubSpot, and although he's arriving late to the party, he has taken a small salary and loaded up on stock options. He doesn't need to be super rich. He just wants to make enough money to pay off his mortgage, buy a vacation house, and "put enough money in the bank that I just don't have to take shit from anyone," he says.

Trotsky is a wildcatter. Hire him, and he'll work your oil field and see if he can strike it rich. If he doesn't, he'll move on. Silicon Valley is filled with people like this who spend their careers jumping from one tiny dysfunctional company to another, chasing a pot of gold. "I was stunned when I was doing recruiting in the Valley," a former software executive recalls. "Everyone is a mercenary. Every resume you'd look at had all these stints of a year here, a year there. Like if they didn't hit the jackpot in a year, they'd go place a new bet."

I think of this as a kind of mental disorder—the Start-up Disease. I know the symptoms, because I am suffering from them myself. But Trotsky has an even more severe case, and he's been afflicted for a lot longer. Trotsky says the clock is ticking down on him and his career. He's already too old to be working in tech. If he doesn't strike it rich at HubSpot he'll get one more chance, maybe two. By then he will be fifty, and nobody will hire him.

He tells me that his first impression of HubSpot is that it reminds him of *Logan's Run*, the dystopian sci-fi movie where people are killed when they reach the age of thirty, in order to prevent overpopulation. Even Trotsky has never worked in a place that is so exaggeratedly young. He tells me how Penny, the receptionist, who is twenty-three but looks seventeen, told him when she first met him, "I think it's cool that they're starting to hire some older people now." Trotsky was startled both by the sentiment and by her lack of tact. Bemused, he asked Penny what age she considers old. Where is the cutoff between young people and old people? "I guess about thirty," she said.

I tell Trotsky that if he thinks HubSpot feels weird to him, imagine working there at my age. A few months ago I turned fifty-three. When I was fifty-two I could almost deal with HubSpot, because the average employee is twenty-six, and so I was exactly double the average. Now I'm more than twice the average, and somehow this feels worse. "It seems like a line you don't want to cross," I say.

I tell him about Zack and his crazy memos in ALL CAPS about CONQUERING THE WORLD. I kvetch about Cranium's latest management innovation, a service called TINYpulse that bombards us with weekly happiness surveys. TINYpulse also has a feature called Cheers for Peers that lets people send out little praise-gasms for their coworkers. You praise me, I praise you, and we all get happy by reminding each other how *awesome* we are. Our super cheery cheerleaders are wearing this feature out with overuse, sending cheers for everything. Spinner, the former volleyball team captain, has a special place in her heart for Ashley, the youngest member of the blog team. "Ashley for president!" is one of her favorite lines. When Ashley fills in for Jan and runs the blog for a few days, Spinner praises Ashley for being "calm and collective."

Sadly, I have not received any cheers from peers. The women on the blog team have pretty much stopped speaking to me. They also won't acknowledge that my little sub-blog has been generating a lot of traffic. In terms of page views, the five biggest posts over the past ninety days have been from me. One of my articles generated 190,000 views in a single day. In the entire seven-year history of the company only two posts have ever generated more page views than that, and it took months for them to hit the number that my post hit in twenty-four hours. On the other hand, my stuff still isn't converting well. I'm getting lots of traffic, but my readers aren't clicking on the e-book offers or filling out forms.

Nonetheless, Cranium notices the spike in traffic, and one week, at our marketing department meeting, he awards me the Golden Unicorn, a prize for being that week's outstanding marketer. This is an actual tiny statue of a unicorn, in gold. I put it on my desk and take pictures of it. Maybe this is good! Maybe I'm learning how to do this marketing stuff after all.

I'm still working in the boiler room, away from the other bloggers. From Marcia and Jan I hear not a peep. There are no little "You go girl!!!" emails being passed around the department for me. The women who run our email campaigns and social media feeds won't promote my articles to their subscribers. Michael, the copyeditor who just got hired to work on the marketing blog, is not allowed to work on my posts; Marcia and Jan say they can't spare him.

Things are going to change, Trotsky assures me. He tells me that one of the biggest reasons he took the job was because he wanted to work with me. I don't believe this for a second, but all those years of working in PR have taught Trotsky how to deal with journalists: A little bit of flattery goes a long way.

"They're wasting your talent," he says. "You should be doing more than just banging out blog posts. I have some ideas for you. I think you should be doing much higher-profile stuff."

I leave dinner with Trotsky feeling cautiously hopeful. Maybe things really are taking a turn for the better. Maybe I'll do some work that I actually enjoy. Maybe, when April arrives, I won't want to leave.

But soon enough, that changes. Ten days after my dinner with Trotsky, before he even arrives for his first day at work, I manage to shoot myself in the foot, and this time I do it in a very big, public way.

Fifteen

Grandpa Buzz

In the first week of December Spinner sends around an email informing us that Halligan has been written up in an *awesome* new story in the *New York Times*. She wants us all to promote the article on our social feeds and drive some traffic to it. Spinner told me a few months ago that a *Times* journalist, Adam Bryant, had asked to interview Halligan for a feature called Corner Office. That column is usually a puff piece where a CEO gets asked some softball questions, but Spinner was nervous about it, because, as she put it, Halligan has a tendency to stick his foot in his mouth and say stupid things when he gets in front of a reporter.

I offered to help Halligan prepare by conducting practice interviews with him. I've interviewed thousands of people, and the ones who do best are the ones who practice. Bryant wouldn't ask any tough questions, but Halligan should have two or three points he wanted to make and not wander off them. Tech companies often pay journalists to act as media training consultants and help their executives learn to do interviews, but HubSpot already had me working in house, so why not take advantage of this?

I also offered to go to New York with Halligan and Spinner when he was doing the interview. I know Adam Bryant, and I figured it couldn't hurt for Halligan to have a friendly connection tagging along. Spinner did not want my help. Perhaps she saw the interview as a feather in her cap and didn't want to share the credit.

Spinner flew solo, Halligan got no media training, and now the article is out and Halligan, predictably, has blown it. The main point of the Halligan article is that Halligan loves to take naps. "Brian Halligan, Chief of HubSpot, on the Value of Naps," is the headline. Halligan thinks naps are so important that he installed a nap room with a hammock at HubSpot. So far so good. Taking naps is the kind of oddball thing that Corner Office is looking for.

That's the angle that got Halligan in the door. Now he has a chance to tell people—and by people, I mean investors—what HubSpot does. Most people have never heard of HubSpot. Even people who have heard of HubSpot sometimes think it is a marketing agency or a consulting firm.

Halligan should have a very simple brief: HubSpot is a *cloud software* company, selling *marketing automation* software and run by *people from MIT*. HubSpot is a leading player in a very hot market space, and the company is growing like crazy. That's it. That's all he needs to do. Talk about naps and plug the company.

But during the interview Halligan starts rambling and talking about how HubSpot likes to hire really young people. Maybe he sees the interview as a recruiting opportunity, a way to reach Millennials. If so, he's wrong. The *Times* media kit says the median age of a *Times* subscriber is fifty. According to the Pew Research Center, people under thirty make up only one-third of the paper's audience. The college kids Halligan wants to hire get their news on Facebook and BuzzFeed. That's where you go to talk about your fun-loving, youth-oriented culture.

Halligan tells the *Times* that HubSpot is trying to "build a culture specifically to attract and retain Gen Y'ers." Yikes. I understand what he is trying to say, but he is getting a bit too close to saying that he would rather hire young people than old people, which is something you definitely don't want to say in public, even if it's true.

Still, if he leaves things there, he might be okay. I read on. Next, Halligan explains that young people make better employees, especially in the technology industry, where everything is changing so fast that older people just can't keep up.

Then comes the money quote: "In the tech world, gray hair and experience are really overrated."

Only an imbecile would say this. Halligan is essentially admitting that Hubspot discriminates on the basis of age. Age discrimination has become a huge issue in Silicon Valley. Halligan is not the only tech CEO who prefers to hire young people; he's just the only one dumb enough to admit it. Halligan has not just put his foot in his mouth—he has taken his foot out of his mouth and stepped on a land mine.

I don't know if Adam Bryant included these comments on purpose, knowing how incendiary they might be. Surely Halligan talked about all sorts of things in the interview, and Bryant cherry-picked which comments to publish. That's why doing an interview is always risky. That's also why CEOs need media training.

For me, Halligan's comments strike a nerve. Here I am, a guy in my fifties, with lots of gray hair and experience, and I'm being treated like shit by the twenty-something people at Halligan's company. Halligan is giving them his blessing.

I start to post a link to the article on Facebook, along with a wise-ass comment. But then I think better of it and delete what I've written without publishing it. I go do something else. But it bugs me. I go back to Facebook and write another post, taking a different approach. It's still not right. I want something that's funny but has a little bite. I go downstairs and make a cup of coffee. Standing in the kitchen, I think of a post that makes me laugh out loud. I go to Facebook and write out the comment. For a while I sit there looking at it. I think about what will happen if I press POST. The smart move is to delete the comment, shut off my computer, and go for a walk. Take a hike in the woods and shout into the trees. Grumble about this privately but don't say anything in public. That's the smart play.

Instead I say to hell with it and post the comment. I include a link to the *Times* story, beneath this comment:

"In the tech world, gray hair and experience are really over-rated," says THE CEO OF THE COMPANY WHERE I FUCKING WORK. "We're trying to build a culture specifically to attract and retain Gen Y'ers." I feel so special.

This isn't such a big deal. It's the kind of snarky little remark that I made on the Fake Steve blog all the time. But I have no illusions about how it will be received at HubSpot. Cults are not usually filled with people who can take a joke.

Then again, why should I care? These people have made it pretty clear that they don't want me around. Here is the CEO saying pretty much the same thing, in a newspaper. I figure I'm done at HubSpot, but I'm okay with that.

Compared to most people, I have a fairly big audience on Facebook, with more than one hundred thousand people following my posts. Within minutes the comments start pouring in, with people complaining about age discrimination in tech. Some are my friends, but many are people I don't know. My post is being shared, going viral and spreading around the world. A guy from France says in his country, "this would be called discrimination. And lead the CEO to serious trouble." Someone writes an article criticizing Halligan and posts a link to the article in the comments under my post.

My post is blowing up partly because people enjoy seeing the crazy Fake Steve Jobs blogger guy making fun of his boss in public. "Did you get fired today?" one asks.

But I've also tapped into a huge well of anger that I didn't know existed. Apparently, a lot of people have been pushed aside after reaching a certain age, especially in the tech industry. The things Halligan said out loud are exactly what those people suspect their bosses were thinking about them when they shoved them out the door. Officially nobody ever gets fired because of age. Officially, their position no longer exists, or the department is changing priorities. But everyone knows the truth. They're old, and they get paid too much. As my editor at *Newsweek* told me, "They can take your salary and hire five kids right out of college." Now here is some asshole tech CEO who has just blurted that out, in an interview.

On Facebook, Spinner chimes in. She writes an angry comment under my Facebook post telling me I am not a team player: "We're all supposed to be solving for EV," she writes. EV means enterprise value, and "solving for EV" means we're all supposed to be doing whatever we can to pump up the value of the company. Then Cranium jumps into the fray. Instead of apologizing for Halligan he doubles down and defends the remarks. "I give Brian credit for being transparent and upfront," Cranium writes. "A lot of CEOs are hard to read and borderline deceptive. With Brian you know what he is thinking and I think that is awesome."

Yup, it's *awesome* all right. Now people really start piling in. It's a feeding frenzy of angry olds on a Facebook rampage. A fifty-something former marketing executive at IBM dismisses Cranium as a buffoon and a bootlicker, and says HubSpot's board should be meeting right away to replace Halligan: "A CEO who insults potential clients, employees & shareholders in the NYT. You're a marketing company? Your VCs should be recruiting by tomorrow."

The post gets hundreds of likes, dozens of shares, nearly one hundred comments. I can't stop the onslaught. I consider deleting my post, which would also delete all the comments, but that would create the impression that HubSpot forced me to take it down, which could make the company look worse. Besides that, what Halligan said was stupid, and I don't feel sorry for pointing that out.

I leave the post up, and wait for someone at HubSpot to call me to tell me I'm fired. But the phone doesn't ring.

My friends are taking a sadistic pleasure in watching me crash and burn. One, who works in PR, says I should start coloring my hair. "Show up tomorrow as a redhead," she recommends. Another, a former *Wall Street Journal* reporter, suggests I need to change my Facebook photo to something that makes me look younger. I scan an old photo from my First Communion and make it my profile photo. There I am, age eight, wearing my First Communion robe, hands folded in prayer in front of me, looking angelic. "I'm trying to get a promotion at HubSpot," I write. "The 8-year-old version of me has lots of ideas about how to expand geographically while also driving up MRR by pushing into the enterprise." My friend the former *Journal* reporter says the twelve-year-olds at HubSpot better watch out for that old guy with the gray hair. "You misunderstand HubSpot," I tell him. "The twelve-year-olds are running the place and they know best."

This is pure hara-kiri, ritual seppuku. But I figure there is no way to salvage the situation, and if I'm going to go out I should at least do it in style.

Some of my HubSpot colleagues seemed genuinely baffled by my complaint. One of them—white, male, in his twenties—sends me an email asking why I'm so angry. I tell him that in retrospect I am not so much angry as I am disappointed and even amused. Halligan has made a classic Kinsley gaffe, named after the journalist Michael Kinsley, who defined gaffes as those moments when politicians slip up and reveal what they truly believe: "A gaffe is when a politician tells the truth."

Halligan really believes that the best way to build a tech company is to hire hundreds of young, inexperienced people, give them lots of free beer and parties, and turn them loose. He's entitled to his opinion. He may even be right. That doesn't make it smart for him to say it in public.

I ask my young, white, male colleague to imagine that instead of saying that *older* people (gray hair and experience) are overrated, Halligan said that *gay* people are overrated, or *women*, or *African-Americans*, or *Jews*. Imagine Halligan saying, "We're trying to build a culture specifically to attract and retain *white* people, because when it comes to technology, white people do a much better job than black people."

"But he didn't say that!" my colleague responds. "He didn't say anything about gays, or women, or black people!"

As the Bible says: Jesus wept.

In a way I almost feel relieved. I'm sick of HubSpot. I'm tired of trying to fit in. Now at least it's over. It's early December. I can enjoy the holidays and then in January start looking for a new job.

But as the day wears on and the Facebook frenzy runs out of steam, I still never get a call or an email from HubSpot. There's no word from Wingman or Cranium, nothing from Halligan or anyone in HR. The next day is a Friday, and again I stay home, and again I get no word from anyone.

Over the weekend it dawns on me that they are not going to fire me—because they can't fire me.

No doubt they want to fire me. But how does that play out? The CEO of a company makes remarks in a newspaper that sound like he and his company discriminate on the basis of age. An older employee criticizes the CEO's comments, and then gets fired for expressing his opinion.

What happens next? Maybe the older employee makes a big stink in public. Maybe the old guy sues the company. Maybe the judge who presides over the case has gray hair, too. My knowledge of the law is based entirely on what I've learned by watching *Law & Order*, but my sense is that this gray-haired plaintiff might have a case.

Even if he doesn't, the company risks unleashing a shitstorm of bad publicity just as it's trying to go public.

They're not going to fire me. They can't, and they know it.

The great irony is that posting that obnoxious comment has actually made me invulnerable. How can they *ever* fire me, without it looking as if they are punishing me for making those comments?

"I can do anything I want," I tell Sasha, who is clearly worried. "I could go into the office on Monday and climb up on Halligan's desk, pull down my pants, and take a dump on the keyboard of his MacBook Air, and they *still* couldn't fire me."

"Strictly speaking," Sasha says, "I think that's not true."

Of course she's right. Dropping anchor anywhere in the office other than a toilet in the men's room will definitely get me fired, not to mention arrested and sent for a psychiatric evaluation. Which is as it should be.

"I am not saying that I intend to engage in any inappropriate loaf-pinching behavior at the office," I tell her.

She looks at me.

"Or here at home," I say.

"Thank you."

So that's the good news—they can't fire me. The bad news is that they can do what companies often do when there's someone they want to get rid of—which is they can abuse me and make my life a living hell, so that I'll leave on my own.

They won't do this right away. They will have to be clever about it. There's an art to making an employee miserable. But that is exactly the treatment that is hurtling toward me. I'm just too stupid to see it.

I'm not sure if my age has anything to do with how poorly I've been treated at HubSpot. Certainly it makes me stand out, and certainly it is something I have become aware of, something that I think about, constantly. This is new to me. Previously I've worked with people of all ages, and I've never thought about their age, or mine. At HubSpot I'm constantly self-conscious. I feel ancient. At one point I notice that one of the top executives, a guy in his late forties, is coloring his hair. I wonder if I should start coloring mine. As a half measure, I buy a conditioner that supposedly will darken the parts of my hair that aren't gray, and make me look less gray overall. It doesn't work, and it makes me hate myself even more than I usually do, so I stop using it.

As far as I can tell there is only one HubSpot employee who is older than I am. His name is Max, and he's in his sixties. He once owned a company and had set aside enough money to retire. But he got wiped out in the first dotcom crash back in 2001. He never expected to be working at this point in his life, but here he is, teaching small-business owners about inbound marketing. Max and I sometimes go to lunch together in the mall food court. We trade stories about being strangers in a strange land, two gray-haired old dudes surrounded by people half our age and aware that those people do not hold us in high regard. We kvetch about the many humiliations, big and small, that are inflicted upon us. At some point I realize what Max and I must look like to the HubSpotters who see us sitting together in the food court: To them we must resemble those elderly dipshits I see sitting in Dunkin' Donuts wearing VFW windbreakers and bitching about these kids these days. I decide that Max and I should cut back on our lunches, or maybe meet on days when we're working at home and can have lunch out in the suburbs, where nobody from HubSpot will see us.

One of the maddening things about discrimination of any kind is that it is often difficult, if not impossible, to prove that it's taking place. The bias is often subtle, or even subconscious. People at HubSpot rarely talk about age bias, and when they do, they're not talking about older workers being treated poorly. They're talking about how unfair it is that people in their early twenties are not given enough responsibility, just because they're young.

But at work people make frequent references to my age. They speak euphemistically about my *experience*, wink-wink. I am asked whether I know how to use Facebook.

Penny, the receptionist, tells me she wants to get off the reception desk and do something else, but she doesn't know what. What do I think? I suggest a few roles—PR, HR, recruiting—but she doesn't like those.

"What else?" she asks.

I tell her I don't know.

"Well what's the point of having an old guy friend if you're not going to give me any ideas?" she says.

Spinner at one point comes up with an idea to get some publicity. "We should pitch a story about you working here at HubSpot, and how you're learning a whole new thing," she says. "We can call it 'Old Dog, New Tricks.'"

I look at her as if to say, *You must be kidding*. She tries to backpedal, saying she didn't mean it as an insult. She thinks it's really cool that I've joined this company with such a young culture and I've done such an *awesome* job of fitting in.

I want to believe she means well. I tell her I'll think about it.

One day the women on the blog team spot an article by an "old guy" (Mark Duffy, age fifty-three) who works at BuzzFeed. WHAT IT'S LIKE BEING THE OLDEST BUZZFEED EMPLOYEE is the headline. Duffy depicts himself as a clueless doofus and illustrates the article with pictures of Benjamin Button, Grampa Simpson, and the crazy bald senior citizen from the Six Flags commercials, the one who wears a tuxedo and giant eyeglasses and dances around like a halfwit.

The blog women think this BuzzFeed article is *hilarious*.

"Dan, you should write something like that for us," Jan says.

"Yeah!" Ashley says. "Like, 'What It's Like Being the Token Old Guy at HubSpot.' You'd be *totes awesome* at that!"

"I hope you die a hundred pounds overweight, surrounded by cats that feast on your corpse"—is not what I say.

What I do say is, "Wow, cool idea. That's something to think about."

I smile. I laugh along with the joke. I'm *old*! I'm so goddamn *old*! I should totally write something funny about what it's like to be this *old*!

At one point I'm working on a project in the brand and buzz department, and one of the twenty-something bros coins a new nickname for me: "I'm going to call you Grandpa Buzz," he says. Everyone laughs. I laugh too, because why not? Grandpa Buzz! It's hilarious! Jimmy, the bro who made up the nickname, doesn't know what I did before coming to HubSpot, and even if he did he would not care. He has probably heard of *Newsweek*, but I doubt he has ever read it. It means nothing to him. He's a recent graduate of the New Hampshire state college system, and though he works in media production, he has never heard of the *Drudge Report*, and when I refer to George Martin as the "fifth Beatle," Jimmy says, "Oh, is he the one who joined after McCartney died?" Sigh.

Maybe I sound thin-skinned. It's just a few wisecracks, after all. These are not bad people. For the most part they're not trying to be mean about my age. It probably never occurs to them that any of this is hurtful to me.

Of course I'm not going to mention any of this to the HR department. It would only make me seem nuts and paranoid and, worst of all, *old*, which is the last thing I want to be. This is no doubt why older workers tend not to complain about age discrimination. Who wants to sound like a whiner? My guess is the same applies to people who feel discriminated against based on race and gender. How do you prove that you didn't get that promotion because you're female, or black? And once you've complained, you're branded a troublemaker.

Yet I know what I feel. I know that when I look around, there are not many people like me. Sure, I'm not being picked on or actively persecuted. And these tiny slights and offhand remarks are not very significant when taken in isolation. But when you put them together they add up to . . . something.

The biggest effect of being older than everyone else is simply that it keeps me from being able to fit in. At tech companies like HubSpot, fitting in is not just something that's nice to do—it's essential to your success. It is perhaps the most important thing. Start-up people talk a lot about the importance of "culture fit." Wingman brought this up during our very first meeting, over lunch at the Thai restaurant, where he told me that he tries to hire people that he would like to meet for beers after work. In tech, the concept of culture fit is presented as a good thing. Unfortunately what culture fit often means is that young white guys like to hire other young white guys, and what you end up with is an astonishing lack of diversity.

HubSpot's problem isn't just about age. The company also has issues regarding gender and ethnicity. There are plenty of female employees, but the company's top ranks are stacked with men, almost all of them white. The sixteen-member management team includes two women. Of the eight directors, two are women, and aside from Dharmesh, everyone is white.

Across the ranks of ordinary employees, as far as I can see there are zero black people. The first time I go to an all-hands company meeting I'm taken aback: It's an ocean of white people, all of them young. It's not just that everyone is white, but that they're all the same kind of white. Klan rallies probably comprise a broader swath of the Caucasian population. It's like stumbling into some weird eugenics lab, where people get hatched from pods, already dressed in J.Crew, Banana Republic, and North Face. The women have the same shoulder-length haircut, and when it rains they all show up in knee-high Hunter boots. The guys are former jocks and frat bros, with buzz cuts, salmon-colored shorts, backward baseball caps, and boat shoes. It's like a reunion of the Greek system from some small college in New England. It's like Cape Cod has barfed up all of its summer inhabitants under the age of thirty, and they've landed in the same building in Kendall Square, still wearing their Black Dog Tavern T-shirts.

From what I can tell, HubSpot employs a handful of fifty-something people, a slightly larger number of people in their forties, a few dozen people in their thirties, and then that huge army of twenty-somethings. Later I will be told by a fellow HubSpot alumnus, a guy in his late thirties, that when he left HubSpot the company had seven hundred employees, only seventy-five of whom were over the age of thirty-five.

"Young people are just smarter," Facebook founder and CEO Mark Zuckerberg once said, when he was twenty-two years old. No doubt after that someone coached him not to say things like that anymore. But it hasn't changed his hiring preferences. In 2013, the average Facebook employee was twenty-eight years old, according to PayScale. Out of thirty-two tech companies surveyed by PayScale, eight had a median age under thirty and only six had a median age above thirty-five, the *New York Times* reported, in an article headlined, TECHNOLOGY WORKERS ARE YOUNG (REALLY YOUNG).

"Silicon Valley has become one of the most ageist places in America," Noam Scheiber proclaimed in a March 2014 article in the *New Republic*, aptly titled THE BRUTAL AGEISM OF TECH. The article introduces a San Francisco cosmetic surgeon who claims to be "the world's second biggest dispenser of Botox," and describes the plight of forty-year-old men who desperately seek out cosmetic surgery so they can hang on to their jobs. WE WANT PEOPLE WHO HAVE THEIR BEST WORK AHEAD OF THEM, NOT BEHIND THEM, reads a technology job advertisement Scheiber cites.

The tech industry's ageism is blatant and unapologetic. It's wrapped up in the mythology that has sprung up around start-ups. Almost by definition these companies are founded and run by young people. Young people are the ones who change the world. They're filled with passion. They have new ideas. Venture capitalists openly admit they prefer to invest in twenty-something founders. "The cut-off in investors' heads is thirty-two," Paul Graham, who runs an incubator called Y Combinator, once said, adding that, "I can be tricked by anyone who looks like Mark Zuckerberg." John Doerr, a legendary venture capitalist and partner at Kleiner Perkins, once said he liked to invest in "white male nerds who have dropped out of Harvard or Stanford and they have absolutely no social life. When I see that pattern coming in, it [is] very easy to decide to invest."

Companies prefer the same thing. Forget about getting booted out when you turn fifty. In Silicon Valley that happens when you turn forty. Jennifer Young, a single mother, sued her former employer, a tech company called Zillow, for age discrimination, at the ripe old age of forty-one.

In her complaint, Young says Zillow maintained a "frat house" culture with binge drinking and lewd behavior, and that she endured harassment by her younger male colleagues, who made snide comments, such as "Younger people are faster," "Are you too old to close?" "Do you even know how to work a computer?" and "You can't keep up with the rest of us." According to her complaint, Young had a successful career in sales and was "lured to Zillow with the promise that Zillow had an exceptional workplace." Once she was there, "It was commonplace at the Zillow office for managers to inform employees, including Ms. Young, that if you do not 'drink the Zillow kool-aid' there would be no opportunity for career advancement," Young's complaint reads.

Young claims Zillow runs a high-pressure sales operation that sounds a bit like the boiler room at HubSpot. At one point the stress of her job caused an old back injury to flare up. She claimed that while she was in the hospital, Zillow fired her for "job abandonment."

Another Zillow employee, Rachel Kremer, sued Zillow complaining of "sexual torture" in an "adult frat house" and said the company had "a pervasive culture of degrading women." Kremer says she received harassing text messages, like this: "Call me. Matt is showering. Thinking 333 dinner drinks and your smooth vagina." In another exchange, Kremer asks a coworker, "Wanna go join a gym and work out tonight?" His response: "Wanna blow me and have sex tonight?" No thanks, she tells him.

The lawyer who filed Kremer's discrimination lawsuit says the harassment was the result of the male employees "being brainwashed by this corporate culture." That culture, the attorney says, was basically the culture of a frat house. Zillow's CEO, Spencer Rascoff, is a thirty-something former Goldman Sachs investment banker. The company's nine-member management team includes seven white men and two white women. Its board of directors comprises ten white guys. If you think that a frat house serves a good model for how to run a

company, consider that Zillow went public in 2011, posted modest profits in 2011 and 2012, then reported losses in 2013, 2014, and the first
nine months of 2015. Despite that, Zillow's market valuation is about
$4 billion, and its founders and investors and CEO have made a fortune.

Grow fast, lose money, go public, get rich. That's the model.

I understand why venture capitalists like to invest in young founders.
Building a company is hard work, and you're trying to do this as cheaply as
possible. Also, inexperienced founders sometimes can be tricked into agree-
ing to terms that are advantageous to investors. Stories of such VC trickery
abound. Another reason to fund young people is that a lot of new tech
companies are not really about technology. They are doing social media, or
games, and that business is a lot like the entertainment business. If you were
running a record label, would you invest in a new rapper who is fifty-five
years old? Would you make a movie about a sixty-year-old superhero?

The entertainment business is built around pop stars who get hot for
two years and then disappear, and TV shows that run for five seasons.
The game is about maximizing profit in a short period of time and then
moving to something else when the first thing fizzles out. The same
now goes for tech investors. "We're in the hits business," Chris Dixon,
a partner at Andreessen Horowitz, has said.

"Making the movie" is the term that a venture capitalist friend
applies to the process of building a start-up. In my friend's tech-
company-as-movie analogy, the VCs are the producers and the CEO
is the leading man. If possible, you try to get a star who looks like
Mark Zuckerberg—young, preferably a college dropout, with maybe a
touch of Asperger's. You write a script—the "corporate narrative." You
have the origin myth, the eureka moment, and the hero's journey, with
obstacles to overcome, dragons to slay, markets to disrupt and transform. You invest millions to build the company—like shooting the
movie—and then millions more to promote it and acquire customers.

"By the time you get to the IPO, I want to see people lined up
around the block waiting to get into the theater on opening night.
That's what the first day of trading is like. It's the opening weekend for

the film. If you do things right, you put asses in the seats, and you cash out." My friend has made a fortune for himself and his partners. He's like a movie producer who keeps making the same movie again and again, and keeps raking in money at the box office.

Venture capitalists will insist that they don't engage in "pattern matching" and are not just looking for people who look like Mark Zuckerberg. But they are, and this makes perfect sense, because that's what mom-and-pop investors want to buy. Investors in the public markets want to get in on the ground floor of the next Facebook. So that's what venture capitalists in Silicon Valley try to make for them, selecting "college dropouts with insane ideas going after tiny markets with no idea how to monetize," as venture capitalist Ben Horowitz of Andreessen Horowitz once put it.

At one time, venture capitalists who invested in a tech start-up with a young founder would insist on bringing in "adult supervision," meaning an experienced executive to help build the business. But today the conventional wisdom among venture capitalists is that it's better to leave a young founder in charge and give him (and it's almost always a *him*) free rein.

Compounding the problem is the fact that Silicon Valley now attracts a different kind of person—young, male, amoral, perhaps not as evil as Patrick Bateman, the investment banker serial killer antihero of *American Psycho*, but cut from the same cloth. Guys who once would have gone to work on Wall Street hoping to get rich now move to San Francisco, where venture capitalists entrust them with millions of dollars and tell them to do their worst. "In all too many cases, what venture capitalists are investing in is assholes," Sarah Lacy, editor of the tech blog Pando, wrote in a 2014 essay that was widely read and shared in Silicon Valley.

Give millions of dollars to young entitled assholes, provide no adult supervision, and what happens next is predictable. You get Gurbaksh Chahal, the CEO of a start-up called RadiumOne, relieved of duty after being charged with domestic violence for allegedly beating up his girlfriend. (Chahal maintained his innocence and pled guilty to two misdemeanors.) Chahal previously appeared on the reality TV show *Secret Millionaire* and posed sitting on his bed, which had a headboard with gold trim and a gold crown over a golden initial G.

You get Mahbod Moghadam, co-founder of Rap Genius, booted out of his own company after posting tasteless jokes about a murder spree on the UC Santa Barbara campus. You get Whitney Wolfe, the female co-founder of Tinder, suing the company for sexual harassment, claiming she endured months of harassment in a frat-house culture where she was subjected to racist, sexist, homophobic, misogynistic and insulting texts, including one calling Wolfe a "whore." (The lawsuit was settled.)

You end up with GitHub, a tiny start-up, raising $100 million and using the money to create a replica of the Oval Office, and Tom Preston-Werner, the president of GitHub, resigning after a female employee complains about sexual harassment and retaliation. You get Snapchat founder Evan Spiegel, age twenty-three, raising $850 million and needing to explain emails he sent in college urging his frat brothers to "have some girl put your large kappa sigma dick down her throat."

Along with personal misbehavior there have been allegations of misbehavior at the corporate level. Facebook was accused of invading people's privacy and made a settlement (admitting no wrongdoing) with the FTC. Path was caught using people's personal information without their permission, and apologized. Zynga forced some employees to give back stock options just before the IPO. Apple has been criticized for using complex accounting structures to avoid paying taxes in the United States, for exploiting underpaid workers in China, and for colluding with Google to prevent poaching employees; in the collusion case the two companies settled with workers who were suing for lost wages. An Uber executive reportedly threatened to spy on journalists. Groupon's initial IPO paperwork used misleading financial metrics that the *Wall Street Journal* called "financial voodoo," and which the SEC forced them to change. In 2012 Groupon had to restate its financial results after under-reporting its losses, attributing the mistake to "material weakness in its controls." The two co-founders of Secret, a mobile app maker, raised a $25 million round of funding, put $6 million into their pockets, then nine months later shut down the company. "It's like a bank heist," one of their pissed-off investors said. (The investor later walked back that comment, saying it was a "poor choice of words.")

Start-ups seem to believe it is okay for them to bend rules. Some, like Uber and Airbnb, have built their businesses by defying regulations. Then again, if laws are stupid, why follow them? In the World According to Start-ups, when tech companies cut corners it is for the greater good. These start-up founders are not like Gordon Gekko or Bernie Madoff, driven by greed and avarice; they are Rosa Parks and Martin Luther King Jr., engaging in civil disobedience. There's also a sense among start-ups that it's okay for them to break the rules because they're underdogs competing against huge opponents; they're David, firing his slingshot at Goliath. Another argument is that the big guys break just as many rules as the little guys. Everybody cheats, and only suckers drive inside the lines.

Presumably the venture capitalists in Silicon Valley know what will happen when they invest in young, inexperienced founders, and they simply don't care. Sexual harassment scandals are easy enough to fix: Fine the founder, fire the founder, issue an apology, settle the lawsuits. From the perspective of the investors, this still works out best. If you just want to build something quickly and cash out, this probably all makes sense.

What's great for VCs may not be so great for the rest of us, however, especially as these companies make their way into the public markets. The last dotcom bubble led to a crash that wiped out the entire stock market. This time the amounts are even bigger. When AOL paid $10 billion for Netscape at the very peak of the dotcom mania, it seemed that the world had lost its mind. Yet Uber has raised more than $8 billion in private funding and is valued at more than $60 billion. By the end of 2015, Facebook's market value stands at $300 billion, more than Walmart, Johnson & Johnson, and Wells Fargo, and about the same as General Electric. Twitter, which has yet to report an annual profit, is nonetheless valued at $16 billion, about the same as Fiat Chrysler, which makes an actual profit by selling actual cars, and more than stalwarts like Alcoa and Whirlpool.

Just like last time, lots of smart people in Silicon Valley keep insisting that this all makes perfect sense and there's nothing to worry about. This time it's different. This time these are *real* companies with *real* businesses.

Sixteen

Ritual Humiliation as Rehabilitation

Two weeks after my Facebook fiasco, in which I blasted Halligan for saying that gray hair and experience are overrated, it's time to face the music. It's the middle of December, a week before Christmas. Trotsky sets a meeting with me, in a conference room on the fourth floor. I assume this is the end. Cranium never likes to fire anyone himself. It would be his style to wait for Trotsky to come on board and then have Trotsky do it. But Trotsky assures me this is not the case and that I'm not being fired. I find this hard to believe.

"I'm sure they want me to leave," I say. "Maybe they can't fire me, but my guess is they want you to have a talk with me and start paving the way for me to get out of here. The sad thing is, I really wanted to make a go of it here. And I was looking forward to working with you. Anyway, it's my own fault. I should have just kept my mouth shut about the Halligan thing."

"Why do you keep talking in the past tense?" Trotsky says. "You're talking like your time here is over."

I've been reading *Going Clear*, Lawrence Wright's book about Scientology. The first rule in a cult is that you don't criticize the cult. You can screw up again and again, and make one mistake after another. You can churn out terrible parody videos and invent things like the Blog Topic Generator, and none of that matters, as long as you're (a) enthusiastic and (b) loyal.

If you're disloyal, no amount of talent or ability matters, and what's more, I don't have any special talent for this work anyway. I'm never going to be content marketer of the year. I can't write for Marketing Mary, or for Ollie the Owner, or for Enterprise Erin.

Trotsky doesn't want to hear it. As a matter of fact he has a big project for me. He wants to create a special series of e-books built around my "personal brand," where I can write for a high-level audience. Also, he is going to move me out of the boiler room and set me up with a desk in the newly renovated space on the fourth floor, in a quiet room with lots of sunlight.

"There's just one thing I need you to do," he says. He pauses. He closes his laptop and looks at me. "I need you to apologize to Spinner."

Ever since the Facebook incident, Spinner has been giving me the silent treatment. If I walk past her desk and say hello, she will look away and not respond. If someone sets a meeting and I'm on the list, Spinner refuses to attend.

"You have to make things right with her," Trotsky says. He tells me he can broker a deal where I will send Spinner a meeting request via Google Calendar, and she will accept my request, as long as she knows that the purpose of the meeting is for me to apologize.

"I don't have any problem with Spinner," I say.

"Great," he says. "So just apologize to her."

"Apologize for what? I never said anything about her. I could understand if Halligan wanted an apology, but why Spinner?"

Oddly enough, Halligan does not seem angry at me. I've run into him in the hallway, and we traded hellos as if nothing happened.

Trotsky says I need to learn how PR people see the world. "Spinner just got her boss profiled in the *New York Times*. That's a big deal for a company like this. It's probably the biggest story that Spinner has ever worked on. Then you ruined it. You came in and peed all over her shoes."

In the world I come from, there's no way that someone in editorial would grovel before someone from PR. Apologizing to the PR person who set up the interview is like apologizing to Halligan's administrative assistant. Is Halligan's admin angry, too? Does she need an apology?

"How about the Uber driver who picked up Halligan at LaGuardia and drove him to the *Times* building? Is *he* disappointed? He drove all the way out there, and all the way back, and then I ruined everything. Should I call *him* up and apologize to him too?"

Trotsky sighs. "Look," he says. "I get it. But trust me. You should apologize. It's the smart thing to do."

Fair enough. Trotsky is my new boss. I want to make him happy. I want to show that I'm a team player. If he tells me to do this, I'll do it. If he thinks this is the smart move for me, then I'll trust his judgment. He's spent years working in companies like this. He knows more about office politics than I ever will.

"Fine," I say. "I'll get on her calendar."

If groveling has to be done, I will at least put some effort into it. As soon as everyone gets back from the holiday break, in January, I go online, order a dozen gourmet brownies, and have them delivered to Spinner, with a note that says, "Can we be friends again please? If you want to yell at me for a while first, I understand. I'm married, and used to it."

She loves it. The whole team sees her get the gift box and open the brownies, and then everyone wants to know who sent the brownies and why, which means Spinner gets to tell everyone that I'm apologizing to her for being such a jerk. She puts the brownies out on a table so that everyone can share and so that everyone walking by will see them.

When the two of us sit down for our meeting, I start by saying that I'm really sorry, but that before I say anything I want to just listen and hear her out. We're in a tiny little meeting room, just big enough for two people, with a glass wall, so that everyone walking by can see us in there.

She talks. Words come out of her mouth. I have no idea what they are. The parenting books that I've read suggest that to help a kid work through a tantrum you should start by listening empathically. So that's what I do. When she's done, I fall on my sword. I tell her that I respect her and admire her, and that she is an amazing PR person and a remarkable human being. My biggest regret is that this dumb thing that I have done might come between us, because gosh, if nothing else, Spinner is someone I hope will be my friend for the rest of my life. Our friendship really matters to me, I tell her.

She nods as I speak, and says, "Agreed. Totally. Absolutely. Likewise. Absolutely. Totally," in her vocal fry voice.

The whole thing takes only a few minutes. The content of our conversation is not what matters. This was all about the gesture. This was about Spinner making *me* apologize to *her*, and having Cranium and Trotsky take her side.

Now that she has gotten her way, we can move on. That is what I believe, anyway. I leave the meeting thinking that this bit of kabuki theater has made things right between us. As I will learn, Spinner still has a knife out for me.

Seventeen

A Disturbance in the Farce

My stand-off with Spinner isn't the only trouble that winter. Trotsky's hiring has thrown a lot of people off balance, including Wingman. Half of Wingman's job involves overseeing the content team. But now Trotsky will be doing that. Suddenly, Wingman has lost half of his direct reports and half of his responsibilities.

What's worse, Wingman is a director, while Trotsky has been hired in as a vice president and thus outranks him. Why should Wingman have a lower title than the new guy? Sure, the new guy is a decade older than Wingman, has more experience, and was a vice president at his last two jobs. But Wingman has more experience *here*. He's been at HubSpot for more than three years! He is Cranium's trusty sidekick!

Cranium has a simple solution: He promotes Wingman to vice president, too. In a memo to the department, Cranium explains that Wingman earned the promotion by being a "yes man," then adds that he's not saying Wingman is a sycophant. What he means is that whenever he asks Wingman if something is possible, Wingman says yes. Can we double the number of leads we generate every month? Could HubSpot build a rocket and be the first marketing automation company to establish a base on the moon? Is HubSpot the greatest company ever? Yes, yes, and more yes!

Cranium says Wingman's willingness to give up half of his job in order to make room for a new guy shows that he's putting the company first, ahead of himself. Wingman reminds me of Chauncey Gardiner, the simpleton hero played by Peter Sellers in *Being There*, who rises to become an advisor to the president of the United States, and at the end of the movie appears headed for the Oval Office himself. Wingman isn't a simpleton, but he's not overly burdened with intelligence, either. He was in the right place at the right time. Now he is a vice president at a company that soon will be publicly traded, and for what? Just for being there.

Zack, however, will not be as lucky. His entire job involves running the content group. But now Trotsky is doing that. Zack literally has nothing to do. Nevertheless, we get a memo saying that Zack is safe, that he is not leaving the company, that he will be assuming a new role and remains a valuable member of the team.

But that's bullshit.

"He's dead," Trotsky tells me, in one of our first meetings. "He's gotta go."

Trotsky explains that there is no way he can join a new company, take away a guy's job, and then let that guy hang around. It's not personal, but Zack has to go.

"How are you going to get rid of him?" I ask. I find this stuff intriguing. I know nothing about office politics.

Trotsky leans back on his beanbag chair. "I'm going to help Zack understand that he would be happier somewhere else," he says.

He smiles. He loves this shit, and I get the sense that he's good at it. Sure enough, two months later, in March, we get an email from Cranium informing us that Zack is "graduating" in order to look for his next adventure. The whole thing is handled with a smile and a hug. Trotsky's fingerprints are nowhere to be seen.

Trotsky's appointment also spells trouble for Marcia and Jan, the two women who run the blog. For years they have operated their own little fiefdom, pushing people around, ignoring orders, and playing favorites.

They bullied Wingman and dismissed Zack. Trotsky makes it clear that he's going to change the way they do things, and that, unlike Zack, he has real authority and is not afraid of them. One change has to do with e-books. The blog writers are supposed to coordinate their efforts with the e-book writers. If the e-book team creates a book about, say, how to use Snapchat to sell pet food, the blog should generate articles about Snapchat and pet food, and use those posts to promote the e-book.

Instead, Marcia and Jan do whatever they want. They might write articles about Snapchat and pet food, or they might not. Some of it comes down to whether they like the person who wrote the e-book. Some of it hinges on whether they feel the e-book people were polite enough to them or gave them sufficient notice. If Marcia and Jan refuse to promote the e-book, the e-book just dies, because nobody finds it unless it gets mentioned on the blog. Over and over, the e-book writers crank out books only to see them die on a virtual shelf, because Marcia and Jan refuse to play ball.

That bullshit is over, Trotsky says. The blog women might not like his decisions, but Cranium has brought him in to break up the log-jam and dysfunction, something that Wingman has been unable to do. Trotsky doesn't shy away from conflict. He actually likes it. The blog women immediately start pushing back on everything he suggests, pointing out reasons why such-and-such won't work. They sit in meetings with sourpuss expressions on their face.

"I can't believe this place," Trotsky tells me one day, when we're having our biweekly one-on-one meeting, which is supposed to be a sort of status update but usually involves just hanging out on beanbag chairs and shooting the shit.

Unlike just about everyone else here, Trotsky has actually worked at companies other than HubSpot. He's having a hard time adjusting.

"Do you realize that the girl who runs the email campaigns can just refuse to do something that I tell her to do?" he says. "She's twenty-two years old, and just graduated from college. I'm a vice president. But I can't give her an order. All I can do is ask. And she can say no. And she does! She tells me she's too busy!"

Welcome to my nightmare, I tell him. "I thought maybe all companies are like this," I say.

"Yeah, well, they're not," he says.

Trotsky is not overly impressed with HubSpot. He thinks the culture is ridiculous, and the people are precious. Cranium doesn't communicate at all and has been completely ignoring Trotsky, giving him no guidance or direction. Wingman is a dimwit and an insecure hack. Spinner is a lousy PR flack and has no sense of humor. The women on the blog team are obstinate and have an overly inflated sense of their abilities. For annual performance reviews, HubSpot asks employees to rate themselves across several categories, on a scale of one to five. I give myself a set of threes. Trotsky tells me that one of the blog women—he won't tell me which one—has given herself fives across the board. He can't believe it. "These people really think they're the shit," he says.

I'm relieved to hear him vent like this. For months I've been walking around HubSpot thinking that the place is nuts, and then questioning my sanity because everyone else seemed to have no problem. Now here is Trotsky, and he sees things the way I do—or at least that's the impression I get from our conversations.

In the first quarter of 2014, people start disappearing. For all of 2013 HubSpot was on a massive hiring spree, especially in sales and marketing, but now the company is reversing course. I suspect this has something to do with the fact that the company recently hired a new chief financial officer who has experience running publicly traded companies. Max, my old-guy buddy, says he's hearing rumors about an IPO. Maybe the new CFO wants to reduce costs and spruce up the financials so that HubSpot can go public.

For whatever reason, people are getting booted out. It's like living in Argentina during the 1970s. Every week someone else is no longer sitting at their desk, and we get an email from Cranium telling us that so-and-so has graduated, and hey ho, let's all wish them well. One guy, who worked with Trotsky at his last company, and whom Trotsky recruited, lasts only for a few weeks and then gets the axe when someone decides they don't need him after all.

So many people are being let go that at one of our weekly marketing department meetings someone submits an anonymous question to Cranium: "Over the last two months, we have lost at least one male employee every week. Are the remaining males safe?"

Cranium tries to make a joke of it. He assures us that HubSpot is not cutting costs, that companies make adjustments all the time. He says he is actively *hiring*, and the company is *growing*, and everything is *awesome*.

In our next one-on-one beanbag chair bull session, I tell Trotsky that it seems to me that the company is trying to cut costs. I realize that I'm probably being paid more than most of the young people in our department, and if makes sense to cut me loose, I will understand. "All I ask," I say, "is that you give me a little bit of warning. I'm asking this not as an employee, but as a friend. Just give me a little time, and I'll go find another job. I'll get out of your hair." Trotsky assures me there is no pressure on him to cut his budget, but if things change, he will let me know.

For a few months in the first half of 2014, things actually get better. I'm now working up on the fourth floor, in a newly renovated space, a world away from the ring of hell that is the telemarketing room. I'm writing e-books aimed at venture capitalists and chief marketing officers, which isn't as fun as being a columnist at *Newsweek*, but it's better than explaining HTML to Marketing Mary. I'm also helping write an update to *Inbound Marketing*, the book that Halligan and Dharmesh published in 2009.

On the side, I've started picking up some freelance work, writing articles for *Newsweek Japan* on topics like robotics and artificial intelligence. Sure, there are still days when I go home and tell Sasha about some astonishingly stupid thing that some bozo has done, but most of the time I can just tune things out.

The best thing is that I no longer have to work with Marcia, Jan, and Ashley, the women on the blog team, or Wingman. The only person I deal with is Trotsky, and he and I are becoming pals. I like Trotsky so much that one weekend I invite him and his family to a cookout at my house. I cook steaks and our kids play together. At work, Trotsky sometimes swings by my desk just to talk.

Apparently the women on the blog team have noticed that Trotsky and I are getting to be friends, and this bugs them. They don't like Trotsky. Neither does Spinner, for that matter. Spinner complains to Cranium that Trotsky and I are getting too friendly. Cranium tells Trotsky that he needs to stop hanging out with me at work. That, anyway, is what Trotsky tells me.

"The women on the blog team don't like it," he says.

I can't believe it. "What is this, middle school?" I say.

"Well," he says, "it's not just that."

Spinner has told Cranium that some of our banter is making the women who sit near me uncomfortable. One woman who overheard one of our conversations felt it was inappropriate. Trotsky won't say which woman complained, but he does tell me which conversation it was. We were talking about child care. Trotsky's wife works full time. They've tried day care but are thinking about hiring a nanny. We've dealt with the same issue, and first hired a nanny and then resorted to getting au pairs to live with us and watch the kids. It turns out that having a nineteen-year-old German girl living in your house is maybe not the greatest idea. Nothing inappropriate ever happened, but it drove my wife nuts, I tell him. Trotsky says no way would his wife even entertain having an au pair live with them.

This conversation has made someone uncomfortable. That person confided in Spinner, who reported us to Cranium.

To me the whole thing seems stupid. But Trotsky takes it seriously. "You can get fired for almost anything and survive," he says. "But the one thing you cannot survive is getting fired for sexual harassment. If that happens, you'll never work again."

From then on I steer clear of Spinner and the women on the blog team. I say hello when I come to work and goodbye when I'm leaving, and that's about it.

Trotsky's trouble with Spinner is just beginning, however. For whatever reason, she has decided that she hates him, and she's waiting for another reason to pounce. One night, foolishly, he gives her an opportunity.

It starts when Trotsky writes a Facebook post about the Ban Bossy campaign that Facebook COO Sheryl Sandberg is promoting. Sandberg wants everyone to stop using the word *bossy* to describe girls. Trotsky says that instead of using her bully pulpit to pursue something as trivial as the word *bossy*, Sandberg should dedicate herself to more important issues, like the plight of the African elephant, which is on the verge of extinction.

Trotsky loves elephants. He's always ranting about the awful poachers who kill them for their ivory. I have no idea how elephants became so dear to him, or how his mind makes the illogical leap from Sheryl Sandberg's feminist crusade to the issue of elephant poaching. I also don't care.

Spinner, however, does. She goes ballistic. Instead of bringing the issue up at work and talking to Trotsky privately, she leaps into Trotsky's Facebook post and starts adding comments bashing him for not taking women's rights seriously enough. She says Trotsky needs to think about the message he is sending to the talented and intelligent women who work for him at HubSpot. What will they think when they read his post? They will feel neglected. They will feel that he cares more about elephants than he does about them.

This is insane. It's also a strange move for a PR person to make. We're all supposed to be "solving for enterprise value" and protecting the brand at all costs. Why attack your company's newest vice president, a guy who is two levels above you in the org chart, and do it in public, on Facebook? What is she thinking?

I'm starting to suspect that Spinner might be a little bit unhinged. I definitely think Trotsky is unhinged. He gets into fights on Facebook, and goes on and on, like a dog with a bone. But this is even better, because just like Trotsky, Spinner loves to fight and will never back down.

For two days they go back and forth, trading insults on Facebook. It's like watching monkeys throw their shit at each other. It's ugly, and stupid, and the best thing ever. Spinner lectures Trotsky about feminism, and Trotsky scolds Spinner about elephants. Soon other people—some from HubSpot, some just friends of Trotsky or Spinner—start chiming in, taking sides and egging them on.

The argument degenerates to the level of seventh graders trading insults in the schoolyard. Neither one of them will give up. Every time you think it's over, one of them lobs another grenade. Trotsky sends me email and tells me he's done, he's not going to take the bait anymore. But then I guess he sits at home, fuming, or maybe drinking, and finally he fires back. But she can't let him have the last word, so then she fires back.

Finally Cranium has to intervene—not on Facebook, but in real life, at the office. He calls the two of them into a meeting and tells them to knock this shit off, because they are making the company look bad.

I love this. I think this is great. I wish they would fight every day. I have dreams where Trotsky and Spinner are dressed up in *lucha libre* costumes, stepping into an MMA octagon while the women on the blog team throw candy at them and jeer.

Eighteen

A House of Cards?

One Thursday morning in the first week of April 2014 Trotsky pulls me aside in a hallway and shares a secret: HubSpot has filed its IPO paperwork. "It's not public yet, and I'm not supposed to tell anyone," he says, practically whispering. We're about to go into a meeting. We're waiting for the people in the conference room to finish up and get out. "But they're hoping to start trading in June."

In the past few months I've started having doubts about whether HubSpot can pull off an IPO. I first started worrying after Halligan called that come-to-Jesus meeting in October and told us he was booting out the head of sales. "The machine is just not working that well" is his quote that has stuck in my mind.

But here we are. The deal is on. HubSpot is going to sell its shares to the public, and we're all going to cash out. It's really going to happen.

Only it doesn't. The problem is that HubSpot files its paperwork right after another tech start-up, Box, announces its own plans to go public. Box is a high-profile company in Silicon Valley. It's seen as a bellwether for other cloud computing companies, including HubSpot.

Box has a charming, charismatic, twenty-something CEO, Aaron Levie, and everyone has been under the impression that the company is doing a booming business. But now it has published its financial results and the numbers are underwhelming. Sales are growing, but Box is spending way too much on sales and marketing, and losing huge amounts of money. To be sure, that's the case for most of the other cloud software companies. But even by the relaxed standards of the second tech bubble, Box's results are disappointing.

Meanwhile, for some reason, shares in cloud computing and "software as a service" companies are starting to swoon. One index of thirty-seven publicly traded cloud-related companies loses $58 billion in market value over the course of two months. Salesforce.com, our rival and role model, drops 25 percent. Workday, another cloud company that's comparable to HubSpot, drops 40 percent.

On May 1, the *Wall Street Journal* reports that Box has decided to delay its IPO, since "investors' love affair with cloud software is waning at the worst possible time."

That's tough news for HubSpot. Trotsky tells me, again on the sly, that management has decided to shelve our stock offering and hope the market picks up again in the fall. The good news is that, unlike Box, HubSpot has kept its IPO plans secret. No one will ever know that we held off, and we can try again down the road.

HubSpot has been able to do this thanks to a provision in the 2012 JOBS Act that lets "emerging growth" companies, with less than $1 billion in sales, keep their IPO paperwork private until the very last minute, when they are ready to start pitching their stock to investors. The provision was meant to boost the economy after the recession by making it easier for companies to go public, which in theory would create new jobs.

An unintended but perhaps predictable consequence of this provision is that it allows companies to squeak into the public markets without being subjected to as much scrutiny. Some people fret that this is leading to bad outcomes, as described in a September 2014 *Wall Street Journal* article: "It is an increasingly common story: a company makes scaled-back disclosures about itself before going public and gives investors scant time to digest the information. The shares sizzle in their first weeks of trading but start to fizzle within a year."

Venture capitalists and start-up founders love anything that makes it easier to flog their shares to the public. They can sell during the sizzle and run away before the fizzle. Mom and pop maybe should be paying more attention, and if I were still a journalist, I would certainly be warning them to beware of wobbly, money-losing companies floating shares to the public. But I am not a journalist. I am now on the same team as the VCs and founders, and hoping, like them, for a chance to foist off my shares. We can use all the help we can get.

I'm curious about what we will discover when HubSpot finally does make its financial information public. At the meeting in October Halligan talked to us about revenue, churn, and customer acquisition cost, but he said nothing about our profit, or lack of profit. I assume we're losing money, but I have no idea how much. When you work at a privately held company you really only know what management tells you. Officially, the word from Cranium is that everything is *awesome*.

But I'm getting the sense that HubSpot's financial results might not be very good. Two months before this, in March 2014, I had breakfast with Gordon, a venture capitalist who knew some of HubSpot's investors. Gordon was not a fan of HubSpot. He told me he had met with Halligan and Shah when they first put the company together and were trying to raise money. "I went back and told my partners, 'I wouldn't put a penny into that place. They're selling snake oil.' Since then I've had to eat my words, because they've done pretty well."

Gordon had an engineering background. Before he became a venture capitalist he had built and sold a tech company. He asked me if I believed that HubSpot's software did what the company claimed. "Do you really think some small-business owner, like a plumber, is going to come home at the end of the day and then write a blog? Do you think that happens?"

"I don't know." I shrugged.

"Even if people use the software, do you think it actually works?"

I had wondered the same thing. One of the consultants told me it was a mixed bag. Some customers buy the software but don't use it, because they're too busy to write a blog. They're like people who sign up for a gym membership then never go to the gym. Among those who do use the software, results vary. There are some places where the stuff just doesn't work very well, the consultant told me. "And then there are about 10 percent of customers where it's absolutely magic," he said. "It's like you've given them a dowsing rod, they've found a well, the town is saved. It's magic."

Gordon says Halligan and Shah are good at telling stories and generating hype, but he doesn't think much of HubSpot's engineering team, and he is particularly dismissive of Shah. "He's not really an engineer anymore," Gordon says. "He's a blogger. He writes a blog. He makes PowerPoint decks."

Gordon was equally contemptuous of Cranium: "Everyone tells me he's some kind of marketing genius, but I don't see it. I've asked him several times to explain the product to me. He couldn't do it. I still don't understand what the product does. I've met a bunch of people at HubSpot and nobody there impresses me. None of them seems that smart."

After breakfast, we stood outside. It was a chilly Cambridge morning, with a cold wind blowing off the Charles River. Gordon told me I should stick around through the IPO, then find something better to do. "The place is a house of cards," he told me. "I'm just hoping they can get to an IPO so the guys who invested can cash out before the whole thing collapses."

Those were pretty strong words, especially to use around a former business journalist. I don't think Gordon meant that HubSpot was a flimflam operation. Obviously HubSpot had a real business, and was selling a real product, to real customers, and generating real revenue. I think what Gordon meant was that he didn't think the business was sustainable, that sooner or later a strong wind would come along and blow the place down.

Later, in August, when HubSpot publishes its financial results, I will think back to this breakfast and Gordon's comment about the "house of cards." Because it turns out the numbers are not so great. In seven years the company has accumulated losses of more than $100 million. It has burned through its cash and is borrowing money against a line of credit.

If the market bounces back, HubSpot will be able to go public and its investors will get a return. But if stocks remain depressed, or if, God forbid, the bubble pops and the market crashes and HubSpot can't sell shares to the public, then its fate will be uncertain. In the worst possible scenario, its investors could lose a lot of money.

That's what is at stake. That, I believe, is why Halligan has seemed so freaked out, why he pushed out his head of sales, and why the new CFO has been cutting costs.

Nevertheless, back in the furniture factory, the party continues.

In mid-May I write to a friend describing the atmosphere at work: "Monday was tequila tasting day. Today is a kayaking adventure starting at 2:30 followed by a pizza party. They just renovated the second floor and put in yet another kitchen, this one with beer and cider on tap. Expense is justified because 'recruiting.' They've raised $100m and I suspect have burned all or most of it."

I'm right to suspect that, because in truth they have burned through pretty much all of their money. But at this point I already have one foot out the door—I've been offered a job in Hollywood.

Nineteen

Go West, Old Man

Four years earlier, in 2010, back when my life was good, when I was writing for *Newsweek* and developing a cable TV show based on my Fake Steve Jobs book, I was sitting at my desk one day when my iPhone rang and it was Ari Emanuel. Ari is the head of William Morris Endeavor, a big Hollywood talent agency. He's the real-life person that Ari Gold, the character in *Entourage*, is based on.

I couldn't believe it. This was Ari. *The* Ari. Calling *me.*

"Who are you?" Ari asked. "How come we haven't signed you yet?"

Larry Charles, my collaborator on the cable TV show, was represented by WME. Larry Charles is a big deal in Hollywood, and apparently he had sent an email to Ari saying good things about me. Now Ari wanted me to leave the United Talent Agency, where I had been represented, and come to WME.

Who says no to Ari? I jumped agencies, figuring I had just taken my first step toward becoming a big player in Hollywood.

Except then my show got killed, and pretty soon I stopped hearing from WME. I figured they had forgotten all about me.

But no: Now it's March 2014, and I'm roaming around the Adobe Digital Marketing Summit in Salt Lake City, fantasizing about hurling myself over the railing of the convention center and wondering whether the fall to the first floor would kill me or just leave me paralyzed, when I get a call from the 310 area code.

It's an assistant at WME. He asks if I can please hold for a guy named Ryan, whose name I remember. Back in 2010, Ryan was the assistant who placed the calls on behalf of the agents.

Now Ryan is an agent. He's *my* agent, apparently. Ryan says there is a new show on HBO called *Silicon Valley*, and they're just about to start airing the first episodes, and my old pal Larry Charles has told the showrunner on *Silicon Valley* about me, and if the show gets picked up for a second season would I like to come to Los Angeles and join the writing staff?

"Dude, I wish you could see where I am right now," I say. I'm looking at a horde of hungry marketing schmucks who are shuffling down the sides of a buffet table, stacking their plates with pasta salad and various kinds of meat in various kinds of gravy. "If you could, you would not even need to ask."

Yes! I'm in. I'm *so* in. Ryan says it's not a sure thing, and I will have to interview with the showrunner, Alec Berg, and we'll have to see if the show gets renewed for a second season, but he thinks it will. Great. Whatever. I call Sasha and tell her what just happened. I'm feeling dizzy. Back in my room, I write an article for the HubSpot blog about some presentation that I just sat through, but in my mind I'm already seven hundred miles away, sitting on a beach in Santa Monica. As soon as I finish the article I start looking at guesthouse rentals in Laurel Canyon.

I can't believe this. The gig feels like a gift from the gods, or maybe a cruel practical joke that one of my friends is playing on me. I feel like George Bailey in *It's a Wonderful Life*—I was just about to jump when an angel appeared. Ryan, my new agent, is that angel. He's my Clarence. God bless you, Ryan.

I talk to Alec Berg. We hit it off. The show gets renewed. Ryan negotiates my deal. As soon as it's official, I set a meeting with Trotsky. Taking the gig at *Silicon Valley* means I'll have to quit HubSpot, but who cares? That's fine by me, and in fact it gives me a way to slide out of HubSpot while saving face.

We plunk down on our beanbag chairs and I tell him what I've been offered: fourteen weeks on an HBO show. It's an entry-level staff writer job, but it's a foot in the door to a new career writing in Hollywood—"a potentially life-transforming opportunity" is how a friend of mine, a novelist who has become a big-shot millionaire TV writer, has put it to me.

"You have to take it," Trotsky says.

"No shit."

I'm ready to give my notice, but Trotsky asks me to hang on for a couple of days and let him get back to me, because he has something else in mind. He comes back with an offer: I can take an unpaid leave of absence from HubSpot for the fourteen weeks, and then return to work. I'll keep my health insurance coverage. I'll also continue vesting my shares.

It's an amazing deal for me. Trotsky reckons it's a great deal for HubSpot too. The local press and the tech bloggers in Silicon Valley are bound to write articles about their journalist buddy getting hired to work on a TV show. HubSpot will look cool and get some good publicity.

Trotsky sets up a meeting with Spinner and Tracy, the woman who runs brand and buzz. Cranium doesn't attend. Before the meeting Trotsky tells me, via email, that Spinner "is eager to put heads together to discuss how HubSpot can derive value from your HBO gig." In the meeting, Spinner expresses astonishment that I've been recruited to work on a TV show. "How did this happen?" she says.

She seems to know nothing about my background or what I did before coming to HubSpot. I'm pretty sure I've told her that a few years ago I developed a TV show for a cable network. I told her this because Cranium was tossing around the idea of having HubSpot make a documentary film, something along the lines of *The Naked Brand*. I asked if I could be involved with the project, since (a) I'm friends with the guy who made *The Naked Brand* and could ask him for advice and guidance, and (b) I have some experience working in TV. No one was interested.

Spinner believes HubSpot can milk some favorable publicity out of the news that I'm going to work on the show. She also wants to do some horse trading with HBO. Can we get them to plug HubSpot on the show? Could Halligan get a cameo? Not likely, I tell her.

Trotsky makes a big deal of reminding me that he is the one who cut this great deal for me with HubSpot. He also seems oddly dismissive of what I'm doing, as if I'm some kind of eccentric.

"Not many people would do what you're doing," he says.

I don't know if he really means that, but in the world I come from, people would give their left nut to be a writer on an HBO show. Maybe he's jealous. He's a huge movie buff, and supposedly he once hoped to become a novelist. He has all those crazy tattoos on his arms, and refers to himself as "a creative." I find it hard to believe that he wouldn't leap at the chance to work in Hollywood.

The plan is I will leave in May and return in September, just in time for the Inbound conference, which is great timing, because I can give a talk about storytelling and my experience working on a TV show, or something. Maybe I can get one of the stars from the show to give a talk as well. Or we could do a panel.

Sasha and the kids come to Los Angeles with me. We rent a little guesthouse in Topanga Canyon, way up in the woods, far from civilization. The kids go to surf camp at Zuma Beach in Malibu. Sasha rides horses at a ranch in Topanga. In the morning we hike in Topanga State Park, where mule deer graze in the tall dry grass. At night Sasha and I sit on the deck vaping cannabis oil—I've obtained a prescription—and listen to coyotes howl. HubSpot seems very far away.

I'm working on the Sony lot in Culver City. It's a classic Hollywood Golden Age lot, built in the 1920s, with huge soundstages and big gates and people zipping around on bikes and golf carts, the place where Metro-Goldwyn-Mayer made *The Wizard of Oz*. On my first day at work, I stop across the street and snap photos of the archway over the Madison Avenue gate. I walk to the gate, give my name to the security guard, and she actually lets me walk in. Our offices are in the Rita Hayworth building. I want to pinch myself.

One big difference between this and HubSpot is that I'm back in the world of grown-ups. I'm no longer working with people half my age, with a boss who believes gray hair and experience are overrated. Here my boss is Mike Judge, age fifty-one, who created *Beavis and Butt-head*, *King of the Hill*, and *Office Space*. My other boss, Alec Berg, is in his mid-forties and was a top writer on *Seinfeld* and *Curb Your Enthusiasm*. The others have worked on *30 Rock* and *The Office*, among other shows.

Here, you are allowed to tell dirty jokes and to be a cynical, sarcastic prick. In fact, it's encouraged. There are ten of us, and it is an intense room. The writers are smart and funny, but they're also a lot friendlier than people at HubSpot. For more than a year I've had to bottle up my disgusting sense of humor. I've even started to feel ashamed of it. Here, everyone is disgusting. We sit around trading the worst poop-related stories we've ever heard, and pitching jokes about enormous cocks. We get paid to do this. It's bliss.

My commute home every night takes me past the beaches in Santa Monica, then up a long switchback road into the Santa Monica Mountains to Topanga, a place where the sixties never ended, full of unreconstructed hippies and stoners. I am a long way from home, and I love it. I don't want to go back.

I'm not sure I can become a TV writer, or even want to become one. But the longer I stay in Los Angeles, the more certain I become that there's one thing I definitely cannot do, and that is work at HubSpot. I cannot return to work among those earnest, upbeat kids who spend their days sending Cheers for Peers on TINYpulse—*Ashley for president!!!!!*—and who would never, ever sit in a meeting and pitch jokes about someone's enormous horse cock.

I'm still in touch with Trotsky. We trade emails and talk on the phone. I've been helping out with the Inbound conference. I've persuaded a friend of mine who runs a PR agency in New York to give a talk about dealing with the press. A producer for *Silicon Valley* has agreed to do a presentation.

But I'm losing heart. Maybe Trotsky picks up on this, because on a Tuesday morning in August, about a month before I'm due to return to HubSpot, I get an email from him, sent from his personal account:

Consider this question as coming from a friend:
Why do you want to work at HubSpot? I am pretty
sure you aren't crazy about the leadership, the
"culture," or the business. I would be surprised
if you enjoyed the work. I think the novelty
aspect—doing marketing, seeing how marketing
works from the inside—has its appeal; and there's
probably a voyeuristic pleasure in drawing back
the curtain on how a business runs. The IPO could
be a feather in your cap—from a variety of per-
spectives (some $, the professional experience,
and a great item on a future resume)—and the salary is reasonable. But other than those things,
combined with the relatively small Boston market
for one like you, what's keeping you here?

I remember how Trotsky got rid of Zack, by "helping him understand that he would be happier somewhere else." Right away I call him
and ask him if that's what he is doing to me. Is that what this is about?
He insists that's not the case. But I'm pretty sure he's lying.

As soon as we hang up I start sending email messages and hunting
for a new job. I'll leave as soon as I can find one. Until then, I will stay
at HubSpot, if only for the paycheck. I would like to get out quickly
and make a graceful exit, politely and painlessly. Unfortunately, that
won't be possible.

Things are about to get ugly.

Twenty

Glassholes

For the past few years one question has hung over Silicon Valley: Are we in a bubble? Some say yes, some say no. Some argue about what the term *bubble* even means and how to define one, and no matter which camp you're in you can cherry-pick examples that support your case. I'm in the camp that says *bubble* refers to a period when valuations of companies are no longer connected to their financial performance, and that we are now in such a period. Silicon Valley has officially become unhinged from reality for the second time in two decades, and even the smartest, savviest investors have thrown in the towel and are admitting that they can no longer tell good ideas from bad ones and have simply begun throwing money at everything, hoping some of their millions might land on a winner. *Spray and pray* is the actual term used by investors in Silicon Valley for this roulette-wheel approach. Some people embrace this philosophy and even celebrate it. "A lot of it is luck" is how blogger-turned-investor Michael Arrington once described the art of investing in tech start-ups.

In April 2013, Google Ventures published a photograph that captures the essence of the second Internet bubble. The photograph appeared on countless websites, but when I asked Google for permission to use it in this book, the company asked what context I would be using it in, and when I told them, they refused. So instead of running the full photograph, I will just show you two of the people in it:

The one on the left, with the cone head, is Marc Andreessen of Andreessen Horowitz. The one on the right is John Doerr of Kleiner Perkins Caufield & Byers. Look how smug they are, how sure of themselves! These two grown men wearing the hideous face computer called Google Glass are two of the most respected investors in Silicon Valley, and they represent two of the most important venture capital firms.

The photograph from which these images are taken was released as part of the announcement of the Glass Collective, a special fund created to invest in companies that would develop applications for Google Glass, which Andreessen and Doerr described as a "potentially transformative technology." Glass had a tiny computer display embedded in a box in front of your right eye and would display information as you walked around. You could check the weather, get directions, take photos, record video.

These glasses were going to change the world! That's what all of the smart money in Silicon Valley believed, and all of the smart money was wrong. Google shut down Glass in 2015, but not before gullible suckers all over the world dished out $1,500 to walk around looking like idiots and inciting people in bars to throw things at them. In the summer of 2013 I had the pleasure of spending a day at Google's headquarters in Mountain View, California—the Googleplex—with a bunch of dorky visitors who all wore Glass and acted as if this were a perfectly normal thing to do. Glass Explorers, they called themselves. Everyone else called them Glassholes. One thing I noticed during that day at Google was that none of our hosts—a bunch of executives from Google's mobile phone division—wore Glass. That's when I knew the gizmo was doomed.

The suckers who plunked down good money for Glass can perhaps be forgiven for being naïve, but Andreessen and Doerr have no such excuse. They manage billions of dollars and are paid enormous sums of money because supposedly they know what they're doing. Not coincidentally, Andreessen and Doerr also played leading roles in creating the new tech bubble, by (a) paying too much for investments, forcing other investors to overpay in order to keep up, and (b) investing huge resources into generating hype.

Stock market manias are heaven for venture capitalists. Eugene Kleiner, a co-founder of Kleiner Perkins Caufield & Byers, the legendary VC firm where Doerr works, once said: "Even turkeys can fly in a strong wind." Kleiner Perkins was founded in 1972 and is one of the oldest, most respected VC firms in Silicon Valley. Kleiner's maxim about flying turkeys is one of ten "Kleiner's Laws," a set of rules that people all over Silicon Valley still live by. Pump money into sales and marketing, generate enough hype, and you can sell almost anything if the market gets frothy enough. "I love bubbles," Tom Perkins, another co-founder of Kleiner Perkins, once declared. "We made a lot of money in bubbles."

You can't blame VCs for feeling this way. They are in the business of making money. Most, however, at least try to play the game with a certain amount of subtlety. Not so Andreessen and Doerr.

Doerr joined Kleiner Perkins in 1980 and has been called "the Michael Jordan of venture capital," a hall-of-fame moneyman, one of the best ever to play the game. Doerr's big hits include Sun Microsystems, Amazon, Netscape, and Google. But somewhere in the 2000s he seemed to lose his touch, making bad bets on so-called cleantech (renewable energy) start-ups while missing out on big hits like Facebook, Linked-In, and Tesla. "Doerr made (Kleiner) the gold standard of venture firms" but he "is also largely responsible for the firm's fall," tech blog Pando wrote in 2013.

Doerr has a degree in electrical engineering from Rice University and an MBA from Harvard. My theory is that when investing in start-ups required the ability to understand technology, he was without peer, but when the Valley turned its attention to social networks, photo filters, and games for teenagers, Doerr was out of his element, and so he started chasing fads. In 2008, when the iPhone became the cool new thing, he announced the iFund, to invest in app makers. In 2010, when Facebook got hot, he announced the sFund, to invest in social media companies. Doerr even started wearing a T-shirt and hoodie, just like Mark Zuckerberg. Forming the Glass Collective in 2013 was just another attempt to latch on to something trendy.

In the end Doerr got nothing out of Google Glass except some publicity, but maybe that was the point all along. In the old days, Silicon Valley venture capitalists embraced a California version of clubby East Coast white-shoe culture. All of the top VC firms literally sit beside one another on the same street, a big boulevard called Sand Hill Road in Menlo Park. For decades these firms resembled snooty private gentlemen's clubs—in the British upper class sense of the word. They were almost exclusively male and were run by former engineers who shunned publicity and quietly voted Republican.

Today generating hype has become a central part of the venture capital business. There are so many new firms and so much new money floating around that VC firms feel pressure to raise their profile. They make kooky videos, just like start-ups. They hire publicists. They launch blogs and podcasts, and hire former journalists to run them. Every year only a handful of Silicon Valley companies deliver big paydays. If you're a VC, you *must* have money parked in those companies. But getting into those deals is not so easy. Investors actually have to *compete* to get into hot deals. How do you get that entrepreneur to take your money? How do you stand out? You generate publicity. You have your picture taken wearing Google Glass and call yourself a visionary, someone who can "see around corners," as they say in Silicon Valley. Even as valuations climb to record levels, you insist that you are not overpaying. "It's not a bubble; it's an unprecedented, long boom," Doerr told *Bloomberg* in June 2015. Then again, Doerr is in the business of selling companies to the public markets. What do you expect him to say? Asking a venture capitalist if private companies are overvalued is like asking a car salesman if he thinks you're paying too much for the new Mercedes he's selling you.

When it comes to getting publicity, Doerr is a piker compared to Andreessen. Think of Rodney Dangerfield's character in *Caddyshack*— big and loud, throwing money around—and you get the idea of how Andreessen has elbowed his way into the clubby world of venture capital: by paying more than everyone else and drawing a lot of attention to himself. In 2009 Andreessen was just another guy with a new venture fund, albeit a guy with a famous name. Six years later he is probably the best known and arguably the most influential investor in Silicon Valley. "Guys running start-ups love him. They all want to meet him," one Boston-based venture capitalist says. "Every time I meet with a start-up, the first question they ask me is, 'Do you know Marc Andreessen? Can you introduce us to him?' He's like a rock star." Says another venture capitalist: "If you take money from Andreessen Horowitz, your valuation doubles or triples just because they're involved. Why? Because they're Andreessen Horowitz."

Andreessen is a physically imposing man: six feet, four inches tall and heavyset, with an enormous shaved head. He's an avid Twitter user, sometimes posting more than one hundred tweets a day, pontificating and picking fights. When Warren Buffett expressed skepticism of Bitcoin, a technology in which Andreessen has invested heavily, Andreessen called Buffet "an old white man crapping on tech he doesn't understand."

Andreessen was quite literally the poster boy for the first dotcom bubble, posing for a February 1996 *Time* cover sitting barefoot on a throne, a millionaire boy king, twenty-four years old. The first bubble,

I believe, became a formative experience for Andreessen and shaped his behavior when he entered the venture capital business. As an entrepreneur, Andreessen had a mixed record. Netscape got crushed by Microsoft and started losing money but nevertheless was acquired by AOL for $10 billion. After Netscape, Andreessen founded Loudcloud, which went public when it was only eighteen months old and had barely any revenues. Later, Loudcloud became Opsware, was split into two pieces, and sold for $1.6 billion, despite never reporting an annual profit. In 2005 Andreessen co-founded Ning, a social network that fizzled out.

At some point it seems to have dawned on Andreessen that the people who make the most money in Silicon Valley are not the ones who found companies or run them, but rather the ones who put up the capital. (At Netscape, he reportedly made as much as $100 million, while his investor and co-founder, Jim Clark, made $2 billion.) In 2009 Andreessen and his friend and former business partner Ben Horowitz launched Andreessen Horowitz, or a16z, as it is known. (The name is a "numeronym," a way of shortening a word or phrase by using a number to represent the number of letters that have been left out. *A*, then sixteen letters, then *Z*. Tech geeks love stuff like this.)

Andreessen and Horowitz developed a reputation for overpaying to get into deals, offering valuations that I've been told were 30 percent higher than what other venture capitalists would pay. They also recognized the value of publicity. One of the first partners they hired was Margit Wennmachers, a veteran Silicon Valley public relations specialist known for her sharp elbows. They've since hired more PR people, as well as journalists and researchers who produce blog posts, podcasts, and market analysis reports—their own little content factory.

Horowitz wrote a book about his experience as an entrepreneur and posed for a *Fortune* magazine cover with his hands wrapped like a boxer, though he apparently does not actually box. He hangs out with rappers and spouts rap lyrics, cultivating a streetwise image—though in fact he was born in London and grew up in Berkeley, and his father is David Horowitz, a well-known author and conservative commentator.

As the tech blog Valleywag summed it up, "Ben Horowitz Is Desperate for You to Think He's Cool."

Andreessen and Wennmachers assiduously court the press. Andreessen has even invested in online publications that cover the tech industry, like Business Insider and Pando Daily. The result has been mostly favorable coverage for Andreessen Horowitz and the start-ups in its investment portfolio. When Andreessen put money into Rockmelt, a middling start-up with the lame idea of developing a new kind of web browser, the tech press went into a frenzy; a few years later, when Rockmelt was sold for scrap to Yahoo, nobody held Andreessen's feet to the fire. When Andreessen Horowitz piled money into Bitcoin-related companies, the tech press began writing that Bitcoin was the next big thing.

Nobody blinked when two companies in Andreessen's portfolio, Instagram and Oculus, were acquired by Facebook, where Andreessen sits on the board of directors. These deals were even more remarkable than the Netscape and Loudcloud acquisitions, since while those earlier companies were sold for billions while not turning a profit, Instagram and Oculus were sold for billions without even generating *revenue*. Andreessen has made it clear that he recused himself in the Instagram and Oculus deals because of his conflicts of interest. To be sure, such conflicts are probably unavoidable for someone as well connected as Andreessen.

Andreessen did take heat for a deal involving eBay, where he also once was a director. In 2009, during Andreessen's tenure on the board, eBay decided to sell Skype, the messaging service, which it had acquired in 2005; eBay paid $2.6 billion for Skype and sold it four years later in a deal that valued the company at $2.75 billion, not much of a gain. The investors who bought Skype included a private equity firm called Silver Lake Partners—and Andreessen Horowitz.

As with Instagram and Oculus, Andreessen found himself on both sides of a deal, working as both buyer and seller. Eighteen months after buying Skype, Andreessen and his partners sold the company to Microsoft for $8.5 billion—three times what they paid. To some,

Andreessen's role as both an eBay director and an investor acquiring an asset from eBay seemed like a problem. "Andreessen, he's screwed more people than Casanova, for Christ's sake, and yet he goes and takes this attitude that he's on the high moral ground," activist investor Carl Icahn said on CNBC. Icahn complained that eBay had sold Skype for less than what it was worth and that eBay's investors had been short-changed. Andreessen said Icahn was "making up a fake conspiracy theory out of thin air." The tech press sided with Andreessen. The story went nowhere.

Andreessen is relentlessly optimistic and pounds away on the same message, which is that no matter how high the valuations of start-ups might go, this all makes sense. In May 2015 Andreessen explained to Tad Friend of the *New Yorker* that there was nothing to worry about. Sure, things got out of hand in the first dotcom bubble, and we had a crash, and now we were on the upswing again, but that didn't mean another crash was coming. The crash of 2000 was an "isolated event," Andreessen said, and the economy was heading into a "sustained boom," almost the same phrase Doerr would use in Bloomberg a month later.

Andreessen Horowitz has invested in some of the Valley's most highly valued companies, including Pinterest, Airbnb, and Box, and enlists its publicity machine (both its own internal operation and its friends in the tech press) to further its interests. In the spring of 2014, when "software as a service" (SaaS) stocks went into a slump, and when Box was still hoping to go public but had started to look wobbly, Andreessen's content factory sprang into action.

The firm produced blog posts and podcasts explaining that SaaS companies were misunderstood. Investors failed to understand how profitable these companies were going to be. The podcast was loaded up with a dizzying barrage of jargon and acronyms and metrics that SaaS companies have invented to measure their own performance. Software as a service is still something of a new business, and it is difficult if not impossible to compare the performance of any one SaaS company to the others.

The bottom line from pro-SaaS believers is that because SaaS companies use a subscription model, they will eventually become enormously profitable, despite incurring big losses in their early years. Whether that theory will be proven true remains to be seen.

By June, shares in SaaS companies stopped plunging and started to claw their way back up, along with the rest of the market. This was good news for HubSpot, which by the summer of 2014 was borrowing money to pay its bills. The market wasn't on fire. Shares in Salesforce .com, our rival and the best-known SaaS company, were still well below the levels they had reached in February. It was far from certain that HubSpot could actually pull off a successful IPO. But the company didn't have much choice. Its funds were running low. Perhaps it could raise another round of venture funding, but the terms might be onerous.

On August 25 HubSpot announced it was making a run at the public markets. When that happened, HubSpot published its prospectus, the document that contained all of its financial information. Things were not pretty.

Twenty-one

Excuse Me, but Would You Please Get the Fuck Out of Our Company?

On the same day that HubSpot files its IPO registration statement, just hours before the announcement, and without any knowledge that this is about to take place, I happen to post a very small joke online. This very small joke will lead to a huge, blown-out-of-proportion fracas, and it will mark the beginning of the end for me at HubSpot.

It begins when I'm sitting on my deck in Topanga, drinking my morning coffee, watching hummingbirds hovering in the branches, scrolling though my news feed on Facebook, and I make a little quip that's a veiled jab at Spinner.

But it's not a good day to be making jokes. Unbeknown to me, HubSpot is hours away from announcing its IPO plans. No doubt everyone in Cambridge is feeling edgy, especially Spinner and Cranium. But I have no idea. I'm three thousand miles away, sitting in the woods. It's Monday. The *Silicon Valley* showrunner has given us the day off. It's also the last day that the kids will be with me in California, and I'm planning to take them to Six Flags Magic Mountain. Tomorrow they fly home to Boston.

The joke that I make on Facebook is a reference to something Trotsky told me a couple weeks ago. It involves a friend of mine, Barbara, a journalist who wrote a story about executives leaving HubSpot. The first to leave were David Cancel, the chief product officer, and Elias Torres, the VP of engineering, and losing them was a big deal. A week later two more people quit—one was Atticus, the creative director, and the other was the "director of user experience." Four key people were quitting a company just as it was supposedly getting ready to go public. Barbara wrote up a story with the headline HUBSPOT TO LOSE TWO MORE EXECS AS IT PREPS ANNUAL SHINDIG AND IPO.

Spinner was incensed. She demanded that Barbara change the headline and rewrite the story, because, strictly speaking, Atticus and the other guy were not *executives*. Barbara argued that they sounded pretty *executive* to her, and anyway, she was busy and on deadline and she didn't have time to get into a debate about semantics with Spinner. Trotsky knew that I was friendly with Barbara, and he called me, apoplectic. "Spinner just ruined a good relationship with an important reporter. Barbara has been good to us. Now she'll never write about us again," he said.

When I called Barbara and asked her about it, she just laughed. Sure, Spinner had been a pest. Maybe she figured that if she just annoyed Barbara enough, Barbara would relent and change the headline, dropping the word *executive*, if only to make Spinner go away and leave her alone. Barbara tends to dislike PR people in general, but especially so when they start telling her which words she can and cannot use. But to Barbara this was not a big deal.

That's the backstory. The news today, as I sit with my coffee in Topanga, is that Atticus has joined a new company, and the Boston Business Journal has done a story with a headline describing him as a "former HubSpot exec." Atticus posts a link to this on his Facebook feed. That's where I post my little wisecrack: "Atticus," I write, "I'm happy for you, but you're not an *executive*. I'm going to demand a correction!"

It's an inside joke, a little wink at a tiny shitstorm that only a half dozen people in the entire world even know about. In my comment I tag Barbara. Other than Atticus, she's the only person outside of HubSpot who will get the joke.

That's it. That's all it is. I post my little comment and keep scrolling down through my Facebook feed.

Within minutes, a text message pops up on my phone. It's from Trotsky. We need to talk. Right now.

All of HubSpot is on red alert, he tells me. My comment is a huge deal. A grave error. Someone has seen it—he won't say who—and alerted Spinner and now Spinner is going ballistic.

"I'll just delete it," I say, and just like that, I zap my comment. It's gone. All told, the little joke was probably online for thirty minutes at most and could not have been seen by many people. Most people who saw it wouldn't even know what it meant.

Yet Trotsky insists this is a terrible thing that I've done. Spinner is livid. She's making a huge stink. Cranium is also furious. "He told me to tell you that as far as he's concerned, this is strike two against you," Trotsky says. Strike one, presumably, was when I criticized Halligan over his comment about gray hair and experience. "You're not fired," Trotsky says, "but you're about as close to fired as you can get. It's bad."

I'm flabbergasted. Fired? Really? Over a Facebook comment? This makes no sense.

"I'm going to talk to Cranium and see what he wants to do," Trotsky says. "I'll get back to you."

Later in the day Trotsky starts badgering me to get on the phone with him. I'm with my kids at Six Flags, and it's their last day in California, and I'd really like to spend the day focusing on them but Trotsky insists on talking now. I'm still reeling from Trotsky's earlier remark about me being as close to fired as you can get without being fired. Early in the afternoon I see the news that HubSpot has filed its IPO registration paperwork. I realize that this might have something to do with why everyone is so hyped up. We agree to talk at four o'clock my time, seven back East.

I call Trotsky from the car, inching along on the 405 freeway in stop-and-go traffic. The kids are in the backseat, wiped out. I'm talking on earbuds so they can't hear what Trotsky says. I figure it won't be pleasant. For all I know he's going to fire me, and if so, I would just as soon they didn't hear that. I'd rather wait until tomorrow to have this chat, so I would not have to do this in front of my kids, but Trotsky won't relent.

He enumerates the problems my joke has caused and how it demonstrates poor judgment on my part. His tone is officious. He seems to be choosing his words carefully, as if he has written down everything he is going to say and is working his way through a list. Instead of Trotsky, my pal, the guy with the raunchy sense of humor, the one who was so friendly with me that the blog women complained about us, now there is a new Trotsky, and this one is telling me, in a very serious and solemn voice, that I have committed a grievous crime against the Cult of the Orange People, a near mortal sin as far as HubSpot is concerned.

Maybe it's because I've been spending weeks on end sitting in a room with writers who talk about huge cocks and dry vaginas, but really, honestly, my little comment on Atticus's post does not seem like a big deal to me.

But it is, Trotsky says. This thing I have done is very, very serious. It is very bad. This is a huge problem. It is going to take a lot of hard work for me to earn back the trust of my colleagues.

"You've dug yourself into a hole," he says. "I'm not sure you'll ever be able to climb back out of it."

I don't argue with him, or mention that it's creepy to have people watching what I post on Facebook and then threatening to fire me over it. I've resolved to just hear him out, listen to everything he says, and find out what happens next. No matter what he says, I stay calm and respond with as few words as possible, remembering that my kids are in the backseat, listening to every word. "Okay," I say. "I see. Sure. Okay. Yes, I see your point."

But this is incredible—literally. As in, I literally do not believe that Trotsky actually means a word of what he is saying. Hardly anyone saw the comment I posted, and I deleted it only minutes after posting it.

What's more, Trotsky is the one who called and told me how Spinner had behaved like an imbecile with Barbara in the first place. If Trotsky were saying, *Look, we both know Spinner is an idiot, but you can't make jokes about her,* I might believe he's sincere. But that's not what he is saying. He is saying that Spinner is right, that she has a legitimate grievance. He's saying that he agrees with Cranium, that I probably should be fired. This is stunning. I don't know how this has happened, but Trotsky has changed—utterly. It's like the final scene from *Invasion of the Body Snatchers*, where you think Donald Sutherland is still human, but then he points and opens his mouth and you realize he's become . . . *one of them.*

This all feels like a pretext, as if Trotsky has been looking for any excuse, no matter how small, to make a stink and start driving me out of the company. I remember the email he sent me earlier in the month, asking me, *as a friend,* why I wanted to continue working at HubSpot. Trotsky had insisted otherwise, but that message had felt like a not very subtle clue that he wanted me to leave. Maybe he was hoping I would write back and say, *Hey, you're right, this isn't working, and I'm not going to return from my leave of absence.* Instead I called and told him that I wanted to keep working at HubSpot. It's true that I have been losing heart, and I have decided to start looking for a different job, but in the meantime I'd like to keep getting a paycheck.

Now we have gone to the next level: Trotsky is using his manager voice and running through a list of things I have done wrong. Really I've done just one thing, and it's just a small comment, and for that matter whatever slight or insult Spinner is claiming to have suffered, it's nothing compared to the open battle that Trotsky and Spinner engaged in on Facebook a few months before, when he was ranting about elephants and she was accusing him of being a woman hater. That argument didn't lead to anyone getting threatened with firing. Yet somehow my little comment, with no names mentioned, constitutes a firing offense, something that we need to spend a whole day going back and forth about, and which has put me into a hole so deep that I might never dig out.

I'm sorry, but I'm not buying it.

When Trotsky finishes working through his list, I say, "Okay. So what do you want me to do?"

He doesn't know. We'll have to keep talking. "Do you have any questions for me?" he says.

"Well," I say, "the one thing that puzzles me is I kind of think you're blowing this out of proportion. I guess the only question I would have is why you guys are making such a big deal out of this. I understand there's extra sensitivity today because of the IPO announcement. Obviously I didn't know that was happening. I'm sorry about the timing. But it all seems like such a small thing and I'm taken aback by the response."

I ask him if the HR department is going to get involved. He says he doesn't know. They might be.

"Are you filing an official report about this to HR?" I say. "Is all of this going to be documented somewhere, in my employee file?"

"I don't know," he says.

"Well I'm concerned because the way you're handling this feels like you're starting to build some documentation that can be used to support a case for firing me. Is that what HubSpot is doing? Are you starting a file on me, a sort of paper trail that you can use later if you want to fire me?"

That's when Trotsky delivers a line I will never forget: "The company," he says, "doesn't need a reason to fire you. The company can do whatever it wants."

A week later, on September 2, the Tuesday after the Labor Day weekend, Trotsky forwards me an email that Cranium has sent around to everyone in the marketing department. We're all getting an amazing gift: customized Bose QuietComfort 15 headphones.

"Congratulations for earning your place as the best marketing team in the world," Cranium writes. "Workday, NetSuite, Salesforce, Rackspace, LinkedIn, and Facebook all look up to you and want to do marketing like you do (all of those companies have asked me to teach them how you guys do it)." Cranium says he knows everyone is working long hours getting ready for the Inbound conference, which takes place in two weeks. "We have a lot to do and a lot of pressure. But I know you guys can do it and once again prove you're the best marketing team in the world. With your help we can rock INBOUND, crush the product launches, and exceed our revenue goals in Q4."

What scares me is that I don't think Cranium is just saying that stuff to get people whipped up. I think he really believes that he runs the best marketing team in the world, and that all of those big companies in Silicon Valley want him to come teach them about marketing.

The headphones are painted bright orange and are customized with the HubSpot logo and each person's last name. Cranium claims they're a "limited edition" and worth $900. They're incredibly tacky. No one in their right mind would wear them in public.

"Yours are sitting here at my desk," Trotsky writes to me.

I'm a bit confused. A week ago Trotsky was telling me that I was on the verge of being fired, that I had dug myself into an impossibly deep hole and I had two strikes against me. I was probably also on thin ice, but he left that one out. A week ago, Trotsky was making me get on the phone so that he could dress me down in front of my children.

Now we're back to being pals, and he thinks I'm going to be motivated to come back to work because I'll get a pair of Bose headphones, in orange.

On the same day, Trotsky sends me a separate email saying he has even more big news. "You've got a new job," he says. "Very high profile. Hugely important. On my team, but a new function. It's awesome. Great way to wipe the slate clean with kick ass output. When can we talk?"

I'm sitting in the writers' room on the Sony lot. We're working. It's my last week in Los Angeles. I write back and tell him I'll call him later in the day, but meanwhile what's the new job? "We need to get a podcast off the ground. You will own it, entirely," he writes.

Doing a podcast isn't exactly a leadership role at HubSpot, but it sounds fine to me. I know how to do a podcast. A few years ago I did a weekly podcast with a partner, and we drew a pretty good audience. I like interviewing people, and I'm not bad at it.

"I even have a really nice professional-quality microphone," I tell him when we get on the phone. "And some good headphones and some sound-canceling foam that I can put around the microphone. I have video stuff too if we want to do a video podcast. I know the guys at YouTube who work with the video bloggers. I can talk to them and get some advice for how to set things up. I'm thinking maybe we could do an opening segment where I riff on the news of the week in marketing, and then I can bring in a guest and do an interview."

There's a pause, and then Trotsky explains that I'm not going to be the *host* of the podcast. The host is going to be Cranium. I am just going to be booking the guests and handling the promotion and marketing, making sure the podcasts get edited and loaded onto the iTunes Store.

Basically, I'm going to be a secretary.

In fact the role Trotsky is giving me is one that Cranium originally intended to give to his administrative assistant. He even paid for her to take a podcasting course.

Now it's my job instead. Trotsky doesn't say that I'm going to be a secretary. He says I'm going to be the "executive producer."

"It's a really big role," he says. "It's very high profile."

"Sure," I croak. "That's great. I can't wait to get started."

An hour or so later, Trotsky sends an email telling me that the reason I am getting this highly coveted podcast secretarial job is that he vouched for me with Cranium. Cranium apparently wanted to just fire me—but Trotsky went in there and fought for me, defended me, and saved my ass.

"I thought of this scene," he writes, and then includes a link to a YouTube video. It's a scene from *Donnie Brasco*, where Al Pacino plays a gangster and Johnny Depp plays an undercover FBI agent who has infiltrated the mob. In the YouTube clip, Pacino confronts Depp about being a rat. He says he put his reputation on the line for Depp, and if Depp turns out to be a rat, Pacino is a dead man.

I understand the implication: Trotsky and I are gangsters. He has vouched for me with Cranium, the *capo di tutti capi*. If I don't turn myself around, Trotsky's own career is in peril. Trotsky is Lefty, the aging hit man, putting his life on the line! He's still not sure whether he can trust me, but he wants to trust me, and he's going to help me become a made man. And me? I'm Donnie Brasco, and I'm really an FBI agent, but now I've been spending so much time around these wise guys that I'm starting to become just like them. How dramatic is this!

Or maybe we are just two dickheads working in a marketing department, and one of us wants that to seem a little less banal than it really is.

Three days later, on Friday, September 5, and still operating in *Donnie Brasco* mode, Trotsky writes an email saying he needs me to make him a promise: "It's really important that I get a clear answer on your future intentions: are you 'all in' with HubSpot? If I am going to give you ownership of the entire podcast program, I need to know that you are all in."

I write back and assure him: "I'm all in."

This is ridiculous. The guy has already started trying to drive me out of the company, but now he wants me to commit to being all in? What's next? Are we going to prick our fingers and burn drops of blood on a picture of Saint Peter, like in *The Sopranos*?

I am not really lying to him. I am *all in*—for now. I've prepared my panels for the Inbound conference. I've started emailing people who might be good guests for the podcast. Sure, when I find a better job, I will leave HubSpot, and I hope that happens soon, but who knows how long it will take? Until I find something else, I need a paycheck. So I will say what I'm expected to say. I'll wear my stupid Bose headphones and be a team player.

But the truth is that eleven days ago, when Trotsky made me get on the phone in front of my children so he could berate me—that day it was over. I should have quit right then, and I feel like a coward for not doing so. But I still remember how I felt in those months after I got laid off from *Newsweek*, when I was out of work and calling around, cap in hand, willing to take anything. No matter how bad things get at HubSpot, at least I'll have money coming in. Having a job, any job, makes it easier to find another one.

So I'll stay, and I'll look for another job, and I'll try to remain on Trotsky's good side. That's the plan. But unfortunately before I can even return to work, Good Trotsky turns into Bad Trotsky and pounces on me again, making a huge deal out of a tiny thing and then unleashing a torrent of abuse over a manufactured pretext. This time it has to do with the Inbound show, HubSpot's annual customer conference.

Twenty-two

Inbound and Down

nbound takes place in Boston the week of September 15, 2014, and it's a huge deal for Hubspot—it's our version of Dreamforce, the four-day orgy that Salesforce.com puts on every fall in San Francisco. We're a fraction of the size of Salesforce.com, but we're trying to flex our muscles and look big. This year the show is an especially big deal because we have just announced our IPO plans. Strictly speaking, we're supposed to be in a "quiet period," when the Securities and Exchange Commission requires companies to avoid doing things that might artificially pump up the price of the stock. Halligan can't get up on stage and start telling everyone to buy shares, but let's be honest—the timing could not be better. HubSpot is about to throw a party for ten thousand adoring fans and customers just before its management team launches a road show where Halligan and Shah, along with their bankers, will pitch to institutional investors.

Inbound is a way to demonstrate HubSpot's market momentum. But also—and I'm sure the top management of HubSpot realizes this—the ten thousand people who attend the show are exactly the kind of people who will buy HubSpot's stock when it starts trading. These are our customers and business partners, they're part of the movement, and they feel an almost religious devotion to the company. Better yet, most of them don't know anything about investing. They don't know how to read a prospectus, or scrutinize an income statement or a balance sheet. All they know is that they love Brian Halligan and love Dharmesh Shah, and those guys are up on stage telling them that business is booming, HubSpot is growing like crazy, and everything is *awesome.*

Cranium knows that he has to go big this year, and he has pulled out all the stops. He's splurged and hired Malcolm Gladwell and Martha Stewart as featured speakers, along with Guy Kawasaki, an author and former Apple marketing "evangelist" who is a big name in the marketing world. This year's show is so big that HubSpot has been forced to move from the Hynes Convention Center in the Back Bay to the Boston Convention and Exhibition Center, a bigger venue. Janelle Monáe, an R&B singer, has been hired to perform at a party.

Inbound also marks my return to HubSpot after my leave of absence. I've been helping out with the show even from Los Angeles. I've convinced a producer from *Silicon Valley* to come give a presentation about the show. I'm moderating a panel of venture capitalists, including three who are members of HubSpot's board of directors. I've also persuaded the head of a public relations agency in New York to do a presentation with me where we will offer tips about how companies can deal with the press. The PR woman, Julia, is a friend of mine.

The week before Inbound, Julia emails me and says she's never heard anything from HubSpot about her travel arrangements. Do we still want her to come? The last I knew, Trotsky was going to take care of this. I figure it's just an oversight. The two women who handle logistics for the conference probably forgot. I assure her that I'll take care of it.

Monica and Eileen are the organizers. I write and tell them that Julia needs a plane ticket up from New York and a hotel room the night before her talk.

Monica says nobody ever asked them to make arrangements for Julia.

"This should have been done ages ago," I respond.

She says it's too late to do anything about this now. There are no hotel rooms available in Boston, and, anyway, HubSpot doesn't cover travel costs for speakers like Julia.

I've never heard of anything like this. I've given dozens of speeches all around the world, and nobody has ever asked me to pay for my own travel. Booking a room and a plane ticket seems like the least you can do when you ask someone to come give a talk at your event.

But this is HubSpot. We do things our own way. Our company is so cool that people will pay to get coveted speaking spots at our conference. I tell Monica and Eileen that I'll just pass word to Julia that she will have to pay for her own airfare. If she needs a place to stay, I will offer to put her up in the guest room at my house.

Julia is appalled and cancels. She sends an email saying we seem to have gotten our wires crossed, and she wishes everyone the best and hopes they have a great conference.

Monica and Eileen have started cc'ing Spinner and Trotsky on our messages. Spinner leaps in and says she will try to make things right with Julia. Then Trotsky jumps in, too, commenting in the thread that we're all on. Separately, he writes an email just to me, telling me I'm being hostile and aggressive, and that I need to cool down. He says my email messages have deeply offended Monica and Eileen. They've been working really hard on the conference, and now I've started berating them.

I think Trotsky's assessment of the situation is way off, but I nonetheless send a fawning, groveling email to Monica and Eileen, saying I'm sorry if I have caused them problems and I know how hard they are working on the show, and I'm sure we can make things right.

I send a copy of the apology to Trotsky so he can see what I wrote. He throws the apology back in my face. It's no good, he says. No apology will ever make up for how I have behaved toward these women.

What else can I do, I ask Trotsky. He says there's nothing.

"That ship has sailed," he says. "You've alienated them. There's no way you're ever going to make things right with them."

Trotsky is making a big deal out of nothing, just like the thing with my little comment on Facebook about Spinner demanding a correction. He goes on and on, telling me that I'm a lousy person, that now I have dug myself into an even deeper hole. Instead of earning my way back into the good graces of the company, I'm making things worse.

I show these emails—my own and Trotsky's—to a friend who has been a C-level executive at a tech company. I ask her to be honest. I know I can be blunt sometimes, and even rude. Maybe I used a tone with Monica and Eileen that's not appropriate in a corporate setting. My friend assures me that my emails were fine. But she is shocked by the harangues I'm getting from Trotsky. Trotsky is a loose cannon, she says. His emails are over the top and abusive, unprofessional and unacceptable. No boss should communicate to an employee in this way, she says.

I tell her about what happened in Los Angeles, with the email from Trotsky asking why I wanted to work at HubSpot, then the harassment he delivered over that tiny joke on Facebook, and his warnings about me being as close to fired as you can get. I tell her that I suspect Trotsky is just trying to make me miserable and drive me out of the company.

"You could go to HR and report him," she says. "Show them the emails he's sending you."

"I know," I say, "but I don't know if I trust HR. My guess is they won't do anything to Trotsky, but they'll tell him that I complained, and that will only piss him off even more. He'll ramp up the harassment."

"So try to talk to him," my friend suggests. "You guys were friends at one point, right? You don't have to make a big deal of out of it. Just say hey, maybe we can get a coffee and clear the air and do a kind of reset. Keep it casual."

It could be that Trotsky is just stressed out. The IPO has everyone on edge. Everyone is under pressure to make sure things go well at Inbound. In addition, Trotsky's wife just had a baby. Maybe he's not getting much sleep and his nerves are frayed.

In the end, Inbound goes well. Julia flies up for the day, and she's ter-rific on stage and lovely to everyone. I moderate a panel with a bunch of HubSpot board members, who thank me afterward for doing a great job. I feel like I've redeemed myself.

The week after Inbound, when we all get back to the office, I stop by Trotsky's desk and ask him if we could grab a coffee at some point and have a talk about how things have been going.

"My calendar is online," he snaps. "Go find a time that works and send me a calendar invite."

At the appointed date and time, we set out for Starbucks but end up taking a long walk around a little canal near the office. Trotsky tells me he's unhappy at HubSpot. Cranium is riding him, hard. The IPO is looking like a bust. He only took this job because he wanted to make a score on the stock. Word is that HubSpot is trying to price the shares in the range of $19 to $21. That's above the strike price that Trotsky and I both have—our options are priced at $13. But Trotsky says it's not enough.

"Unless the stock gets to $40, it's not even worth it for me to stay here," he says.

We go to Starbucks and get our coffee. We walk back to HubSpot and sit down on the couches in the lobby on the first floor.

At last I ask why he seems so angry at me.

"I feel like something must have happened, and I don't know what it is," I say. "If I did something to piss you off, I just want to know, so I can apologize and make things right."

I'm hoping he'll soften up a bit and remember that we're friends. But unfortunately that doesn't happen. Trotsky sticks to his guns. He says that he *is* angry at me, and that I'm doing a shitty job, and I have a shitty attitude. I'm not showing enough team spirit, and I don't respect him enough.

"I'm the only person here who gives a shit about you," he says, prac-tically seething. "I don't think you realize this, but I'm the only reason that you still have a job here at all. If it weren't for me, they would have fired you a long time ago."

"How would they fire me?" I say. "Fire me for what?"

"They'd call it an experiment that didn't work out. They hired a journalist, but it wasn't a good fit."

"Jesus. So Cranium wants to fire me?"

"You've shown me no gratitude, and no respect. I've gone out of my way to help you. Over and over, I've tried to help you. I wanted to help you. But frankly, right now, I'm a lot less inclined to help you anymore. That's just the truth."

He gets up. I get up too. We walk to the elevators and share an awkward, uncomfortable ride up to the fourth floor and back to our desks.

I write to my friend, the C-level executive, and tell her that her suggestion about going out for coffee didn't work out as well as I'd hoped.

It turns out the abuse from Trotsky has only begun. From this point on he will be looking for any possible reason to tell me that I've done something wrong. One day I have a lunch set up with a local tech CEO, a guy who might be a good guest for the podcast. To make the lunch I have to miss the marketing department meeting, but this is no big deal. Cranium holds this meeting every Monday. It's not mandatory. Sixty or so people attend, but it's just a way to get an update on what's happening in the department. People miss it all the time.

Nevertheless after the meeting I get an angry email from Trotsky demanding to know why I wasn't at the department meeting. I remind him that I had a lunch with a CEO and that I had cleared it with him in advance.

Back comes an angry, argumentative email saying that I'm being standoffish and not making enough effort to demonstrate my loyalty to the team. I send a list of things I've done in my first week back to reconnect with my colleagues. He fires back with an email saying he does not accept my explanation and offering point-by-point rebuttals to all of the items on my list.

Now that we're on the subject of my loyalty, he has some other questions for me. How many sessions did I attend at Inbound? He doesn't recall seeing me there. I send him a list of the panels I attended and the people I spoke to, which includes several of HubSpot's board members and investors, one of whom, Lorrie Norrington, thanked me for doing a good job moderating the panel on which she appeared. I tell him the name of everyone at HubSpot with whom I've had coffee or lunch as part of my effort to reintegrate myself at the company.

Okay, Trotsky says. But that's not all. Why did I remove any mention of HubSpot from my profiles on Twitter and Facebook when I was away in Los Angeles? Why have I still not put the word *HubSpot* back into my profiles there? Why did I skip the Thursday night after-party at the Inbound conference? Do I not like to socialize with my colleagues?

I explain that I don't drink, and I don't like going to parties where people drink too much. Also, I have two young kids, I've just spent part of the summer away from them, and when given the choice of spending a night home with my family or going to a keg party with a bunch of twenty-two-year-olds, I'm probably going to choose my family. Is this really a problem?

It is. All of these little things, Trotsky says, are adding up to create a picture of an employee who just doesn't care enough about the company. Each one makes it a little less likely that I will earn my way back into the company's good graces.

"These are setbacks," he says.

I keep expecting the old Trotsky to appear, burst out laughing, and say, "Shit, buddy, I'm just kidding! Oh my God, you should have seen the look on your face!" If that doesn't happen I'm hoping he will at least pull me aside and say, "Look, I have orders from above to just give you loads of shit and make you miserable so you'll leave. I don't want to do it, but it's my job, and I have to. I know it sucks, and I'm sorry."

But neither of those things happen. As far as I can tell, Trotsky really, sincerely means everything he says. Never in my life have I had someone turn on me so completely.

The abuse continues when I start my new secretarial job on the podcast. Whatever I do, I'm falling short. Trotsky wants to know, what is my marketing plan? My marketing plan is to make a great podcast and over time it will build an audience. No! We're marketing people. We need to do marketing! We need to create an email campaign and send spam to thousands of people urging them to click on a link and subscribe to the podcast. If enough people do that, we can trick Apple into thinking that we have a huge audience, and Apple will put our podcast near the top of its ratings.

Numbers: We need them! How many listeners will we have in six months, and in a year? Where will the podcast rank in the iTunes Store? How soon will we get into the top ten? At what point can I promise that this will be the number-one business podcast in the entire world? These are projections that I need to make, and once I make them, I have to hit them—or else!

As far as my career at HubSpot goes, everything is riding on the podcast.

"It's a very simple situation," Trotsky says. "If the podcast succeeds, you keep your job."

"And if it doesn't, then what? I get fired?"

Trotsky scowls. "Just make sure it's a success," he says.

Left unspoken is how we will define success. My guess is success is whatever Trotsky and Cranium decide it will be, and no matter what I do, I will never achieve it.

Meanwhile, Trotsky rides me. Constantly. Why haven't I scheduled meetings with a dozen different people across the marketing department to get them on board with the podcast? Why have I not solicited their help? So I do have those meetings. The question then becomes, Why didn't I do that sooner? When is our deadline? When do we go live? Why can't we start sooner? Do I not realize that I am now a project manager, responsible for every step of this project?

Why have I not sent Trotsky a full report on my progress, in writing? Why have I not created a full podcast marketing campaign document and shared it via Google Docs with everyone in the marketing department so they can read the marketing plan and add comments? Once I do create that document, why am I not responding to comments immediately? Where are my responses to the list of comments that Trotsky has placed into the document?

We're creating a dedicated web page for the podcast. It looks great, but the designers miss their deadline and ask for a few extra days. I tell them that's fine. Why did I do that? Why did I tell them they could have those days? Why did they miss the deadline in the first place? Did I fail to communicate the deadlines clearly enough to them?

There's a person I think would be great as a guest on the show. I send an email to Cranium asking him what he thinks. Trotsky leaps in: Why am I writing directly to Cranium? Why am I asking him to get involved in minor details like this? Do I not understand the protocol of how to deal with a C-level executive?

A conference in Peru wants me to come give a talk. A HubSpot user group in San Diego wants me to come out. I say yes, of course, I want to help promote the brand. But no! Trotsky says I've screwed up again! Why am I accepting invitations to speak at conferences when I'm supposed to be hunkered down and focusing on the podcast?

It's all just crazy-making. The podcast is not a big deal, it's not hard to do, and frankly nobody is ever going to listen to it, since it will be hosted by Cranium. I'm guessing he will draw about the same size audience as he used to attract with his HubSpot TV video podcast, meaning no one.

This is basically a vanity project for our boss, and I'm happy to do it, but there's no point in getting carried away and believing this jackass is going to be the host of the biggest business podcast in the world. There is also no point in setting unrealistic goals that will almost guarantee that I will fall short and fail, unless that's the whole point, which I suspect it is.

I try to distance myself from the abuse. I pretend I'm an anthropologist. How does the tribe behave when the chief has decided that one of the members must be driven off? I imagine that I'm a research psychologist and that the HubSpot marketing department is a laboratory exercise, a corporate version of the Stanford prison experiment or the Milgram experiment at Yale.

I imagine that I am studying the way a corporate department goes about getting rid of an unwanted employee, using myself as the subject of the experiment. I've heard horror stories about people who have gone through this, but I've never experienced it myself, and I don't know how it is done, specifically.

I study Trotsky's tactics and techniques, the way he will make a point of ignoring me—he sits only a few desks away from me and will sit there without acknowledging my presence. I admire the way he berates me without raising his voice and in fact takes the opposite approach and speaks more softly than usual, in a lower register, sometimes adopting the paternal tone of a teacher admonishing a student. He'll wait until no one is around and then will pull up a chair, lean close, and explain to me that I'm really trying his patience with my behavior. Why did I ask him that question during that meeting? Was I trying to embarrass him in front of the others? He really wishes I would shape up and stop being so aggressive and hostile.

Another of his tactics is to tell me that someone else in our department is furious with me and that he has fielded yet another complaint about me. Oddly enough, when I apologize to those people, they have no idea what I'm talking about. One person I've allegedly offended is Roberta, Cranium's administrative assistant. Trotsky says she's boiling mad because she booked a hotel room for me during the Inbound conference and I never used it, which wasted money and deprived someone else of a room. I can't imagine why the company would book me a hotel room in Boston, since I live here. But I tell Roberta that I'm really sorry that she booked me a room and I didn't use it.

She looks at me as if I'm nuts. "It's no big deal," she says. "Nobody gave it a second thought."

I tell her I've heard she is really upset.

"That's ridiculous," she says.

The same goes for Monica and Eileen, the women who handle logistics for the conference. Supposedly they were so angry with me that I could never repair the breach, no matter how many times I apologized. This, too, turns out to be complete bullshit.

"Neither of us was upset with you," Monica will tell me, months after I leave HubSpot. I tell her I was told that she was furious with me. "That," she says, "is complete news to me."

A public relations guy in Boston writes to me and says Trotsky has been getting into vehement arguments on Facebook, posting angry screeds and ad hominem attacks on people. "Is this guy really your boss?" the PR guy asks, having noticed that Trotsky works at HubSpot, where I also work. "How do you tolerate him? He seems to have a psycho streak in him. He comments on posts in a manner that I would classify as almost nuts. He comes off as insufferable. A first-class douchebag."

I've never had an abusive boss before. I've worked for a few colorful characters, including an editor at *Forbes* whom I once called a "fucking asshole" and who laughed and told me that this was why he loved working with me. I always found a way to get along with my colleagues. No one in my adult life, at work or elsewhere, has ever spoken to me the way Trotsky does. No one has ever berated me and insulted me, or expressed such hostility and contempt for me. Maybe I've just been lucky. Maybe this kind of treatment is what most people experience at work. But I've worked in some rough places, from a textile mill to a Hollywood writers' room, and I've never experienced anything like Trotsky.

I never got bullied in school, either, but I imagine this is what it feels like. Some guy is tormenting me, and I'm afraid to tell anyone, because I'm pretty sure that telling someone will only make things worse. That fear, in turn, sends me down a different rabbit hole and I start to hate myself for being such a coward, for being afraid to stand up for myself. I feel ashamed of myself. This guy is using me as his punching bag, and I'm not doing anything to stop him. It seems to me that if I can just keep it together, eventually he will realize that I won't fight back and he will get bored with harassing me. Instead the opposite happens. When he realizes that I will not fight back, he becomes even more aggressive. It's as if I've given him permission to beat the shit out of me.

In a strange way, I almost admire Trotsky. As the subject of a psychology experiment, he's fascinating. The problem is that this is not a psychology experiment, and despite my attempts to pretend that it is, the abuse begins to take a toll on me. I dread going to work. The office seems surreal, almost Kafkaesque. Trotsky has become my jailer, and I live in fear of doing something that will arouse his ire, but I have no idea what those things might be. Anything can set him off. I feel overpowered and helpless.

Spinner sits around the corner from me, braying like a donkey at her own jokes. I'm surrounded by happy, upbeat young people who are all having the time of their lives in this adult kindergarten. Their latest innovation is a random lunch date generator, created by the women who work for Jordan, the creator of Fearless Friday: Sign up, and once a week you'll be paired up with another HubSpotter for a getting-to-know-you-better lunch. The cheery atmosphere doesn't offset the bleakness that I feel but instead makes it worse. I would love to work from home, but the podcast job requires me to be in the office, and anyway, Trotsky says I need to come into work to show that I'm a team player and that I'm "all in."

For weeks I put up with Trotsky's abuse. No matter what he says, I respond in a calm, measured way. It takes a huge amount of energy to maintain that composure—and eventually I can't do it anymore. One day I lose my temper and tell him to get off my back.

It's a Friday afternoon in October. In what has now become our regular little routine, Trotsky comes over to my desk, pulls up a chair, leans close to me, and in a voice that's just above a whisper, starts complaining about something I said to him earlier in the day, which he says felt like an insult.

This time I cut him off.

"Look," I say, "are you trying to make me quit? Because if so, it's working. You've been riding me ever since I came back to work, or since before that even. You're constantly giving me shit, and being hostile to me, and I don't understand why. But I really wish you would stop."

He sits back. After a moment he says, "You know what? You're right."

To my amazement, Trotsky admits that he has been hounding me. He even explains why he's doing it. He says it's because I unfriended him on Facebook, back in August. He knows it's silly, but he felt insulted by this. I explain that after the fiasco over my Spinner joke, I severed my Facebook connections with everyone from HubSpot—not just him. I want to put a big space between my personal life and my work life. "I'm only using Facebook to post pictures of my kids and talk to my friends," I say.

Trotsky says he understands. He says he knows he can be thin-skinned and that he has a short temper. He gets offended too easily, and when he does he tends to go cold on people and write them off. Maybe that's what has happened here, he says.

"I'm going to get off your back," he says. "I'll give you some space."

Remarkably, he does—for a few days. But then he comes back, having found a way to turn my complaint against me.

"You know," he says, sidling up to me one day, like Lumbergh, the smarmy boss in *Office Space*, "now that you're being all defensive, this is causing a problem, because now you're putting up a wall, and this makes it harder for me to do my job and be your manager. If I try to give you feedback, I'm worried that you'll say I'm being hostile, or that I'm harassing you. Do you see what I'm saying?"

Yes, I do: He's saying that when I told him to stop harassing me, *I* was being hostile to *him*. I have to admit, it's a good play on his part.

My friend, the former C-level executive, the person who previously suggested I talk things over with Trotsky over coffee, now gives me new advice: Get out.

"There aren't any other options," she says. "The guy has it in for you."

As if to add insult to injury, one day in a meeting of the entire content team Trotsky announces that he has come up with a big, bold idea. He is going to launch a new publication—a high-end online magazine, with feature articles aimed at investors and CEOs. It will be separate from the blog. It will have its own website, with beautiful illustrations and photographs, and feature-length articles.

This is the exact idea that I pitched to Wingman when I first joined, and which he rejected. It's the idea that I then took to Halligan and Dharmesh, and which they approved, but which Cranium refused to put into effect.

Trotsky knows that I pitched this idea. He knows the whole story. Now he has just taken my idea and made it his own.

But there's more: "Some of you know we've been talking to Sandra Bale," he says. "She gave a talk at Inbound, and everybody loved her."

Sandra Bale runs a blog for a venture capital firm in San Francisco. She's thirty years old and briefly worked at the *Wall Street Journal* before going into public relations.

"We're not sure we can get her, but we're pitching her really hard," Trotsky says. "If she takes the job, we're going to put her in charge of the new publication and have her build it for us. She's a rock star. It would be a huge deal if we can get her."

Meanwhile, I will be the podcast secretary. What the hell? After the meeting, in private, I remind Trotsky that the idea he is proposing, the project he wants to hire Sandra to run, is the exact idea that I pitched months ago.

Trotsky nods. He seems to be mulling this over.

"I'll tell you what," he says. "If Sandra comes on board, and if she needs any help, I will definitely want you to work with her."

At this point the message could not be more clear. Trotsky is doing everything short of hiring a skywriter to scrawl GET OUT, DAN in the airspace above HubSpot headquarters.

I will be happy to oblige him. I'm making some progress in my job hunt. But I don't want to leave until I've found a new position. I'm the sole breadwinner in our household, and we depend on HubSpot's health insurance.

From this point on, however, I find it pretty much impossible to take HubSpot seriously. One day I come back from lunch to find that

Keytar Bear is performing in a conference room near my office. Keytar Bear is a busker who performs in Boston subway stations, wearing a bear costume and playing an instrument that blends a guitar and a keyboard. He's here because it's Tracy's birthday—she's the vice president of brand and buzz—and the people in her department thought it would be fun to have Keytar Bear serenade them while they eat birthday cake. They invite me in, so I stay and have a piece of cake and take a bunch of photos of them. At Halloween I do the same thing, roping people in for photographs, snapping away as they strike crazy poses and act like they're the shit.

Along with his constant stream of happiness surveys, Cranium asks us to submit suggestions (anonymously) for new ways we could all have fun at work. "Sundaes on Mondays" is one of my ideas—every Monday, Cranium should truck in a huge supply of ice cream and toppings so we can all make sundaes. Another week I suggest that we should take the hammock of out of the nap room, replace it with a massage table, and hire full-time massage therapists. Neither idea succeeds.

In meetings, where previously I would say as little as possible, I now pitch the most ridiculous ideas I can think of, while keeping a straight face. One day Trotsky convenes about a dozen of us with the goal of coming up with big, new, outside-the-box ideas, revolutionary approaches to marketing that will put HubSpot on the map. He says he's looking for a "Thom Yorke moment," referring to the singer from Radiohead, who in September 2014 sidestepped the entire music industry and put out a new album as a bundle on BitTorrent, got millions of downloads, and earned $20 million, without having to deal with a record label.

We've had a week or so to come up with our own ideas that are as revolutionary as the one Thom Yorke had. When it's my turn, I pitch this: "We take five thousand one-dollar bills, and we stamp the word *HubSpot* on each one, in big red letters, along with our web address. We take the dollar bills to a city—let's say it's Cincinnati, because my brother lives there, but it doesn't matter which city. We scatter the dollar bills—all over the city. It's a metaphor for marketing. Do you get it?"

They don't. The women from the blog team stare at me with hate-filled eyes. I can't tell if that's because they don't like my idea or because they just hate me.

"Right now the way we get customers," I say, "is we take millions of dollars and we pay people to create content on a blog. Then we hope that some tiny fraction of the people who see our content eventually turn into customers. Our conversion rate is tiny.

"I propose we cut out the middleman—that's us—and just literally give the money away. People in Cincinnati start spotting these bills all over the place. They start wondering what's going on. The press gets wind of it. The local paper does a story. Then we get on local TV. Halligan talks about his crazy marketing scheme. It's free coverage! Let's say, after all this, we get one new customer in Cincinnati. We just spent five thousand bucks and got a customer. That's way better than our current customer acquisition cost."

They're not buying it. But I continue anyway to phase 2 of my plan: scavenger hunts. Lately these have been in the news. Some mysterious philanthropist has been putting hundred-dollar bills in envelopes, stashing them all over San Francisco and New York, and posting clues about how to find them.

"I propose we kick it up a notch. We announce that on a certain day we will hide a bag containing five thousand dollars somewhere in San Francisco, say in Golden Gate Park. Or in Central Park, in New York. We create a frenzy. Imagine you have hundreds, or thousands, of people racing around trying to find the money. They all descend on the park at the same time. They're blocking traffic. They're causing accidents! It's like that old movie, *It's a Mad, Mad, Mad, Mad World*, where all the different teams are trying to find the treasure. The press would be all over this. They'd all do stories about the chaos. They'd do stories about whoever finds the money. They'll do stories about us. We'll be on national TV."

The thing is, this really isn't a bad idea. It's controversial, and maybe crazy, but it's not outside the realm of possibility.

Nobody likes it.

"Okay," I say, "so we could even take it one step further. We build a money cannon. It's a big cannon that shoots dollar bills. You just need a big fan, in a box, and then a tube sticking out. We mount the cannon on the back of a Hummer, with *HubSpot* in huge letters on both sides, and we drive around a city blowing money into the streets. Think of the disruption! People rushing into the streets, trying to grab as many dollar bills as they can. They'd be fighting over the money, like people at Walmart on Black Friday. It would be a nightmare!"

They all just sit there, looking down at their hands. Trotsky clears his throat and says, "Okay—anybody else?"

We spend an hour listening to various lame ideas. One is called Uber-a-Marketer, and it's a ripoff of a promotion that Uber did with a vaccine service, where you could have a nurse with a flu shot driven to your door. With Uber-a-Marketer, you'd pay some money, or win some kind of competition, and HubSpot would send one of its marketing people to your office and teach you how to do marketing. After all, we're the best marketing team on the planet! People would *kill* to have us teach them about marketing!

This idea actually generates some responses. But someone worries that Uber might not want to play ball with us. What happens then? We could go to Lyft, or some other car service.

I chime in, saying that I love this idea but maybe there's a way to kick it up a notch and make it even more dramatic: "Why not have a marketing person parachute in?" I say. "Like Google did at their I/O conference last year, when they had people wearing Google Glass skydive onto the roof of the venue. You win the prize, and zoom—a plane flies overhead and a marketing person comes skydiving out of the plane and lands on your roof. How cool is that?"

Dead stares.

"Or," I say, warming to the topic, "we could fire someone out of a cannon. We could make Spinner do it. I'd pay to see that. Or hey, Fatima would do it." Fatima is an unbearably ambitious and energetic young woman who recently graduated from college, loves HubSpot more than life itself, and would do just about anything to get a promotion. "She's tiny," I say. "We could put her in an orange jumpsuit and an orange helmet and fire her right through an open window and into a cubicle. Bang! There she is! She doesn't miss a beat. She just starts giving a lecture about marketing."

A few people laugh. But then they look around and see that the others aren't laughing, and they stop.

For a moment there's nothing. Crickets.

"You know," I said, "I really think you should consider that money cannon. Because that one seriously would work."

Twenty-three

Escape Velocity

Fortunately, as it happens, my job hunt has been going well. I'm pretty sure I will have an offer lined up soon and can give my notice.

Meanwhile, on October 9, HubSpot manages to pull off its IPO. I'm rich! Not really. My options are worth about $45,000 more than what I will pay to exercise them. Still, I can't complain.

When companies go public they have to file paperwork with the Securities and Exchange Commission and reveal information about their business, including their financial performance. After looking at the HubSpot prospectus I cannot believe anyone would actually buy shares in the company. The losses are huge, and instead of getting smaller, they are getting bigger. Losses in fact are growing faster than revenues.

According to its IPO prospectus, in 2013, HubSpot generated $77.6 million in revenue but lost $34.2 million. In the previous year, HubSpot posted $51.6 million in revenue but lost $18.9 million. Losses are growing faster than sales. From 2009 through the middle of 2014, HubSpot has generated $231 million in revenues but lost $118 million doing it, meaning that for every dollar generated in sales, the company has spent nearly a dollar and a half.

Sure, top line revenue is growing, but HubSpot is accomplishing this by spending more and more money on sales and marketing. According to the prospectus, in 2013 HubSpot spent $53 million just on sales and marketing—that's about 68 percent of total revenues. Sales and marketing represents by far the biggest expense on the income statement. HubSpot spends more than three times as much on sales and marketing as it does on research and development.

According to HubSpot's balance sheet, from the end of 2012 to the middle of 2014, a period of just eighteen months, HubSpot's assets have declined by 20 percent, from $65 million to $52 million. Its liabilities, meanwhile, have more than doubled, from $27.6 million to $57.4 million.

Also revealed in the prospectus is that HubSpot has started borrowing money against a line of credit. In total the company has borrowed $18 million, which will be repaid out of the money raised in the offering. Management hopes to raise $100 million in the IPO.

The prospectus contains a warning: "We have a history of losses and may not achieve profitability in the future." Note this does not say it will take a while to achieve profitability, or that profits will one day arrive but the company cannot predict when this will happen. Rather, the prospectus says the company might *never* become profitable. Sure, this is partly just a way to be conservative. Companies always exaggerate the risks to their business so that they can't be accused later of misleading investors or overpromising.

So what are you getting if you buy this stock? You're not really investing; you're speculating. You're hoping that whatever price you pay, someday someone else will be willing to pay more for it. No doubt there are people who will buy HubSpot shares without ever reading the prospectus or looking at the income statement or balance sheet. They're just buying a story. They're also hoping that the IPO will deliver a little "pop," meaning the stock will go up on its first day of trading, giving them an instant profit.

In the end those people got their wish. In the days leading up to the IPO, HubSpot starts seeing strong enough interest from investors that it raises the price of its stock, from a range of $19 to $21 to a range of $22 to $24. On October 8, the night before HubSpot shares will start trading, the company raises the price again, to $25. The next day, when the market opens, HubSpot shares surge past $30 on the New York Stock Exchange.

Halligan and Shah have overcome tremendous odds to get where they are. In 2006, the year they founded HubSpot, more than 600,000 new companies were launched in the United States, according to the Bureau of Labor Statistics. Fewer than 1,500 of those companies raised money from angel investors and venture capital firms, according to a 2015 report by CB Insights, which tracks the venture capital industry. Of those 1,500 companies, only 1 percent made it to "unicorn" status, achieving a market valuation of $1 billion or more, CB Insights says.

What's most remarkable is that HubSpot pulled this off even though the company had come within a hair's breadth of running out of money. Apparently this happens more often than I realized. "It's called 'Go public or go broke,' and it's not at all uncommon," says Trip, a former investment banker and venture capitalist. "The one thing people do not appreciate is that these companies are incredibly fragile. There is so much less to them than people believe. The difference between success and failure is so much smaller than people recognize. The whole thing is based on companies trying to achieve escape velocity before they blow themselves up."

Trip says pulling off an IPO is "like a caper movie. You know they're going to try to rob the place, but you don't know how they're going to do it, and you don't know if they'll get away with it. There's the promised land, over there, but will they make it?"

Halligan and Shah and their investors have pulled off the caper. HubSpot has gone public. The investors have made a fortune.

On October 9, the first day of trading, Halligan and Shah and a team of top executives go to New York and ring the bell at the New York Stock Exchange. They all wear goofy orange HubSpot sunglasses, like a bunch of clowns. The rest of us gather in the big conference room in Cambridge, watching a live feed from the floor of the stock exchange. Two young women sitting in front of me have loaded the Yahoo Finance app on their iPhones and are trying to figure out how much their options are worth.

Once the stock starts trading, the "reporters" (they're actually PR people) on the stock exchange floor conduct interviews with the executives from HubSpot, asking them if they have anything to say to the folks back in the home office.

The best comment comes from Dharmesh. He owns 7 percent of the company, more than any other individual. At a $30 stock price, his 2.3 million shares are worth nearly $70 million. This windfall has come to him thanks to a single daring bet, one that probably seemed crazy at the time: Back in 2006, he took $500,000 of his own money out of the bank and used it to start HubSpot. He was the only seed investor.

Dharmesh holds the title of chief technology officer, and he wrote the HubSpot culture code, but he doesn't seem to be around much. By October 2014, when the IPO takes place, he is mostly working on a new project, an online community for marketers, called Inbound.org.

But now he's the richest person at the company. I'm anxious to hear what he will say to the people back in Cambridge—the engineers who write the code, the bros in the boiler room who sell it, the grunts in the content factory who generate the leads, the customer service reps who deal with angry people all day.

Most of these people will get next to nothing from this IPO, but their hard work had just made Dharmesh an immensely wealthy man. How will he thank them? He embodies our culture: humble and modest, remarkable and transparent. He's the creator of HEART, the inventor of *delightion*, the pundit who proclaims, "Success is making those who believed in you look brilliant."

This man who has just reaped a $70 million windfall, whose stock will soon be worth more than $100 million when HubSpot shares keep climbing, looks into the camera and says something amazing: "Get back to work."

I will never forget it.

On the way out we each get a mini bottle of Freixenet Brut with a HubSpot logo. Penny, the receptionist, checks names off a list so nobody can duck back and grab a second bottle.

It's perfect.

Twenty-four

If I Only Had a HEART

About a month after the IPO, in November 2014, I get an offer from Gawker Media, a blog publisher in New York with a reputation for doing some salacious stuff but also for doing some good investigative journalism. They want me to write about Silicon Valley on a blog called Valleywag. After months pretending to be an anthropologist at HubSpot, studying natives who have been growing increasingly resentful of my presence, I will return to my own tribe.

By pure coincidence, on the day in November when I am expecting to receive a letter from Gawker that makes their offer official, I also have my annual review with Trotsky. I consider skipping the meeting, because I'm guessing he's going to insult me. The review is pointless, because as soon as I get the letter from Gawker I'm going to give Trotsky my notice. On the other hand, why miss it? I'm sure Trotsky has something special planned. Also, if I'm really going to do this anthropologist thing, I should carry it through to the end.

Trotsky has set the meeting to take place in a tiny room on the fourth floor, a room named after Dustin Pedroia, a Red Sox player. They call it a meeting room but it is about the size of a closet. There are two chairs and a tiny round table between them, big enough to hold two laptops. The room has a glass wall and glass door, so everybody walking by can see inside.

When I arrive, Trotsky is still finishing up with a young woman named Kacie. They're smiling and laughing, having a good time. I walk down the hallway and wait for my turn. After a few minutes, Kacie comes out, beaming. Her review went well! "Hey!" she says.

When I walk in, Trotsky has his laptop open on the table and a pained expression on his face. Clearly this is not going to go well. For some period of time I clung to the belief that Trotsky didn't really mean all of the shitty things he was saying to me, that he was only abusing me because Cranium had told him to drive me out of the company. But lately I have started to think otherwise. Lately I have come to suspect that Trotsky is getting off on this.

He begins by explaining how HubSpot reviews are conducted. We are graded in three categories: job performance, HEART, and VORP. In each category we get a score from one to five. The numbers make the process seem scientific, or, as people here like to say, *data-driven*. At other jobs when I've had an annual review it basically has entailed having a conversation with my boss. But HubSpot likes numbers.

In job performance, "I'm going to give you a three," Trotsky says. He looks up at me, then stares at his MacBook Air, as if as if there is some matrix of numbers on his screen, data that support the score that he has given me.

Three, I suppose, means I'm doing an adequate job. Not great, certainly, and not even good. But not bad, and not awful. I imagine it's like getting a C on a test. It's an average score. Nothing special, but I'm okay.

Trotsky looks up as if he wants me to respond. I shrug. What can I say? I think I've been doing a killer job as a podcast secretary. We've already interviewed some great guests. The podcast website looks terrific. We've been accepted by the iTunes Store. We're actually ahead of schedule. But I'm not here to argue. I'm just here to find out what this assclown has to say. If he's giving me a three, so be it.

Next up is HEART, the acronym that Dharmesh created in his culture code. The letters stand for humble, effective, adaptable, remarkable, and transparent. Trotsky explains the acronym to me with a straight face, as if HEART is something that two grown men, two normal adult human beings, should take seriously and be able to discuss.

In HEART, Trotsky gives me a two. That one hurts. I am not completely lacking a HEART—I'm not the Tin Woodman from *The Wizard of Oz*—but at the same time, at least according to Trotsky, I don't have much of a HEART. There's one in there, somewhere, but it's very small.

Trotsky does not explain how he computed this score, but I wish he would. I'd like him to unpack the acronym and explain what score he gave me for each of the five categories, and then how he added those up and divided by five to arrive at the final score of two. Was it exactly two? Was it two-point-something? Is there a chance he could round the overall score up to three? In which of the five do I need the most improvement? Am I not remarkable? Or transparent? I may not be humble by nature, but certainly I've demonstrated a willingness to be humbled by accepting a job as a podcast secretary after working in Hollywood on an Emmy-nominated TV show. I think I've been effective with the podcast, and I've certainly had to be adaptable.

But anyway, I'm a two. I'm below average. As with my first score, I don't argue with Trotsky or try to haggle or negotiate. I just listen.

The third category is VORP, the scoring system that Halligan borrowed from Major League Baseball. VORP stands for value over replacement player. VORP is a cruel, heartless metric, and it's weird to set it right alongside HEART. It's like putting a photo of Gordon Gekko next to a photo of the Dalai Lama. VORP is the opposite of HEART. It's the anti-HEART. It's HEART-less.

In this category I figure I will get a one, or a zero, or even a negative number, if that's possible. I'm being paid a lot of money to do a job that a summer intern could do, a job that originally was created as a part-time assignment for Cranium's administrative assistant. Scheduling people for a podcast and fetching glasses of water for Cranium and his guests in the studio are not challenging tasks. My salary is pretty high. It's actually higher than Trotsky's, because he was clever enough to take a small salary in exchange for getting more stock options. Anyway, I'm getting paid like a top executive, and I'm doing secretarial work. My VORP must be the lowest of any employee in the history of the company.

But Trotsky is benevolent. In VORP, he gives me a two.

He shuts his MacBook Air. He looks at me.

"So," he says, "what do you think?"

I think that I want to burst out laughing. Who can take this rubbish seriously? HEART? Really? I feel like I've fallen into a scene from *Office Space*. How can it be that the two of us are sitting in this ridiculous orange broom closet and talking about such risible bullshit? There is no data behind these scores. Trotsky is just pulling numbers out of his ass.

Maybe he thinks that my feelings will be hurt. But I've just spent four months in Hollywood working with some of the best writers in TV, and I've been asked to come back for next season. In a few hours I'm going get an offer letter to write for one of the best-known tech blogs in the world. Trotsky can give me a score of negative one zillion and I won't care.

"Well," I say, "those scores all sound very fair."

I'd really like to leave now, but the scores are only the beginning. Trotsky has a few more tricks up his sleeve. I'm starting to feel as if I am being detained by the police and subjected to interrogation without legal representation. Shouldn't I get one phone call? Or something?

In his very solemn voice, the one he uses when he's really going to say something mean, and when he wants me to know that he really feels sorry that he has to tell me something so terrible about my character, Trotsky says there is another part to the performance review. For every review, he is required to get feedback about an employee from his or her peers.

Oh shit. Here it comes. I figure he's going to open his laptop and read some quotes about me that are going to go straight through my rib cage and into my heart. Maybe they really did come from a peer, or maybe he will have just made them up. Either way, this is going to suck. I steel myself.

"So I asked two people," he says. "I asked two people who work with you to give me comments about you. I sent them email, and they didn't respond. I emailed them again, and asked them a few times, but they never responded."

"Oh," I say. "Do you think maybe they just forgot to do it?"

He winces, and shakes his head. "I don't think so," he says.

He waits. I wait. I'm not quite sure what to say.

"So I got no feedback at all about you. What do you think that says about you?"

This sounds like it could be a rhetorical question, but from the look on his face he seems to expect me to say something.

"Well," I say, "I guess it's not good, right?" I slump a little bit in my chair. I let the information sink in. "I mean, if people say nothing, that's almost worse than if they say something bad, right? I mean supposedly the worst thing that can happen to you in the workplace is that you get shunned by your peers, or ignored. So I guess it tells me that people here really do not like me, and they really don't want me here. I mean, not a single person would say even a single nice thing? Really?"

That last line is my attempt to get some sympathy—a chance for him to say that, oh, things aren't that bad, and he's sure that some people here like me.

Instead, he nods in agreement. "Hmm," he says, with a sympathetic expression on his face, as if to say that he knows how hurtful this must be, and he's really sorry that he has to be the one to tell me.

"Who did you ask?" I say. "Which two people?"

"I can't say," he says. "The reviews have to be confidential." Then, after a pause, he says, "Well, one of them was Tracy."

Tracy is the vice president of brand and buzz, the woman who had Keytar Bear playing at her birthday party. She's a tiny woman in her thirties, with jet-black hair. She sits three desks away from me, and I really like her. I consider her a friend. I cannot believe she would refuse to comment for my review.

Somehow this gets to me. The low scores I can deal with. But this bit of information really stings. Until now I've been laughing up my sleeve at this charade. I was able to not take it personally. But now that's changed. As much as I want this not to hurt, it does.

I'm upset in part because of what Trotsky is saying to me—but more so because I've put myself in this position in the first place. What was I thinking when I took this job? Why have I subjected myself to this for so long? How have I ended up trapped in a room with this tattoed sadist, playing out this psychology experiment?

Like an idiot, I start talking. I babble. I spill my guts. I tell Trotsky how disappointing this is, how nothing like this has ever happened to me before, and by *this* I mean the whole thing, the whole shitty year and a half at HubSpot. For twenty-five years my career went up and up. I went from one job to a better job. I got promotions, and raises. And I was happy! I loved my work. I made good friends—lifelong friends, people I still talk to all the time.

"Maybe I'm not cut out to work in marketing," I say. "That's fine. But I've never worked in a place where I didn't make friends. I've never been in a place where everyone makes it so clear that they don't like me, or want me around. Some jobs you like better than others, but I've never felt lonely at work. That's how I feel here."

I've gone through my entire life feeling that I am basically a likeable person, someone who can make friends and fit in. But here I have stumbled into a world where I am really and truly not wanted. Some of that may have to do with my personality, and some of it has to do with my age. Apparently I have crossed some invisible line, and I now live in the Land of the Old. That's what's hitting me here. That's what this job has forced me to confront: I'm old. A few months ago I turned fifty-four. One hundred years ago that was the average life expectancy in the United States. At this age, I would be getting carted off to the cemetery.

Instead, I'm here. What's really depressing is that this is entirely my fault. If I'd managed my life better, I would be retired now. I would have stayed on the track to become a doctor, which was my original plan and the one my parents urged me to follow. Most of my high school friends became doctors. They're retired now, or working part-time. They're coasting. They've made their money, and they're all set. Meanwhile I'm still working my ass off, still needing to earn a paycheck. I've reached a point in my life where I should not have to put up with being degraded like this, punched around by some buffoon like Trotsky. But here I am.

"The whole thing is depressing," I say.

Trotsky smiles. I've given him an opening. He says he wants to tell me something about that comment I made about always making friends at work.

"When I first took this job," he says, "I knew I was going to be working with you. So I got in touch with someone who knows you, a person you worked with. I asked them what you're like. You know what they said? They said, 'Smart guy, but acerbic.'"

He looks at me, expecting a response.

"Everybody knows I'm acerbic," I say. "It's what I'm known for."

"I guess I'm not making this clear," Trotsky says. "What I mean is, when you say that you always made friends at your past jobs, maybe that's not really how it was."

"I always left on good terms. I have friends from *Forbes*, people I've known for fifteen years, and we're still really good friends. Same at *Newsweek*."

"Well," Trotsky says, "I'm sure that *you* liked *them*. But I'm suggesting that maybe your perception of those situations was not the same as the perception that other people had about you."

"So what are you saying? That people at those places didn't like me either? That I've been walking around for years thinking that people are my friends, when really, behind my back, they all don't like me?"

He does a sort of shrug and smile, as if to say, *I guess so.*

"Who did you talk to? Who told you I was acerbic?"

"I can't tell you that."

"Okay. Fine. But you know, telling me that story is a pretty sick move on your part. Because now I'm going to walk around all day wondering who that is. Who would say that to you? Who's the person that I think is my friend but who actually talks shit about me behind my back? You know what I mean? That's going to gnaw at me."

"I know," he says, with a huge grin. "Consider that my gift to you."

I walk out to the lobby, feeling numb. We're up on the fourth floor, overlooking the atrium. Down below, on the ground floor, twenty-something HubSpotters are sitting at tables, drinking coffee and having meetings. Suddenly there's a burst of laughter—three people cracking up. Their laughter rises up through the atrium and rings off the skylights.

I stand there, reeling. My heart is racing. My face, I'm sure, is flushed. All that stuff Trotsky just told me about the people who don't like me—is any of that even true, or did he just make it up? Is there really some former colleague of mine from *Forbes* or *Newsweek* who goes around telling people I'm a jerk? Did Tracy really refuse to comment for my review? I have no idea what to make of any of this.

I call a friend of mine in New York and tell her what just happened, how HubSpot grades people on HEART and that my HEART has been found lacking.

"Are you serious? That's hilarious!" she says.

"Well," I say, "it is and it isn't."

I start telling her the rest, about how nobody would give me a peer review, and how supposedly everyone at my past jobs hates me, too— and then the door from the north wing of the building opens and there is my good friend Tracy, the peppy vice president of brand and buzz, striding across the lobby with a huge smile on her face.

"Hey you!" she says, and waves, as if she's super-duper happy to see me.

"Hey!" I say, faking a smile.

Maybe she figures I don't know that she stabbed me in the back by refusing to comment for my peer review. Or maybe she does. Maybe she knew that Trotsky was going to tell me this, and she came out here specifically because she wanted to see the look on my face after I found that out. Could she really dislike me that much? Could she possibly be that nasty?

Down in the atrium the kids are still laughing and whooping it up. They're having a meeting! About marketing! This place is so cool! They're having the time of their lives.

I hurry to my desk and grab my jacket. I stuff my laptop into my backpack. My hands are shaking. Out in the lobby, I stare at the elevator doors, waiting for them to open. Finally they do, and I ride down to the ground floor and walk past the security guard, who gives me a lazy wave and says, "Good night."

Finally I'm outside, bundling my coat against the November air, hurrying to my car. It's late afternoon, the daylight draining from the sky. When I get home I call the editorial director at Gawker and accept the job.

Twenty-five

Graduation Day

The next morning I stop by Trotsky's desk and tell him I need to talk to him in private. We find an empty conference closet. Ironically it's the one with the beanbag chairs where we used to have our biweekly one-on-ones and shoot the shit about the morons we were working with.

I tell Trotsky that I've been offered a new job, and that I've accepted it. It's Thursday, November 20. I won't start until January, but I am giving him six weeks of notice. Next week is Thanksgiving, and then there are three weeks when everyone will be working before the Christmas break.

I'd like to remain at HubSpot through the end of December. That will give me time to get the new podcast up and running smoothly. I'll manage a smooth handoff to whichever person will be running it after I leave.

Trotsky acts surprised. "Why are you leaving?" he says.

"Are you serious?"

"I thought things were going well," he says.

"Well, that performance review yesterday didn't go very well. I got pretty bad scores."

"I didn't think the scores were so bad," he says, and he really, sincerely seems to mean this.

He asks me if I will reconsider. I tell him that in addition to the Valleywag job, my agent in Los Angeles has told me that I'm probably going to get hired back on *Silicon Valley* if the show gets renewed. So I would be leaving HubSpot anyway, and I may only be working at Valleywag for four or five months, until I go back to Los Angeles.

Trotsky suggests I could just stay at HubSpot instead of going to Valleywag. The podcast job will be easy. It won't take up much of my time. I can coast and collect a paycheck. He's back to being my buddy. He says the whole idea for giving me the podcast was to set me up with a cushy, easy gig, as a way to help me out.

This is a whole new level of crazy. Trotsky has spent the past three months making my life a living hell, putting me through the worst experience of my life. Now he's acting as if he is not even aware of that. He thinks we're pals.

I tell him I appreciate the offer, but I've made up my mind.

"Fair enough," he says.

He wishes me the best. We shake hands. I go back to my desk, get my stuff, and go home. I send an email to the HR department, telling them what I just told Trotsky, that I'm resigning effective December 31, 2014. The woman from HR writes back and copies someone else from HR who will "set you up with an exit interview."

Later in the day Trotsky emails me and asks if I could come in tomorrow, on Friday, so we can start processing the paperwork to make things official. I figure we will talk about the podcast transition plan, and maybe he will walk me through the things I need to do over the next few weeks like scheduling an exit interview with the HR department.

But on Friday, when I get to the office, I skim through my HubSpot email inbox and see that on Thursday afternoon, a few hours after I gave my notice to Trotsky, Cranium sent an email to the entire marketing department, including me, informing everyone that today, Friday, will be my last day at HubSpot. This is news to me. Cranium never called me to tell me this. Neither did Trotsky. This email to the whole department has been sitting in my inbox since yesterday afternoon, but

I haven't been checking that account because I've busy dealing with people at Gawker.

I'm stunned. Until this moment it's been my understanding that I will continue working at HubSpot for another six weeks, until December 31. I can't believe that this is how I am discovering when my last day will be, by reading an email that has been sent to the entire department.

Worse, Cranium worded the memo in a way that sounds as if I've been fired:

> After a lot of conversations about career paths and what we are looking for out of our content team, as well as a lot of thinking about what he wants to do with his career and where his passions lie, Dan has decided to take his career back into the media industry. His new job is running the website Valleywag, part of Gawker Media. We wish Dan lots of luck in his new role! (And hope he doesn't have any photos of the IPO party...haha.) His last day in the office will be tomorrow, so reach out to Dan if you want to connect with him in person.

I go to the meeting with Trotsky. He plunks down a stack of paperwork with a cover letter that says I've been terminated, effective immediately, signed by the director of "people operations." I have ninety days to exercise my vested stock options, or they will expire. My pay ends today. My health coverage ends in a week. So much for all that stuff about being *lovable* and *remarkable* and *HubSpotty*, and treating people with HEART.

Trotsky says the company can offer me something a little better. I can keep my insurance through the end of December, and I can even continue to get paid for those weeks, but only if I sign a "release and waiver of claims" agreement that's attached to the termination letter. Signing the release form prohibits me from ever bringing any kind of legal claim against the company. It also includes a nondisparagement clause.

I tell Trotsky I want to take the paperwork home and look it over, and maybe have someone review it for me.

"Sure," he says. "That's fine."

He asks me a few questions about the podcast and where things stand. There's something I need to look up, so I open my laptop and start to search for the file—but he stops me.

"I'm not supposed to let you do that," he says.

Trotsky takes my laptop. He also takes my ID bracelet. I'm speechless. I really can't believe this. I gave these guys six weeks of notice and wanted to make a smooth transition, and in exchange for that courtesy, they're firing me.

Before we leave Trotsky says he wants to tell me something: "I'm your friend," he says. "I've always been your friend. I know that right now you don't think that's the case. You think I've been out to get you. But the truth is that I've always been on your side, and I still am."

He also gives me some advice. He says that in his last two jobs he clashed with his managers. He left feeling angry. But in both cases, after he calmed down a bit, he reached out and tried to make amends with them. One boss refused to talk to him. The other met him for coffee and Trotsky believes they patched things up.

"No matter how angry you are right now, you should take a little time, and then reach out and try to make things right," he says. "If someone says no, well, fine, at least you made the effort. You've taken the high road."

I'm not sure which people he thinks I need to apologize to. He says Spinner is one example. I should reach out to her, ask her to have coffee, try to repair our relationship. I get the sense that he's also talking about my relationship with him. His idea seems to be that I should go home and cool off, and then at some point reach out and apologize to him.

This is nuts. This guy has just spent three months harassing and abusing me, and now he's handing me paperwork that cancels my health insurance in a week—and he wants me to know that he's my friend? He wants me to make an effort to be nice to him in the future? I really don't know how to respond to that.

"So what do we do now? Am I supposed to go talk to someone in HR?" I say. "They emailed me and said someone was going to set up a time for me to do an exit interview."

"Do you want to go to HR?" he says.

"Isn't that what I'm supposed to do?"

Trotsky says the conversation we're having right now can serve as my exit interview. He says he asked HR to let him be the one to give me the paperwork and explain everything to me, because we're friends.

"But if you want to go talk to HR as well, we can do that," he says.

I think about it for a moment, then decide that if there is no need for me to go to HR, then I'll just leave.

We go back to our desks. I get my coat and backpack. Trotsky puts my laptop on his desk.

It's mid-morning on a Friday, but there aren't many people working in my area. I wonder if the room has been cleared out. This is something HubSpot does when they fire an employee, presumably to let the person save face. They did it to Paige, when they fired her on Fearless Friday.

On my way out I walk past Tracy, the vice president of brand and buzz, the woman who supposedly refused to give me a performance review. She gives me a big smile and wishes me all the best.

Trotsky walks out to the lobby with me, and we ride the elevator down to the first floor. I shake his hand, and say, "Thanks for everything."

I start for the men's room. Trotsky stands there.

"What is it," I say. Then it dawns on me. "Do you need to make sure that I actually leave the building? Are you going to wait here while I go to the bathroom?"

That is, in fact, what he is probably supposed to do. He seems embarrassed. He says no, I can go to the bathroom unsupervised. That's the last time I see him.

I never sign the nondisparagement and nondisclosure exit paperwork. But I do manage to negotiate a better severance agreement. The company agrees to keep paying me through the end of the year and to continue my health insurance coverage. Halligan and Dharmesh send me nice email messages thanking me for my service. Cranium says nothing.

It seems shabby and half-assed that I never got a real exit interview and that Cranium never bothered to talk to me. I don't like the way the termination letter was worded or the way Trotsky gave me the bum's rush out of the place. Cranium's email memo to the department, written to make it seem like I was fired, felt like a little kick in the shins on the way out the door.

But I suppose Cranium is just trying to protect the brand. At every turn, he needs to make sure that HubSpot appears to come out on top. I didn't break up with them; they broke up with me. Or, we broke up with each other.

A few weeks later, just before Christmas, I'm home with Sasha and the kids, around dinnertime, when the doorbell rings. It's a FedEx guy with a huge cardboard box addressed to me. The kids are all excited. What can it be? Inside the box there's an enormous wicker picnic basket with a lid and a latch. The basket contains delicacies from Dean and DeLuca: nuts, sun-dried tomatoes, fancy cheeses, smoked meats. I'm sure it cost a fortune.

My first guess is that it's a Christmas gift from my dad. But when I open the note I find that the basket comes from Cranium—the guy who in nearly two years never held a one-on-one meeting with me, who had just spent the past few months, through a proxy, making my life miserable, and who, when I did finally leave, did not bother to speak to me in person, call me on the phone, or even send me an email.

The note says Cranium is happy for me and wishes me well as I return to the media business.

Trotsky, meanwhile, starts reaching out, sending me email messages asking me if I will meet him for coffee. I wonder if this is all still part of some game he is playing. Maybe he got off on tormenting me, and he misses it. He's hoping I will keep playing along. We can go have lunch and hang out, and for a while he'll be nice, and then he'll turn on me again, and he'll see how much I will tolerate.

For a while I ignore his messages. In early January he emails me again, saying, "You've unfollowed me on Twitter, blocked me on Facebook, and haven't replied to email. I get that things weren't great after you returned from LA, but I would like to talk." He says we can bury the hatchet, or if I just need to vent, he'll sit and listen. If I don't want to talk to him at all, "that'd be a shame, but I'll respect it. I always liked you, considered you a friend. It'd be unfortunate if...if...if poof, that's all over because we didn't find a professional groove after your return."

This time I write back: "Hey! Great to hear from you. I've been crazy busy. Hope you had great holidays and will enjoy 2015!"

A few weeks later, I publish a blog post announcing that I'm writing a book about my time at HubSpot. I never hear from Trotsky again.

Epilogue

A few weeks after I delivered a first draft of this book manuscript to my publisher, things took a weird, dark turn. On July 29, 2015, late in the afternoon, HubSpot issued a press release announcing that Wingman had been promoted to chief marketing officer.

Buried in the second paragraph was a bombshell: Wingman had been promoted because HubSpot had fired its longtime CMO, Mike Volpe, the guy called Cranium in this book. Volpe was terminated for cause because he had "violated the Company's Code of Business Conduct and Ethics" in his "attempts to procure" a manuscript of a book involving HubSpot, the release said.

Furthermore, Joe Chernov (Trotsky) had resigned from HubSpot "before the company could determine whether to terminate him for similar violations." Brian Halligan, the CEO, had been "appropriately sanctioned" but would not be fired.

Given the very public manner in which Volpe was fired and Chernov left the company, I decided to name them here. I left their nicknames intact in the main text of the book because, frankly, the fake names are a lot more memorable.

The press release did not say what Volpe and Chernov had done. It said only that HubSpot had hired an outside law firm to conduct an investigation, and that after reviewing the law firm's report, the board had voted to fire Volpe. Also, the board had "notified the appropriate legal authorities about these matters." The press release did not specify that the book in question was my book. It just referred to "a book involving the Company." I figured it was my book, but I couldn't be sure.

This kicked off a speculative whirlwind in Boston. What was the book? What did it say? What had Volpe and Chernov done? Why were legal authorities involved? Soon after the release was issued, a reporter from the *Boston Globe*, Curt Woodward, started calling Spinner and trying to get an interview with Halligan or Shah. When Spinner didn't return his calls, he showed up at HubSpot headquarters and was let into the lobby. Spinner called security. Woodward was asked to leave.

The story made front-page news in the *Globe* the next day and was splashed across all of the local tech blogs. Most people speculated that the book in question was mine. The supposition seemed to be that Volpe and the others had engaged in some kind of hacking.

HubSpot did an abysmal job of managing the situation. "HubSpot & Crisis Communications: A Lesson in What Not to Do" was the title of a post by Maura FitzGerald, who runs Version 2.0 Communications, a public relations agency in Boston. The crisis itself made HubSpot "look like an arrogant, cowboy culture rather than a company that has been thoughtfully built to last," but the way HubSpot handled the crisis "reinforced the negatives and did little to halt damage to the brand," FitzGerald wrote.

The first mistake was HubSpot's press release, with its headline about Wingman being appointed CMO, which looked like a clumsy attempt to put a positive spin on a situation that could only be viewed as a world of shit. Someone, presumably Spinner, must have argued that putting the "good news" first somehow would soften the impact of the bad news. Instead it made the company look sneaky.

Next was the way HubSpot dealt with the local press. Spinner seemed to think HubSpot could just brazen it out: Put out a press release, then stonewall. Refuse to answer questions. She should have had a director or executive cued up, prepped, and ready to give interviews. Instead, she called security and had a reporter bounced from the lobby.

When that didn't work, Spinner made another blunder. Instead of talking to Woodward, the *Globe* reporter who was covering the story, Spinner called the *Globe* and requested they send Scott Kirsner, a contract columnist who is not a *Globe* staffer and who has been cozy with HubSpot. Companies in the midst of a crisis don't usually enjoy the luxury of choosing which reporters will cover the story, but apparently the *Globe* acceded to Spinner's demand and sent Kirsner.

Kirsner wears kooky bright green eyeglasses and is involved with a company that runs tech conferences, including some events where HubSpot executives have been speakers. One HubSpot employee serves as an advisor to that company. Kirsner tagged his articles about the scandal with a disclosure outlining his potential conflicts of interest.

Even with Kirsner assigned to the story, Halligan and Shah would not answer questions or explain what had happened. Halligan said the board had uncovered some "fishiness" and some "really aggressive tactics." He wouldn't say what those tactics were or who engaged in them.

The first principle of crisis communications is that if you have bad news to divulge, you do it quickly and completely. HubSpot did the opposite. The vague press release, the handpicked journalist, and the refusal to say what happened all reeked of a cover-up. The response to the crisis raised new questions. Why had HubSpot been so worried about the book? Was there some dark secret they didn't want people to know about?

For a few days, the story remained front-page news. I was deluged with calls and emails from reporters. Kirsner entreated me to talk to him, writing, "You are missing the greatest publicity opportunity of all time." Friends started calling, too, wanting to know what happened. The problem was I had no idea. All I knew was what HubSpot had said in its press release, which wasn't much. I didn't respond to any of the reporters. I figured it was best to just keep quiet and hope that eventually the facts would come out.

HubSpot alumni have a Facebook page, and oddly enough, sentiment there was that Volpe was a great guy and should not have been fired, and that I was a jerk for writing a "tell-all" book. The company's own board of directors had fired Volpe and "notified appropriate legal authorities" yet these people simply refused to believe this could be true. They had left the company but still remained brainwashed.

Someone started a #teamvolpe hashtag thread on Twitter, trying to gin up support for this disgraced executive, but only about a dozen people posted tweets taking his side. Among those who expressed support for Volpe was Dharmesh Shah, who posted messages on Twitter and LinkedIn saying in essence that Volpe was a good person who had done a bad thing. Kirsner, the chummy columnist who interviewed Halligan and Shah for the *Globe*, wrote an article quoting local marketing people saying Volpe was great. Kirsner also quoted HubSpot employees, speaking anonymously, saying bad things about me. In addition, Kirsner posted a tweet that seemed to excuse Volpe's behavior: "Q for you: if an employee had signed a confidentiality agreement, then wrote a book about your co, would you try to prevent its publication?"

The stuff about a confidentiality agreement was a smokescreen. HubSpot requires new hires to sign a document saying you can't divulge trade secrets or confidential information, but my book doesn't contain any of those. For that matter, people write books about their work experience all the time. Focusing on a confidentiality agreement was an attempt to distract attention from the real issue, which was that a set of top executives at a publicly traded company had done something that their own board thought might rise to the level of criminal behavior.

HubSpot wasn't the first tech company to get caught doing something ugly. In 2006 Hewlett-Packard was discovered to have spied on reporters. The scandal led to the resignation of Hewlett-Packard's board chairman and general counsel, and to hearings before Congress where people invoked the Fifth Amendment right against self-incrimination. One Hewlett-Packard board member quit the board in disgust after learning what had gone on.

In 2014 there was a huge outcry after an executive at Uber made a comment about being able to investigate a journalist named Sarah Lacy. Uber looked like a pack of thugs. The media frenzy went on for weeks and was covered on national television.

Yet here were HubSpot's top executives doing something that their own board believed might be illegal—and nobody seemed to care. Nobody was outraged that a billion-dollar company might have hacked into a journalist's computer or broken into his house. Wall Street didn't care either. In the days after the announcement, HubSpot's stock price sagged a little bit but remained close to its all-time high.

At first I thought the whole thing was hilarious. What a pack of buffoons! Presumably they had engaged in some kind of hacking and got caught. The episode only served to confirm my depiction of them. To be sure, I also was angry, and in the case of Chernov somewhat disappointed, since we had at one time been friends. I also felt a sense of schadenfreude as I remembered how poorly Chernov and Volpe had treated me. "These guys will never work again," a former HubSpot executive said to me. "You realize that, right? Their careers are over."

Although at first I found the whole thing comical, over the next week I started to get scared. Stuck in my head was one phrase Halligan used with the *Globe*: "really aggressive tactics."

The original HubSpot press release said Volpe had been engaged in "attempts to procure" the book. I tried to parse that language. Did "attempts" mean they had tried to get the book but failed? How had they tried? How had they been caught? The word *procure* might imply a transaction involving money. Had they tried to bribe someone at the publishing company? If so, whatever happened might not have involved me at all.

Most speculation seemed to be that HubSpot had tried to hack my computer. Over the summer my laptop had been having problems. It was a four-year-old MacBook Air, and I had thought the hard drive might be failing. Now I wondered if perhaps it had been hacked.

Other strange things had happened. On June 21 I received a warning from Twitter that someone had been trying, unsuccessfully, to log into my account with an incorrect password. In August I got a warning from Google that someone had tried to log on to one of my Gmail accounts: "Someone has your password," the message said. The hacker had used the correct password but the log-in attempt had come from Germany, and Google's system had flagged it as possibly not legitimate. In August my dad received a strange email from a "fakestevejobs" email account that wasn't mine, but the message contained a list of names from my contacts, with each person's phone number and email address,

as if someone had cracked into my contact list and was sending messages to people on that list. Toward the end of June I had received an
email from a friend asking if I had remained on good terms with people
at HubSpot, because "I happen to know they are keeping an eye on
your Facebook activity." This friend said that Chernov somehow was
aware of what I was posting on Facebook, even though I had blocked
Chernov fram seeing my posts.

Those incidents were strange, but they didn't really prove anything.
I racked my brain trying to figure out what the HubSpot idiots might
have done. I recalled that on my last day at HubSpot, Chernov did my
exit interview himself, instead of sending me to HR. He also confis-
cated my company laptop, a MacBook Air. I was fairly certain that
I had removed my personal Gmail account from the machine before
handing it over. But what if I hadn't? What if my password was still
stored on the machine, and Chernov had been able to restore my personal Gmail account? He might have been snooping into my email for
months.

If HubSpot had gained access to my email, and to my Facebook
and Twitter accounts, they might know which people I talked to during my reporting. These included some current and former HubSpot
employees. I had assured those people I would not use their names.
Now they might be in jeopardy.

One theory was that someone had broken into my house to get the
manuscript. It would be easy enough to do. Our house isn't exactly Fort
Knox. I had printouts strewn all over my office, and versions stored on
my computer and backed up onto a thumb drive.

Most people, however, seemed to believe that I had been hacked.
I shut down my MacBook Air and never touched it again. I bought a
new MacBook and changed the passwords on all of my accounts. But
I still did not feel safe. If someone had hacked me, what else had they
taken? I had to assume that someone had cracked my home network
and obtained not just my book manuscript, but everything.

They might have been in the server where we keep our family photos. They might have gained access to our Wi-Fi router. They might still have access to the router. They could have accessed our bank accounts and credit cards, or installed keystroke logging software on my computer and recorded every letter I typed, discovering all of the passwords to all of my accounts. They might have invaded Sasha's computer as well as mine. They might have gained access to the cameras on our laptops and sat there, watching us, recording us. What about our cell phones? And our home phone? Had someone parked on our street and watched our house, waiting for us to go out so that they could break in?

What if HubSpot had hired outsiders to do the dirty work, and those guys kept copies of what they found? Indeed, a few months before the HubSpot scandal broke, I discovered that my Social Security number had been stolen, and that someone had used it to file a fake tax return, hoping to scam the Internal Revenue Service. Hackers could have put my Social Security number and all of my financial information up for sale on the dark web, a secretive world inhabited by criminals with sites that can only be accessed using special software that cloaks your identity. Pictures of my kids could be floating around in pedophile forums, along with our home address and the name and address of their school.

Unless someone from HubSpot or its board of directors called and explained to me exactly what happened, for the rest of my life I would have to assume that all of these things had happened. Hackers might have started out just trying to get a copy of a book manuscript, but in the end they might have done much more damage, not just to me but to my family as well.

I've grown used to the call from my credit card company telling me that my card has been compromised and they're sending me a new one. But this felt different. This was targeted and personal. The people who did this were people who knew me. This wasn't the same as getting rounded up in a massive hack where bad guys steal millions of credit card numbers and yours just happen to be one of them.

Once, when I was in high school, our house was burglarized. One Sunday night we came home from our weekly dinner at my grandmother's house to find a door broken open, rooms ransacked, jewelry missing. Someone had studied us, learned our routine, and then hit the house when they knew we would be out. We suspected a kid in the neighborhood, but the police could not prove anything.

The worst part wasn't that things were stolen. It was the feeling we had afterward. It was as if until then we had gone through life believing that the locks on our doors and windows could protect us, that danger was something abstract and far away, something that happened to other people but not in our sleepy neighborhood in a tiny town in New England. After the robbery I wondered if we would ever feel safe again. As Chekhov wrote, "However happy [one] might be, life will sooner or later show its claws."

HubSpot had shown me its claws. This company was not just a wacky frat house with Cinco de Mayo margarita bashes and sales bros puking in the men's room and a bunch of clueless twenty-something managers. The people who ran the place were not just a pack of bullshit-slinging charlatans, but something more sinister. It seemed to me that maybe their intent all along had been not only to get hold of the book but to send me a message: *You think you can make fun of us? Just look at what we can do to you.*

The day after HubSpot announced Volpe's termination, a former executive at HubSpot asked me to meet him in a town outside Boston. I thought he knew what had happened and wanted to tell me. At the last minute he canceled the meeting, saying he was afraid I might be followed. I said that seemed a bit extreme, but he responded: "You're fucking with a company that's worth a billion and a half dollars. These people take this shit seriously."

Suddenly the whole thing seemed not funny at all, not even a little bit.

To make things worse, all this was happening just as I was about to leave Boston for Los Angeles, to spend several months as a writer on the third season of *Silicon Valley*. I left with massive anxiety, fearing that Sasha and the kids might be in danger. Sasha assured me that I was worrying about ghosts that didn't exist. If something happened, she had friends and neighbors and relatives nearby. On weekends I would fly home to Boston. Nevertheless, I left for Los Angeles still feeling that that none of us was really safe.

What came next was a kind of police procedural, as I set out to discover what had happened. Beyond the question of *what* HubSpot had done to me lay a second and more intriguing question, which was *why* they had done it. Why would anyone go to such lengths to get hold of a memoir whose essential purpose was to entertain? It occurred to me, and to others as well, that HubSpot might be worried that I had stumbled on some damaging piece of information. What could they be so worried about? Just as I was thinking that the book was pretty much done, I wanted to dive back in and find out what I'd missed.

Lawyer friends told me I should expect to hear from law enforcement and that I should hire an attorney. I retained Steven A. Cash, a lawyer from Washington, DC.

Cash and I started trying to piece together a timeline of events. There were three key dates.

On June 22, Halligan sent me an email asking about the book. I told him it was a funny memoir about being a middle-aged journalist trying to fit in at a company with a kooky culture. He said he was concerned that the word "bubble" was in the title, because he didn't think HubSpot was a bubble company. Sales were growing 50 percent! After a few messages, he went dark.

On July 13, I emailed a draft of the manuscript to my editor.

On July 29, sixteen days after I sent the manuscript, HubSpot announced that Volpe had been fired.

These three dates seemed to form a kind of narrative, but we still had no idea what happened. All we knew was that the board had hired a Boston law firm, Goodwin Procter, to conduct an investigation.

Members of the board had read the report produced by Goodwin Procter, so they knew what Volpe had done.

Perhaps this was naïve, but I hoped that someone from HubSpot's board of directors would contact me and offer an explanation. No one ever did. Bear in mind that I've *met* some of these people. I would not call them friends, but I know them, and they know me. One director lives in my town. We've had coffee together. We have mutual friends. Nevertheless, I heard nothing.

Remember the HubSpot culture code? Remember the stuff about HEART, and how the *T* stands for "transparent"? The culture code deck contains a slide with a paraphrase of the famous Louis Brandeis quote about sunlight being the best disinfectant, and another slide that says, "We are radically and remarkably transparent." When it came to my situation, apparently these principles were no longer operative.

Steven Cash, my attorney, contacted HubSpot general counsel John Kelleher asking for information. Kelleher bounced Cash to Goodwin Procter. A lawyer at Goodwin Procter offered no information and would not even say which law enforcement agencies had been alerted.

Days after that conversation, however, Cash got a call from an assistant U.S. attorney who said she was investigating the case with agents from the FBI's cyber crime division. I met with them in September 2015. Even after the meeting, I still had no idea what HubSpot had done.

Later I would hear some crazy stories. One was that the spying involved "Dumpster diving," meaning that Volpe, or someone working for him, had gone to my house and dug through my trash, trying to find a manuscript. I tried to imagine Volpe out in my driveway in the middle of the night, digging through bags of used cat litter. I didn't know whether to laugh or to cry.

Another story, told to me by several present and former HubSpot employees, is that when Volpe was fired, HubSpot held an all-hands meeting to explain the news to employees, and Halligan and Spinner were sobbing.

I also heard that the scandal began when a whistleblower inside the company ratted out Halligan, Volpe, and Chernov to the general counsel or to a member of the board. I have not been able to find out if this is true, or who the whistleblower might be.

On October 9, 2015, the assistant U.S. attorney told my lawyer that the government did not plan to bring any charges related to the case. The AUSA would not say what her investigation had uncovered. I wasn't sure whether to be relieved or disappointed. At first glance it might seem that since no charges were brought, nothing bad had been done to me. But the AUSA herself told me, during my interview, that the government might find evidence of illegal activity but decide not to invest resources to pursue the case.

Clearly, Volpe did something. Why else would the board of directors fire him? In November, four months after the news broke and a month after the feds told us they would not be pressing charges, I sent an email to Lorrie Norrington, a member of the HubSpot board of directors, asking if she would tell me what happened. Norrington is an independent director, meaning she does not work at HubSpot and does not represent one of the company's big venture capital firms. She was also the only board member quoted in the press release. During my time at HubSpot I'd met her and liked her. In my email asking for an explanation, I told her I was concerned especially because Halligan had talked about "really aggressive tactics." I hoped that perhaps out of the goodness of her heart she would tell me what had been done to me and what steps I should take to safeguard myself and my family. I heard nothing back.

The three characters caught up in the scandal have emerged unscathed. In August 2015 Chernov landed a job at a small start-up in Cambridge whose executives include former HubSpot employees. Chernov is the vice president of marketing. Halligan remains the CEO of HubSpot, and in September 2015, just weeks after the scandal broke and at a time when he was still being sanctioned by the directors, he gave a keynote speech at the Inbound conference in front of thousands of adoring customers.

Volpe for a few months went dark on social media, but on the day that my lawyer got word from the AUSA that no criminal charges would be filed, Volpe apparently got the same news. On October 9 he suddenly surfaced, posting on Twitter a photograph of the HubSpot executive team at the New York Stock Exchange, with this message: "One year ago today I was at @NYSE celebrating HubSpot IPO. Want to build Boston's next pillar company? Hit me up." In November he published a blog post announcing that he would be holding "open office hours" for Boston techies who wanted to talk to him and that he had latched on to a new cause: diversity. "Boston tech can't grow into what it should be without more gender and ethnic diversity," he wrote.

For the record: HubSpot's sixteen-member management team contains two Indian guys—one of them is Shah, the co-founder—plus two white women and twelve white men. On the eight-member board, everyone besides Shah is white, and only two are female.

The biggest beneficiary of the scandal was Wingman. It was remarkable enough when he was promoted to vice president after Chernov was hired as a vice president and Cranium apparently didn't want Wingman, his loyal sidekick, to be outranked by the new guy. Before joining HubSpot, Wingman worked as a social media manager—the guy who sends out tweets. Now he is a C-level executive at a publicly traded company with a $2 billion valuation. The mind reels.

As for me, the journey I've taken over the past three years is not what I imagined when I set out in 2012 to reinvent myself as a marketer. I don't regret that I tried to start a new career or that I went to work for a tech company; I do regret that the company I chose was HubSpot. Even that wasn't all bad. HubSpot shares went up after the IPO, and by the time I sold my options, I cleared about $60,000. Certainly back in 2012 I didn't expect that I would end up writing for a popular TV comedy like *Silicon Valley* and spending part of my time in Los Angeles. I also didn't expect to end up writing a book about being a fifty-something guy struggling to work with Millennials—because I honestly didn't expect this would be such a struggle. I knew life at a start-up would be less structured than life at an eighty-year-old publishing company, but I really thought I could adapt. In the end, I found I wasn't prepared for things like Fearless Friday and teddy bears being given a place of honor at the table during management meetings.

Certainly when I joined HubSpot I didn't think I was going to work for bosses who would engage in activity that might be illegal, or on the verge, or that I would be the target of their actions. I also never imagined that a board of directors of a "radically transparent" company would refuse to tell the full story about what happened.

The board's handling of the scandal raises serious questions about HubSpot's corporate governance. HubSpot has three independent board members who do not represent venture capital firms. Each of them, however, holds shares in HubSpot worth millions of dollars. Instead of coming clean, the directors have released only a tiny amount of information, leaving huge questions unanswered.

HubSpot has vowed to develop a "Company-Wide Code of Business Conduct and Ethics training program." That's a good start, but not enough. The directors should share everything in the Goodwin Procter report, and not just with me but with their public shareholders. The board represents shareholders and is accountable to them, yet is denying them information. Investors who have put money into HubSpot are supposed to have a voice in how the company is run. They are asked, every year, to elect board members and to approve the compensation paid to management, among other things. How can HubSpot's shareholders vote intelligently when the board withholds information from them?

Something happened that was so bad that the board fired a top executive. According to HubSpot's press release, Halligan knew about the behavior and did not report it to the board. Shareholders are entitled to know more than this in order to decide whether he is fit to remain in place as the company's CEO. What was Halligan's role? What did he know, and when did he know it? Why did the board fire Volpe and consider firing Chernov, but not Halligan?

The irony to me is that taking the job at HubSpot has led me back to where I began—back to being a reporter and writer, trying to get to the bottom of a story. As I hit my deadline on this book I am still trying to get answers. In December 2015 I hired an attorney who filed a Freedom of Information Act request seeking the release of documents from the U.S. attorney's office and FBI related to this case. I'm not sure this will work. I've been told it's a long shot.

Meanwhile, I keep thinking about HubSpot's customers, those thousands of people who attended the Inbound conference in September 2015 and cheered for Halligan, even though they knew about the scandal and the criminal investigation. You could not be a HubSpot zealot and be ignorant of Volpe's firing, of Halligan being sanctioned, or that legal authorities had been notified.

The customers didn't care. Many of them truly love HubSpot and feel an almost religious devotion to the company. They've been swept up in HubSpot's narrative about being *lovable* and *magical* and making the world a better place. The same goes for HubSpot's employees. In December 2015 HubSpot was ranked fourth on a list of the top fifty places to work in the United States, based on an employee survey conducted by Glassdoor. Also near the top of the list was Zillow, the real estate website that has been sued by women claiming the company had an abusive, ageist, frat house culture. HubSpot scored higher than even Facebook and Google. A lot of its employees really, truly love the company and are happy there. I understand why. For the right kind of person, it's a great place, with nice perks and a fun culture. Even former employees remain loyal to HubSpot and still love the company.

I had a different experience. Where others saw a fun place to work, I saw a place where "old people"—those over forty, and certainly people over fifty—were largely unwanted, and the company made no secret of it. I saw astonishing uniformity and groupthink, and an incredible lack of diversity, based not just on age but also on race, euphemized as "culture fit." I saw poorly trained managers, haphazard oversight, and an organization that was out of control.

I know that HubSpot can be a fun place to work, that they put on an entertaining show at Inbound, and that at least some customers, maybe a lot of customers, derive real value from HubSpot's software. But I fear that customers and employees are being naïve about the people they're working for and doing business with. HubSpot has fifteen thousand customers. Those companies entrust their private data to HubSpot, things like emails, customer lists, pricing, and billing. HubSpot holds data not just about its own fifteen thousand customers but data from *their* customers as well. If your plumber or pool installer or local appliance store uses HubSpot software, HubSpot may be holding information about you, without you even knowing it.

Yet this is a company where top executives allegedly engaged in a scheme to invade the privacy of a former employee and did something so serious that the FBI investigated. Despite that, those marketers cheering for Halligan at the Inbound conference somehow believe they can trust his company with their data.

The thing is, we all do this. We share our information with companies all the time. We send email through Google or Microsoft. We store files on Dropbox. We shop on Amazon. We buy apps and music from Apple. We hire drivers through Uber, and rent apartments through Airbnb. Companies use Workday for HR, Zendesk for customer service, Salesforce.com for customer tracking, Slack for messaging, and on and on. Most of these companies don't operate their own data centers. Instead, they rent server and storage space from a hosting company like Amazon. Our information gets distributed around the globe, zipped between data centers at the speed of light, stashed on hard drives, backed up, duplicated, replicated, sliced and diced, sold and shared. Even the people who supposedly manage our data have no idea where all of it resides or who has access to it.

Yet we go along. We convince ourselves that nothing bad will happen. We tell ourselves that we're not important enough for anyone to spy on us, or that even if someone did want to spy us, there must be safeguards in place that prevent bad people from snooping. We hear the people who run these online services present themselves as idealistic do-gooders who want make the world a better place.

Even if we don't believe them, we understand that they have a financial incentive not to spy on us. They don't have to be good people, or honest people, or law-abiding citizens. They just have to want to make money. They can't do that unless people trust them. Their own greed will keep them honest—that's the theory, anyway.

So we figure we're safe. We figure we can trust the people who run online services not to snoop on us. I used to believe that. I don't anymore. Halligan, Volpe, and Chernov were not random nerds going rogue in some data center. They were top executives of a publicly traded company. They're the ones who were supposed to be keeping an eye on the others. During my time at HubSpot, I was shocked to see how badly managed the company was and how packs of inexperienced twenty-something employees were being turned loose and given huge responsibility with little or no oversight. In the world of start-ups that is now the norm, not the exception.

The consequences are just what you would expect. Employees at Uber, the ride-sharing company, have used a "God View" feature to stalk people using the service, including a BuzzFeed journalist. Re/code, a tech blog, claims other companies have done the same, including Lyft, a rival to Uber; Swipe, a photo-sharing app; and Basis, which makes a "health watch" that tracks people's heart rates, sleep patterns, and other personal information. In the early days at Facebook, the young employees had a master password to gain access to anyone's account, according to a book by a former Facebook employee. Dirty tricks have become par for the course at these places. In 2011 Facebook was caught running a sneaky smear campaign, hiring a PR firm to spread negative stories about Google—I know because I'm the reporter who caught them and broke the story for *Newsweek*. Facebook's entire business model is based on mining personal data in order to deliver targeted advertising. The same goes for Google and countless other online companies. We have no idea who has access to what.

We also have no choice but to go along. None of us is going to opt out of using the Internet. Nor can we expect that the companies will do any better when it comes to oversight. They're funded by venture capitalists who seek only the biggest and quickest return on their investment. That means hiring kids, cutting corners, breaking rules. It does not mean investing loads of money in order to build safeguards and protect users. There's an adage in Silicon Valley that people who use online services are not the customers. We're the product. As far as companies in Silicon Valley are concerned, we exist solely to be packaged up and sold to advertisers. We should not expect these companies to look out for us.

In March 2015, just five months after the initial public offering of stock, HubSpot went back to the public markets for a second shot of cash.

This time most of the money went not to the company but to a bunch of insiders. The company itself sold only 850,000 shares, while insiders sold 3.2 million shares. Shares were priced at $37, so the company raised $31 million while insiders raised $120 million.

Halligan and Shah each sold shares worth about $6 million. Four of their biggest venture capital investors—General Catalyst Partners, Matrix Partners, Scale Venture Partners, and Charles River Ventures—pocketed just under $80 million, collectively.

HubSpot has created a great deal of wealth—by the end of 2015 the company was valued at nearly $2 billion. But most of the money has ended up in a remarkably small number of hands. After the IPO, in October 2014, nearly 80 percent of the company was owned by five venture capital firms and three insiders—Halligan, Shah, and J. D. Sherman, the chief operating officer, according to the S-1 prospectus filed with the Securities and Exchange Commission. The five venture capital firms invested $100 million and turned it into about $1 billion.

And HubSpot stock kept climbing. By the end of 2015, even after selling some of his shares in the secondary offering, Halligan had a stake worth $63 million. Shah had a stake worth $120 million.

HubSpot itself has never turned a profit. Wall Street analysts estimate that the company will continue losing money at least through the end of 2016. Most analysts recommend buying the stock.

Acknowledgments

I'm indebted to many friends from Silicon Valley who spoke to me when I was working on this book and shared their insight and perspective. For the most part I have not mentioned these people by name, for the sake of protecting their privacy—but you guys know who you are. Also, in some parts of the book I have drawn on reporting and writing that I originally did for other publications, including Valleywag.

My wife, Sasha, offered emotional support and boosted my spirits during the dark time when I was banished to the telemarketing center at HubSpot. She stayed calm when I was freaking out and dealing with lawyers and being interviewed by the FBI and trying to figure out what HubSpot's executives had done to us. Most important, Sasha held down the fort while I was away from home, working in Los Angeles, and when I got back to Boston and was holed up in my office for weeks on end.

My agent, Christy Fletcher, and her associates at Fletcher & Co. read drafts and provided valuable feedback. My editor, Paul Whitlatch, offered wise counsel, as did others at Hachette, including Mauro DiPreta, Michelle Aielli, Elisa Rivlin, and Betsy Hulsebosch. Production editor Melanie Gold and copy editor Lori Paximadis exhibited tremendous grace under pressure, and improved the manuscript immeasurably.

Finally I would like to thank Brian Halligan, Dharmesh Shah, and everyone else at HubSpot for providing me with such rich material. You truly made one plus one equal three.